An Introductory Text Book to Study

GENERAL PSYCHOLOGY

with the Integration of
Theology, Spirituality,
and the
Personal Search for
Truth and Meaning

Dr. David W. Bailey

All bible quotes throughout book are from the King James version.

Cover image © Shutterstock.com

www.kendallhunt.com
Send all inquiries to:
4050 Westmark Drive
Dubuque, IA 52004-1840

Copyright © 2019 by Kendall Hunt Publishing Company

ISBN 978-1-7924-0072-8

Published in the United States of America.

Contents

Preface

Welcome to this first edition of An Introductory Text Book to Study General Psychology with the Integration of Theology, Spirituality, and the Personal Search for Truth and Meaning. After reading this brief preface, you may have a better understanding of why the title of book is so long. It is my hope this will be the first of several editions. But this edition is very special in part, because of you. If you have purchased this edition, it means you are a member of the first group that has ever used this book. And, you will be a part of the process for making subsequent editions. Let me explain.

This book is being offered as both a hard copy and e-Book for a couple reasons:

1. It will help keep the cost down for students. As a college student back in the 1970s, along with most of my friends, money was always on short supply. I suspect that may still be the case for many.
2. In the first few years of using this book, I will be collecting feedback and receiving instruction from you the student on how to improve this book for others. We will even be doing some in class experiments and collecting data that will be included in future editions.

Back to the long title. One unique aspect of this particular text book is that it explicitly includes use of the Holy Bible as a source of inspiration, insight, and discussion for each chapter. I personally believe this book is preeminent over all other books ever written. While many love the Bible, many do not. Perhaps most are not even familiar with it. Whatever your current view is, please keep an open mind as we explore ancient concepts and writings as well as current concepts and writings. Ultimately, you will be making your own conclusions and interpretations of this book and all concepts and books you are exposed to.

What you will study in this book is what I consider to be the meat and potatoes of what you should be exposed to and understand as an undergraduate student being introduced to the study and profession of psychology. I have taught general psychology for many years and in my opinion most introductory psychology books try to cover too much material. In doing so, the student is often overwhelmed or given a lot of information but in a very superficial manner. Truly, each chapter in this book could be expanded into an entire course. If you go on in the field, you will find this out as you take specialized courses in these areas in your undergraduate and graduate level training.

This book will be used to provide structure and a foundation for you to interact with the material and apply it to your own personal, spiritual, and psychological journey. With each chapter, you will also be given supplemental material to watch, read, and interact with. This will be done both online in Canvas (the tool I use) and in class films, experiments, and discussion groups.

As this book is used as foundational information and content of this general psychology class, there some themes and principles that will help us get the most out of this class. While these are will be gone over in class, let me share what I believe to be some of the more important concepts and themes that we will address in class.

Truth does exist and truth is reality. Our perspectives and beliefs about reality may or may not be true, accurate, or in alignment with truth and reality. But each person's belief and perspective is important to that person.

All truth is God's truth and only God Almighty knows all truth. None of us know all truth. But knowing the truth always helps. Ignorance and error never help. The Truth truly does make us free.

Besides encouraging this lifelong pursuit of Truth, I will encourage us to see people, including yourself, as individuals. Not as generalizations, categories, classifications, or labels of any type. Even though diagnoses and classifications and statistical understanding of people will be mentioned in this text, it is important we don't reduce people too much. It is important to respect each person as a creation of God deserving respect. We are constantly growing and changing. We cannot grow and not change. Healthy living is about growing and changing in positive ways.

As we will discuss in class, I will encourage each of us to hate racism, sexism, ageism, and all other "isms" that put people down. Hate these errors, but hate no person. Narrow, generalizing, stereotypical ways of thinking are the roots of all bigotry and is a very immature way of thinking. Unfortunately this way of thinking and viewing people can be done by well-educated people and people in positions of influence. My prayer is that we will be part of the solution on this planet and not part of the problem. As we grow in Truth, Light, Life, and Love we will be part of the growing and healing process that Holy God would have each person receive. This way of Being is ultimately marked by Love and Respect of the Highest nature.

Perhaps not so much in a structured text book way, but during the class you will be given opportunity for self-analysis or what I like to call soul searching. We all have room for growth. This is true throughout one's entire life, and in my opinion even the afterlife. I believe God made you special and wants to give you the true desire of your heart. That you will become your true self. All you were created and meant to be. The desire and purpose of your heart, your destiny is different than every other person on this planet. May in some way this book, this study, this class help you more clearly become your very best self-possible.

God is with us and for us. God is Love. God is Spirit. God is Light Life Love and More. Creator God made you and me and all living things for a great purpose. I will do my best to serve you and help you in any way I can. I look forward to seeing you in person or on line as we begin this class in general psychology.

Sincerely,

Dr. David Bailey

1

Introduction to Psychology: Study of the Psyche

Focus Questions

By the end of the chapter, you should be able to answer the following questions:

- How is psychology defined?
- What are the principal responsibilities of members of the main divisions in psychology?
- What were the key beliefs and contributions of some of the early contributors to the development of psychology?
- What are the identifying characteristics of the scientific method?
- What are some key types of descriptive research?
- How does descriptive research differ from experiments and ex post facto studies?
- What is the correlation fallacy?
- What are some of the main sources of error in interpreting the results of psychological investigations?

Psychology: The Human Puzzle by Guy R. LeFrancois © 2013 Bridgepoint Education. Reprinted by permission.

The purpose of psychology is to give us a completely different idea of the things we know best.

—*Paul Valéry, Tel Quel, 1943*

Inspirational Words

Then the LORD God formed man of dust from the ground, and breathed into his nostrils the breath of life; and man became a living being. Gen. 2:7

And ye shall know the truth, and the truth shall make you free. Jesus in John 8:32

And thou shalt love the Lord thy God with all thy heart, and with all thy soul, and with all thy mind, and with all thy strength: this is the first commandment. Jesus in Mark 12:30

A good, but unexamined life will be high on duty and not likely to celebrate the odd paradoxes, the ironic coincidences, and the humor of being dirt.

C. S. Lewis (Surprised by Joy)

There are no ordinary people. You have never talked to a mere mortal. Nations, cultures, arts, civilizations—these are mortal, and their life is to ours as the life of a gnat. But it is immortals whom we joke with, work with, marry, snub, and exploit—immortal horrors or everlasting splendors.

C. S. Lewis (The Weight of Glory)

1.1 What Is Psychology?

What Psychologists Do

As Figure 1.1 shows, the vast majority of psychologists are involved in the practical application of psychological knowledge.

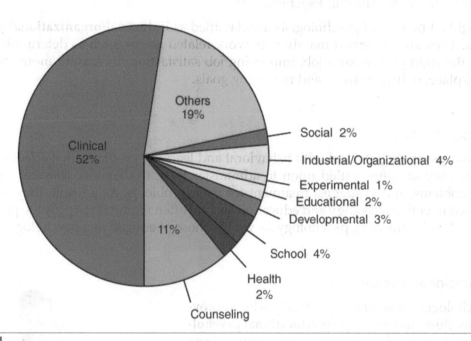

Main Specialties in Psychology

Others 19%
Social 2%
Industrial/Organizational 4%
Experimental 1%
Educational 2%
Developmental 3%
Clinical 52%
11%
School 4%
Health 2%
Counseling

Figure 1.1

Main specialties in psychology. Based on a survey of the American Psychological Association's 90,221 members in 2005. Data from APA Directory Survey 2005, compiled by APA Research Office. Retrieved July 13, 2010, from http://www.apa.org/workforce/publications/05-member/table-3.pdf.

Clinical Psychologists

About half of all psychologists are **clinical psychologists**. These are typically psychologists working in a hospital or clinical setting. They specialize in helping people with psychological problems such as anxiety, depression, addiction, or relationship problems.

Although **psychiatrists** and clinical psychologists often treat similar sorts of problems, their training and expertise are quite different. Psychiatrists are medical doctors with specialized training in identifying and treating mental and emotional disorders. In addition to the various other interventions they might use, they can prescribe drugs, which are now commonly used to treat many disorders ranging from mild anxiety to severe deviations from normality. In most jurisdictions, clinical psychologists cannot write prescriptions.

Counseling Psychologists

A significant number of psychologists are **counseling psychologists**. They, too, treat problems related to emotional and mental disorders. In addition, they also deal with issues such as those having to do with vocational choices, learning problems, relationships, and related concerns. Whereas clinical psychologists often work in clinical settings or in private practices, counseling psychologists work mainly in private practices.

Industrial/Organizational Psychologists

Roughly 4 percent of psychologists are classified as **industrial/organizational psychologists**. They are concerned mainly with work-related issues, such as determining how to hire the right person for a job, improving job satisfaction, increasing motivation in the workplace, reducing stress, and managing goals.

School Psychologists

School psychologists deal with behavioral and learning problems that affect schoolchildren. They are often called upon to administer tests, to diagnose learning and behavior problems, and to suggest treatment for these problems. As a result, they are usually trained in both psychology and education and are often required to apply the principles of clinical and counseling psychology, as well as those of educational psychology.

Educational Psychologists

Psychologists concerned specifically with improving teaching and learning are **educational psychologists**. Unlike school psychologists, they are less concerned with individual behavioral and learning problems than with broader questions relating to how people learn in educational settings. Educational psychology applies psychological principles to classroom management, special needs education, instructional design, and lesson planning.

Developmental Psychologists

Developmental psychologists study systematic changes that occur between conception and death. Some specialize in the study of child development; others are more concerned with adolescent or adult development, or with aging and dying. The findings of developmental psychology are especially important for school and educational psychologists as well as for clinical and counseling psychology.

About half of all psychologists are clinical psychologists specialized in helping people with psychological problems. Unlike psychiatrists, they're not usually medical doctors.

Experimental Psychologists

Much of the content of psychology—and therefore of this text—is based on the work of **experimental psychologists**. They specialize in the use of experimental methods to investigate the puzzles of psychology. Experimental research requires that the investigator control significant aspects of a situation in an attempt to uncover cause-and-effect relationships. (There is more about experiments shortly.)

Other Divisions

There are many other specializations in psychology: *Health psychologists* look at how psychological factors influence health and illness and often work in clinical settings or hospitals to promote wellness; *social psychologists* are concerned with how people relate to and influence each other; *sports psychologists* use psychological research to improve athletic performance; *forensic psychologists* are usually experts in criminal law as well as in psychology and might be called upon to assist in jury selection or as expert witnesses for assessing the state of mind of the accused at the time of the offense or the defendant's competency to stand trial; and *environmental psychologists* look at the relationship between humans and their surroundings, and specifically at the effects of the environment on our well-being (Table 1.1).

Table 1.1 What Psychologists Do	
Some Major Divisions	**Main Concerns and Activities**
Clinical	Diagnosis and treatment of emotional illnesses and disorders, frequently in a hospital or clinical setting
Counseling	Evaluation of and assistance with behavioral, emotional, and other problems not serious enough to require hospital, clinical, or psychiatric treatment; assistance with important decisions such as those having to do with careers, relationships, adjustment, and stress
Industrial/organizational	Applying psychology in business and industry; developing and administering tests to evaluate aptitudes; dealing with motivational, management, and interpersonal issues in the workplace
School	Identifying individual aptitudes and skills among learners in a school setting; developing and administering tests pertinent to school-related abilities; diagnosing and remediating behavioral and learning problems
Educational	Researching the application of psychological principles for improving teaching and learning
Developmental	Studying changes that define growth, learning, and maturation from birth to death; applying findings in educational programs and in child guidance and counseling
Experimental	Using experimental methods to investigate the puzzles of psychology

Regardless of their specialization, many psychologists write books, teach, do research, conduct private practices, work in business and industry, or are employed in a variety of different professions where knowledge of psychology is useful and sometimes even essential. Many are engaged in combinations of these activities.

All that affects human behavior, thought, and emotion falls within the domain of psychology. The chapters in this book represents the most common divisions and interests in psychology: While psychologists are mental health professionals who require an earned doctorate, along with state-specific internships and board examinations, the reader should be aware that you can also be a mental health professional at the master's level of education and training. While each state has somewhat different names and qualifications for licensure, social workers, licensed professional counselors, pastoral counselors, and school counselors (to name a few) also provide mental health services to people in need.

Since spiritual, religious, and personal worldviews and beliefs are part of what makes up the human journey, they will also be looked at and discussed in this book.

1.2 The Beginnings of Psychology

That definition begins with the history of psychology—a history that goes back at least as far as ancient Greece, when the discipline of **philosophy** embraced almost all other disciplines, including what is now psychology. In fact, the term *psychology* has its roots in the Greek language, where the word *psyche* means "soul" and *logos* means "the study or discussion of."

More recently in psychology's history, discoveries in medicine had a dramatic influence on our conception of the human being. When William Harvey discovered that the heart pumped blood into tubes throughout the body, many thinkers became convinced that people were nothing more than elaborate pumping machines. Many suspected that the ability to think originates in the blood. Aristotle didn't merely suspect this—he knew it. If a person's blood were entirely removed, he argued, no evidence of thinking would remain!

Early physics, too, contributed to the development of psychology. The psychological importance of Sir Isaac Newton's observation that apples invariably fall earthward lies in the fact that it illustrates a different way of looking at natural phenomena. The ancient Greek philosophers undoubtedly knew that apples fall earthward. And had they wanted to know why apples fall, they might have thought long and hard about the problem and held learned discourses with colleagues. But their approach would have made little use of the methods of **science** as we now know them. Newton, however, felt compelled to demonstrate and verify the phenomena he observed and to investigate them by means of controlled experimentation. We are products of Newton's generation: Psychology, anthropology, sociology, and other related fields are seldom referred to as the social *studies*; they are the social *sciences* (Figure 1.2).

Recent Origins of Psychology

Scientific psychology is not much more than a century old. Its founder is generally considered to be Wilhelm Wundt, who founded the first psychological laboratory in Leipzig, Germany, in 1879. Many of Wundt's students later established laboratories of their own throughout Europe and North America. Very soon after that, psychology departments opened at all major universities. Typically these began as branches of departments of

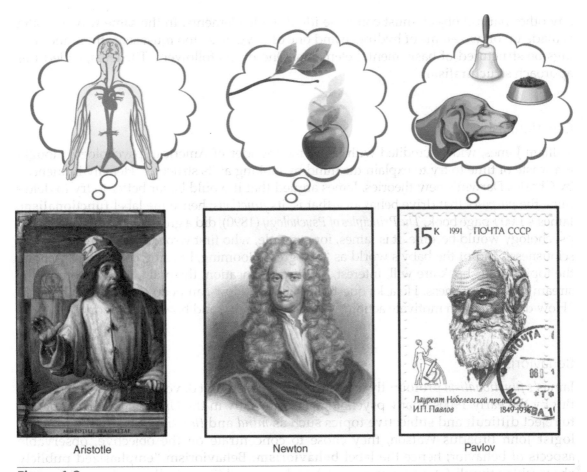

Figure 1.2

Contemplation of their own experiences guided the ancient Greeks in learning about people. The result: the theory that the ability to think originates in the blood. Centuries later, Newton used scientific observation and experimentation to test theories about the physical world. By the 20th century, psychologists were applying scientific methods to animals and people to learn about behavior. The result: psychology as it exists today.

philosophy, but in time the discipline became totally separate. Departments of psychology now claim far more students than do departments of philosophy.

Structuralism

The early history of psychology is marked by the rise—and fall—of a number of different "schools" of thought. The first dates back to Wilhelm Wundt and his followers, whose search for pieces of the puzzle relied on **introspection**. Introspection involves *looking inside* oneself, examining one's own thoughts, feelings, and motives and generalizing the resulting insights to understand the thoughts and feelings of others. Stop, for a moment, and *think about* the words you are now reading. How does a physical **stimulus** such as a word on a page affect you? As you carefully analyze your current thoughts and feelings, you are introspecting.

The goal of introspection as practiced by Wundt and his followers was to understand the *structure* of thoughts, emotions, and motives. They reasoned that the conscious mind, like any other natural object, must comprise identifiable elements. In the same way as water is made up of two atoms of hydrogen and one of oxygen, so too must sensations and feelings be structured of basic mental elements. One of his followers, Titchener, called this approach **structuralism**.

Functionalism

William James, widely credited with being the founder of American psychology, thought it a waste of time to try to explain the mind by looking at its structure. Heavily influenced by Charles Darwin's new theories, James argued that it would be far better to try to determine the *purposes* that drive behavior—that is, its *functions*; hence the label **functionalism**. James's 1,000-page book, *The Principles of Psychology* (1890), did a great deal to establish what psychology would become. It is James, for example, who first wrote of the "stream of consciousness" and of the baby's world as "one great blooming, buzzing confusion." Among the topics in his book are will, interest, emotions, sensation, the brain, and, of course, the stream of consciousness. He asks questions such as "How can people strengthen habits?" "How does intention motivate action?" "What is memory, and how does it work?"

Behaviorism

James's *functionalism* profoundly influenced the subsequent development of psychology. But by the early 1900s, many psychologists, especially in the United States, had begun to reject difficult and subjective topics such as *mind* and *thinking*. Led by the psychologist John Broadus Watson, they chose to concentrate on the objective, observable aspects of behavior; hence the label **behaviorism**. Behaviorism "emphasized publicly observable stimuli (s) and responses (r) and spurned supposedly unobservable, centrally initiated processes like consciousness" (Moore, 2010, p. 143).

Among the most important behaviorists are Pavlov, Watson, and Skinner. Behaviorists tend to study reflexive behavior and the consequences of behavior. As we see in Chapter 4, many scientific experiments can be carried out to investigate these matters. As a result, with the advent of behaviorism, psychology became progressively more scientific. But because of its emphasis on discovering how behavior is controlled by stimuli and by its consequences, behaviorism is sometimes interpreted as denying the existence of free will.

Psychoanalysts are psychiatrists who, like Freud, believe that mental disorders result from deep-seated *psychodynamic* conflicts. The purpose of the couch is to allow the patient to relax so as to facilitate uncovering these conflicts—often through free association or dream analysis.

Psychodynamic Theory

At about the same time that the behaviorists were first popular in American psychology, the Austrian neurologist Sigmund Freud was developing startling new ideas about the mind. As explained in ch. 7, Freud believed that the mind is a little like an iceberg: We see only the very tip, which represents the *conscious* mind; the bulk of it is hidden, *unconscious*. Much of our behavior is driven by unconscious forces: They lie beneath the visible iceberg, beyond our conscious awareness. Freud believed that many of our emotional disorders stem from these unconscious **psychodynamic** forces. There are methods of analysis, of **psychoanalysis**, explained Freud, that can uncover these hidden motives and forces and that can lead to the alleviation of mental disorders.

Cognitivism

Other psychologists rejected the narrow emphases of a behaviorism that limited itself to observable events, but relatively few embraced Freud's psychoanalysis. Many can be described as belonging to the school labeled **cognitivism**. These are psychologists whose main concerns are with intellectual (*cognitive*) events such as problem solving, thinking, information processing, and imagining. Cognitivism provides explanations for behavior based on our ability to symbolize, to uncover cause-and-effect relationships, to determine what goes with what, and to anticipate the consequences of our actions.

Humanism

Some psychologists object to what they see as the overly limited, mechanistic, and *dehumanizing* emphases of behavioristic approaches to psychology. They also reject the Freudian notion that we're driven by dark, unconscious forces over which we have little control. These approaches, they argue, pay too little attention to the positive and healthy aspects of human nature. **Humanistic psychology**, is concerned with the uniqueness, the individuality, the humanity of each person. It emphasizes the development of the "self" and is represented by psychologists such as Abraham Maslow and Carl Rogers.

Humanism arose primarily as a reaction against behavioristic and psychodynamic theories, which Maslow (1998) described as the two great forces in psychology; he labeled the humanistic movement **third force psychology**. His hope was that this third force would become as powerful as the first two and that it might counter the *dehumanizing* influence of a rigorous scientific approach to the study of psychology.

Other Orientations

There are a number of other important orientations in the study of psychology. **Evolutionary psychology** emphasizes biology and genetics as a source of explanations for human learning and behavior. Evolutionary psychologists look at the evolution of human behavior and try to explain human characteristics in terms of historical pressures of adaptation.

Neuroscience is another important and highly current, biologically based orientation. Using powerful new brain-imaging techniques, neuroscientists look to the nervous system, especially the brain, for explanations of consciousness and of mental processes like thinking, imagining, problem solving, and remembering.

Both evolutionary psychologists and neuroscientists make extensive use of **genomics**, the study of genes and how they relate to human behaviors and characteristics.

1.3 Principles of Science

Psychology is a *science*. What does that mean?

In one sense, *science* can mean a collection of information in a field of study. For example, the science of physics is a collection of information about the nature of matter and energy and how they interact. And the science of psychology is a collection of information about human thought and behavior and how they interact.

In another very important sense, science is a way of dealing with information. As such, it is both an attitude and a set of guidelines. It is an attitude that insists on objectivity, precision, and consistency. And it is a set of guidelines meant to ensure that this is the case. As a result, science stands in sharp contrast to those ways of knowing that are based principally on subjective analysis or *introspection*.

Attempts to explain and organize the observations of science take the form of **theories**. Theories are collections of related statements that clarify observations and permit predictions (**hypotheses**).

In spite of science's preoccupation with the objective, many topics of interest to psychology cannot be observed and measured directly, but can only be inferred from behavior or from highly subjective self-reports. Emotions and thoughts, for example, are subjective rather than objective. And even though these might lead to behavior from which an observer might guess the underlying emotion or thought, this is not always so. For example, I might be very angry or very sad because I now know for sure that my dog does not much like me; but you would not necessarily know my emotion from my behavior because I can easily pretend I don't care.

One of psychology's tasks is to devise ways of examining nonobjective events and states as objectively and scientifically as possible.

The Scientific Method

Studying phenomena objectively and scientifically means using what is often labeled the **scientific method**—an approach designed to ensure that observations are as accurate and valid as possible, that they can be replicated by other investigators. The sciences have now been using the scientific method for more than a hundred years to find and assemble pieces of the human puzzle. It can be described in terms of five systematic steps:

1. Ask the question. (For example: Would after-school detention be effective in stopping a group of boys from stealing iPods, MP3 players, and smartphones?)
2. Develop a hypothesis. On the basis of observation and a careful examination of relevant investigations and theory, make a prediction—a *hypothesis*. By definition, a scientific hypothesis is unproven and can be falsified (proven incorrect). Hence the outcome of a scientific investigation can lead to the rejection of the hypothesis. (Hypothesis: After-school detention will be effective in curtailing thefts of electronic devices.)

3. Collect relevant observations. As we see in the next section, science suggests many different ways of collecting observations. The nature of the question being asked, as well as constraints related to money, time, instrumentation, and the availability of suitable participants, usually determines which method is best. (Method: Detain the group of thieves after school; monitor subsequent thefts.)

Although psychology probes and measures things not as easily analyzed and quantified as matter in test tubes, it strives for the same precision, objectivity, and replicability—though perhaps with somewhat more restraint than this mad scientist.

4. Test the hypothesis. Do your observations indicate that the hypothesis should be rejected? And even if they do not, might they be due to chance? Science is very concerned that observations might be just chance happenings—in which case, they don't mean very much at all. For this reason, investigators often use special **statistical procedures** to determine whether observations are *statistically* **significant**. These procedures allow investigators to determine the likelihood that observations are due to factors other than chance. (How many devices disappeared before the detention? How many disappeared after?)

5. Reach and share a conclusion. If science is to progress, the hypothesis has to be *rejected* or *not rejected*. If it is not rejected, it may be accepted as *tentatively* valid (we can seldom be *absolutely* certain). (For example: As many electronic devices disappeared after as before detention. Tentative conclusion: Detention is not an effective deterrent in this case.) The conclusions of the research then need to be shared. This means communicating the findings to others so they can apply them and so continue the research and learning process.

1.4 Sources of Psychological Information

The ways psychologists gather observations vary greatly depending on the topic being researched and sometimes on the psychologist's preferences. What is invariably true, however, is that observation is the source of all psychological knowledge, just as it is the source of knowledge in other sciences. Psychological studies and experiments vary according to who is being observed, when, how, and under what conditions.

Descriptive Research

Descriptive research describes the characteristics of an individual or of a group. It answers the questions who, what, where, when, and how. What is the average age of a group? How common is bipolar disorder? What is current life expectancy in North America?

11

Descriptive research is often based on the results of **archival research**—research that depends on secondary sources such as census data, birth certificates, or other forms of past records. It may also be based on the results of observation, which can be naturalistic or nonnaturalistic.

Naturalistic and Nonnaturalistic Observation

Naturalistic observation is observation that occurs in natural settings rather than in laboratories, hospitals, and other surroundings. Naturalistic observation is well illustrated by the research of Jane Goodall, who, since 1960, has lived among chimpanzees in the Gombe Stream Research Centre in Tanzania, simply observing chimpanzees without disturbing them. The assumption of naturalistic observation is that if the investigator does interfere, the behavior under examination may be affected. For example, chimpanzees that would be playful and bold in their natural state might become anxious and furtive when observed too closely.

Naturalistic observation takes place in surroundings that are not altered by the observer or by the requirements of the observation; **nonnaturalistic observation** occurs in more contrived surroundings such as laboratories. Both are important in psychological investigation. Naturalistic and nonnaturalistic approaches to gathering psychological information can be classified in terms of who is observed and how and when the observations are made. Thus, there are *case studies* (discussed in next section), where single individuals (or single units such as a family) are observed, and *surveys* (discussed after case studies), where large groups of individuals (or larger groups of units such as a number of families) are studied.

Studies may be longitudinal or cross-sectional, depending on when observations are made. When the goal of psychological investigation is to identify changes that occur within individuals or within a group of individuals over time, **longitudinal studies** may be used. A longitudinal study examines the same individual(s) at different times and makes direct comparisons between the individual at this point in time and the same individual at an earlier time. In contrast, **cross-sectional studies** examine two or more groups of subjects at the same time. Cross-sectional studies are much less time-consuming and consequently much less expensive, but they are not always appropriate for answering questions about changes that occur within individuals over time.

Torrance's study of creativity, in which subjects were followed from childhood beginning in 1958 through a period of 50 years, provides one of the better-known examples of longitudinal research in psychology (Millar, 2001, 2010). Investigators kept track of all creative accomplishments of each individual in the group: books written, art exhibitions, software programs, inventions, invited lectures, leadership positions, and so on. This investigation found that highly creative children tend to become highly creative adults. The most highly gifted grew

Naturalistic observation involves as little interference with ongoing activities as possible and occurs in "natural" environments such as schools or, as shown here, playgrounds.

up to be college presidents, inventors, doctors, diplomats, and lawyers. Strikingly, their scores on measures of creativity were far more predictive of their eventual accomplishments than were their scores on intelligence tests (Plucker, 1999).

Case Studies

Descriptive research, as we noted, can be based on **case studies**. A classic example of a case study is that of a young Russian, known to us only as S, who presented himself to a psychologist one day. S was confused and poorly adjusted. He hoped that the psychologist, the very well-known and highly respected Alexandr Romanovich Luria, would help him. His problem was that he had difficulty following ordinary conversations, that his mind was such a jumble of sights and sounds that he was often absolutely overwhelmed and bewildered. From this initial meeting there developed a long relationship between the two, during which Luria conducted intensive and detailed investigations of S's memory. Luria soon discovered that S could remember with incredible and uncanny accuracy. Nor did he remember as you or I might remember, painfully retrieving some isolated bit of information that we have succeeded in storing and protecting from the ravages of time. He could remember in infinite detail, retrieving from his memory not only the item requested of him, but a host of other associations that most people would never have noticed initially, let alone remembered.

As an example, one day Luria presented S with a table of 50 single-digit numbers. S spent three minutes examining the array. He then reproduced the entire table in 40 seconds and could read off any number it contained in horizontal, vertical, or diagonal arrangements. Perhaps even more amazing, when S was asked to reproduce the same table several months later (the table had not once been presented in the interim), he could do so unerringly and just as rapidly. The only difference was that the second time he required a brief period to "re-imagine" the situation in which he had first memorized the table.

As a result of this intensive and prolonged case study, Luria discovered that S didn't simply hear sounds but sensed them as vivid and colorful images; that he could remember the clothing he and Luria had been wearing on a given day years before; that he frequently remembered by "seeing" objects, events, or numbers in mental images of places where he had stored them. Sometimes he would imagine he was walking along a very familiar street in his hometown, and he would mentally place different numbers on various fences, trees, and houses along this street. Later, when called upon to remember these numbers, he would simply imagine the street and read off the numbers as he saw them. On one occasion when he couldn't recall a number he had memorized in this fashion, it eventually occurred to him that he had "placed" the number in question on a dark, heavily shaded piece of broken board and that he simply could not "see" it!

S presents a classic case of what is termed **synesthesia**, a condition where one sensation evokes another related to a different sense. For example, a person with synesthesia might *hear* a color or *see* a taste or an odor. It seems that S's *synesthesia* provided him with an extraordinarily vivid assortment of visual images that later became keys to his memory.

Luria's investigation of S's memory and his subsequent reports of the results of this investigation provide us with a striking example of a case study. Numerous other examples can be found in psychological literature, especially in studies of abnormal behavior. Whenever a psychologist requires extensive and in-depth information about a single individual, a case-study approach is likely to be used.

Surveys

Descriptive studies are often based on surveys. Whereas a case study involves a single individual (or a single unit), **surveys** involve groups of individuals or groups of units. Case studies are often inappropriate when the intent is to describe a group of people. A psychologist who wanted to find out what the average person in the street thinks of a political event could not easily accomplish this by walking up to and questioning an "average" person. In the first place, there is no **average** individual: he or she is an invention. When a researcher refers to the average person, it is never a single person being referred to; it is, instead, the nonexistent, idealized "averaged" result of investigating many individuals.

A survey is a research technique that attempts to discover the qualities of the average person by examining the characteristics of a number of real individuals. What is especially important in doing a survey is that those being surveyed be representative of the entire group to which investigators want to generalize. When researchers wanted to discover the sexual beliefs and behaviors of the average British 16- to 44-year-old, they surveyed 11,161 individuals by means of interviews and computer-based questionnaires (Gerressu, Mercer, Graham, Wellings, & Johnson, 2008). They were then able to state that 73 percent of men and 37 percent of women had masturbated at least once in the preceding four weeks. Had they conducted two case studies instead, one male and one female, and generalized in the same manner, they would have had to state that all men or all women between the ages of 16 and 44 have masturbated at least once, or that none of them have. Either conclusion would have been highly misleading. (See Figure 1.3 for a comparison of surveys, longitudinal research, and cross-sectional research.)

Correlational Research

A great deal of psychological research is intended to find out whether there is a relationship between two variables. Often psychological research tries to answer questions such as: Is hyperactivity related to parental upbringing? Does anxiety contribute to poor test performance? Are attractive people more likely to be successful in business?

Research designed to answer questions such as these typically results in a measure of **correlation** and is therefore called **correlational research**. A positive correlation exists between two variables when a change in one of these variables is reflected in a similar change in the other; a negative correlation is observed when a change in one variable is accompanied by an opposite change in the other. Numerically, correlation is expressed as −1.00 for a perfect negative correlation, +1.00 for a perfect positive correlation, and 0 for lack of correlation (Figure 1.4).

It would seem logical to assume that if there is a high positive correlation between two variables, one must cause the other—and that may sometimes be the case. In fact, if a

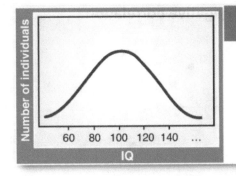

What is the average American IQ?

Surveys reveal information about groups of individuals at a specific time. But a single survey provides no information about change over time and it gives only a composite picture of an idealized "average" individual.

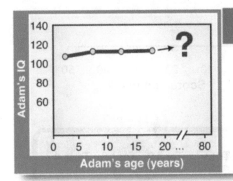

How stable is an individual's IQ?

Longitudinal studies provide information about one or more individuals over a period of time. But they are expensive and time consuming. Many cannot be completed in the lifetime of a single investor.

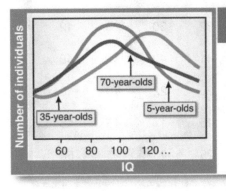

Does IQ peak at different ages?

Cross-sectional studies can provide information about different groups at the same time. But, like surveys, they provide statistical averages and may not take all variables into account. For instance, did the 70-year-olds grow up with the same developmental stimulation as 35-year-olds, or 5-year-olds?

Figure 1.3

Surveys, longitudinal studies, and cross-sectional studies are examples of descriptive research designed to answer different questions.

variable does cause another, there *will* be a correlation between the two. Put another way, correlation is *essential* evidence of causation—but it isn't *sufficient* evidence. The assumption that correlation proves causation is known as the **correlation fallacy**.

For example, there is a high positive correlation between children's shoe sizes and their ability to read. But it would be a *correlation fallacy* to conclude that having big feet helps children read. Having big feet, like being able to read, simply reflects the child's continued development and growth. (The correlation fallacy is explained more fully in a later section.)

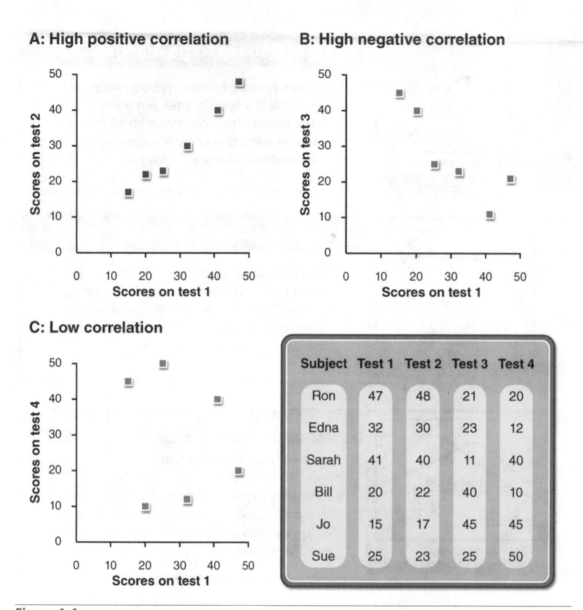

Figure 1.4

Graphic representations of correlation. In A (high positive correlation), those who scored well on test 1 tended to score well on test 2. In B (high negative correlation), those who did well on test 1 tended to do correspondingly poorly on test 3. And in C, there is little relationship between scores on test 1 and scores on test 4.

Experiments

An **experiment** is a research procedure where investigators control one or more of the **variables** in a situation and observe the effects this has on other variables. The experiment is a very powerful tool in science's quest for knowledge because controlling variables makes it possible to observe and measure causes and effects.

A variable may be a measurement, an outcome, or some other way of describing or classifying things such as people, events, or objects. Intelligence test scores, environmental factors, physical characteristics, medications, and so on are all examples of variables. Variables the experimenter controls and whose effects are being investigated are **independent variables**; variables that may be affected by changes in the independent variables are **dependent variables**. Independent variables are assumed to have an effect on dependent variables. Dependent variables are ordinarily measured at the end of an experimental procedure.

As a simple illustration, an experiment can easily be designed to determine whether a new approach to teaching is better than the current approach. The experiment would require that subjects be assigned to one or the other of the teaching methods, that the methods be put into practice, and that subsequent performance be measured and compared. In this case, teaching method is an independent variable; performance, a dependent variable. If teaching method affects performance, it (the independent variable) may be used to predict learning (a dependent variable) (see Figure 1.5).

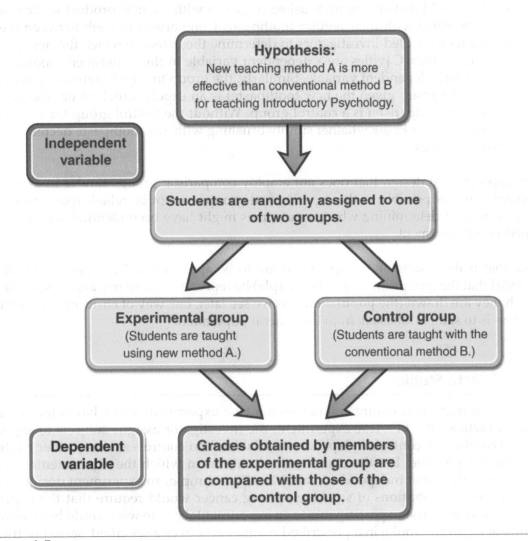

Figure 1.5

A simple experiment designed to test a hypothesis. Note that hypotheses can generally be worded as "if-then" statements. The "if" part of the statement is the independent variable (in this case, the change in teaching method); the "then" part is the dependent variable (in this case, the grades obtained by members of the experimental group).

Note that most experiments can be reworded in terms of an "if-then" statement. What the investigator is saying is "if such and such, then such and such." The if-then statement is the *hypothesis* (prediction) that the experiment is designed to investigate. The "if" part of the statement usually defines the independent variable; the "then" part of the statement is the dependent variable. For example, the hypothesis "rewarding learners will have a positive effect on their learning" can be reworded to "*if* learners are rewarded, *then* they will learn more effectively."

Experimental and Control Groups

The most common experiment is that which makes use of an **experimental group** and one or more **control groups** (sometimes called *comparison groups*). When the manufacturer of some exotic toothpaste assures us that it leads to 40 percent fewer cavities, we are sometimes told that one group brushed regularly with the new product while a second group brushed with their regular toothpaste. Comparison of teeth between these two groups then enabled investigators to determine the extent to which the new product prevents cavities. Cavities are a dependent variable in this experiment; toothpaste employed is an independent variable. Similarly, the group to which something is done (in this case the group given the new toothpaste) is an experimental group; the group that is used for comparison is a control group. Without the control group for comparison, we would never know whether simply brushing with any toothpaste decreases the incidence of cavities.

Any experimental design that does not employ comparison groups similar in as many relevant ways as possible to the experimental groups cannot be relied upon, since we have no way of determining whether outcomes might have been identical without any experimental treatment.

Note that if the results of an experiment are to be applied to a large population, it is essential that the groups involved (the **sample**) be representative of the larger group from which they are drawn (the **population**). As we see later, one way of ensuring representativeness is to sample *randomly* from the general population.

Ex Post Facto Studies

There is an important distinction between a true experiment and what is termed an **ex post facto study**. In a true experiment, the investigator assigns subjects to experimental conditions, controls independent variables, and controls as many other related variables as possible. But there are many situations in which the experimenter does not have control over independent variables. For example, an experiment designed to uncover the contributions of smoking to lung cancer would require that the experimenter randomly assign participants to an experimental group who would be required to inhale cigarette smoke in a prescribed manner and over a specified period of time. Other participants, comparable to the experimental group in all relevant ways, would be required *not* to smoke. Clearly, there are ethical reasons why this experiment cannot be conducted.

In cases such as this, investigators often conduct *ex post facto studies*—literally, *after the fact* studies. These are studies in which participants are selected on the basis of differences that already exist among them, in terms of either dependent or independent variables. For example, instead of assigning participants to smoking or no-smoking groups, people who have a history of smoking or not smoking are selected and compared with respect to the dependent variable, cancer or no cancer. Alternatively, the investigator might begin by looking not at independent variables (smoking or not smoking), but at the dependent variable (cancer or no cancer) and then ask, "How many of those with cancer were smokers and how many were nonsmokers?" They might also ask, "How many without cancer were smokers or nonsmokers?"

Ex post facto studies are highly common in psychology, simply because investigators usually don't have control over many important independent variables such as social class, family composition, mother-infant interaction, where people live, whether they have pets in the home, and so on.

There is one important caution in interpreting the results of ex post facto research. Although these studies can establish the presence of relationships, they don't provide evidence that one variable causes another. An ex post facto study might establish that there is a relationship between father absence in early childhood and delinquent behavior in adolescence, but it cannot prove that father absence causes delinquency because any number of other uncontrolled variables (for example, poverty, mother absence, family size, and so on) might be causally related. Only a carefully controlled experiment can provide sufficient evidence of causation.

For a comparison of research methods that differ in terms of who is observed, when, and how, see Table 1.2.

Table 1.2 Common Types of Psychological Investigations		
Who	Case	Survey, Experiment
	A single individual is observed.	More than one individual is observed.
When	Longitudinal	Cross-Sectional
	The same individuals are observed at different times.	Different groups of individuals are observed at the same time.
How	Experimental	Ex Post Facto
	The experimenter controls relevant independent variables and assigns subjects to groups.	The experimenter selects subjects, but neither assigns them to groups nor exercises control over independent variables.
What	Descriptive	Experimental
	Main goal is to describe the characteristics of what is being studied. May be *archival* (based on existing records), or can be based on surveys, interviews, case studies, longitudinal or cross-sectional research, or correlational studies.	Main goal is to look for causal links between independent and dependent variables.

1.5 Cautions in Interpreting Psychological Research

To what extent can we rely on an experiment such as the toothpaste study described earlier, assuming, of course, that the results were reported accurately? Should we all run and purchase armloads of the new toothpaste?

Would the results be affected, for example, if the control group had been selected from a small rural area where the drinking water is obtained from a questionably clean river whereas the experimental group all reside in an urban area where fluoride is added to the water? Would the results be affected if the dentists who examined the subjects were shareholders in the company that manufactures the new toothpaste and if they knew who was a member of the experimental group and who belonged to the control group? Is it important to know the number of cavities in the histories of members of each of these groups? These questions touch on various potential weaknesses of psychological research, including *experimenter bias*, *sampling bias*, and *subject bias*.

Experimenter Bias

An assortment of rats was divided among two groups of psychology students (Rosenthal & Fode, 1963). The students knew that psychologists had been successful in breeding strains of rats highly different in their ability to learn how to run through mazes—so-called maze-bright and maze-dull rats. In this experiment, one group of students was told that they had been given rats of the maze-bright variety; the second group had to be content with less intelligent rats. In point of fact, however, both groups received randomly assigned rats of presumably equal intelligence.

Students were asked to work with these rats over a period of time and to train them in maze tasks. Amazingly, students who had been led to believe that they had bright rats reported considerably more success in training their rats. In addition, they thought the rats more cooperative, gentler, and generally more pleasant to work with than did students whose rats were labeled dull (see Figure 1.6).

This experiment was among the first of many that have illustrated what is termed **experimenter bias**. It appears that the expectations of experimenters exert subtle and sometimes remarkable influences on their actual observations.

A similar investigation conducted with elementary school children also illustrates experimenter bias (Rosenthal & Jacobsen, 1968). It involved telling teachers that some of their students had been identified as potential "bloomers." "Bloomers" were described as students of average or below average achievement whose potential indicated they could easily achieve at a much higher level. The experimenters led the teachers to believe that they had developed a test that enabled them to identify these students and casually let them see a list of these "bloomers." Astonishingly, although the "bloomers" had been randomly selected, they performed better than other equally intelligent students.

There have been many replications of this investigation since 1968. Some have not supported the original findings (Wineburg, 1987), but many have, although not always with results quite so dramatic (Jacobs & Harvey, 2010; Rubie-Davies, 2010). It seems clear that on occasion

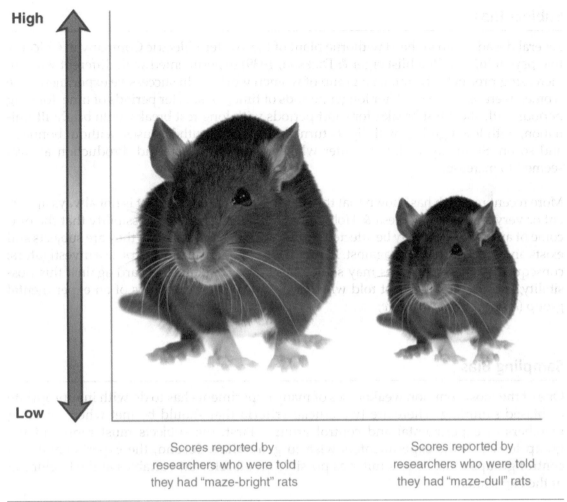

High

Low

Scores reported by
researchers who were told
they had "maze-bright" rats

Scores reported by
researchers who were told
they had "maze-dull" rats

Figure 1.6

How great a role does experimenter bias play in the results of experiments? The smaller rat represents lower scores reported by researchers who were told they had maze-dull rats. Those who thought they had been given the more gifted rats reported significantly higher scores.

the expectations of teachers can affect not only the achievement of their students, but also their performance on objective measures of intelligence as well as their general behavior.

One of the most effective and most common means of guarding against the influence of experimenter expectations is to ensure that those responsible for gathering crucial experimental data not know which subjects are members of experimental groups and which are not. In the toothpaste experiment described earlier, if the dentists examining the children didn't know which children had brushed with the new toothpaste and which were members of the control group, experimenter expectations would not likely affect the conclusions of the experiment. Studies where neither the examiners nor the subjects are aware of who is in the experimental group are termed **double-blind procedures**. In a **single-blind procedure** either the subject or the examiner is unaware ("blind").

Subject Bias

Several decades ago in the Hawthorne plant of the Western Electric Company in Chicago, two psychologists (Roethlisberger & Dickson, 1939) experimented with different ways of increasing productivity among a group of women workers. In successive experiments the women were asked to work for longer periods of time, for shorter periods of time, for long periods with short rest breaks, for short periods with long rest breaks, with bright illumination, with low lighting, with lights turned almost off, with bonuses, without bonuses, and so on. Strangely, it didn't matter what the experimenters did: Production always seemed to increase.

More recent research has shown that this so-called **Hawthorne effect** is not always apparent or very significant (Chiesa & Hobbs, 2008). Nevertheless, the possibility that the outcome of an experiment may be affected by the fact that subjects know they are subjects still exists and must be guarded against. Participants are often anxious to please investigators; consequently, their responses may sometimes be misleading. To guard against this possibility, subjects are often not told whether or not they are members of an experimental group (*a single-blind procedure*).

Sampling Bias

One of the most common weaknesses of many experiments has to do with inappropriate or biased sampling. There are two crucial **criteria** that should be met when selecting members of experimental and control groups. First, the subjects must represent the group to which the experimenters wish to **generalize**. Second, the experimental and control groups must be as similar as possible on all relevant variables at the beginning of the experiment.

If the experimental group is significantly different from other groups, then the experiment will not provide information that can be generalized to other groups. Consider, for example, an experiment designed to compare the effectiveness of two teaching methods. If the experimenter intends to determine the relative effectiveness of these methods for all students in a given school system, it is important that experimental and control groups be as similar as possible to all students in the system in terms of intelligence, achievement, motivation, and other relevant variables. If subjects are selected from a school where students have higher intelligence test scores, the results of the experiment might not be valid for other students.

No matter how large the sample, if its characteristics are very different from those of the population, resulting conclusions will not have general validity. This soccer crowd, for example, might be very different from the mass of humanity who stayed home.

Problems regarding the representativeness of samples are most evident in large-scale surveys where the intention is to generalize to a major segment of the population. Political forecasts would be highly unreliable if only one segment of the population were sampled. For example, it would be difficult to predict how a nation would vote if forecasts were based only on surveys of academic populations or truck drivers.

To ensure that the results of such a survey apply to the entire population, investigators might select their sample so that it matches the population in terms of as many relevant characteristics as possible—a process called **stratified sampling**. If 52 percent of the population is female, close to 52 percent of the sample should also be female; if 23 percent have college degrees, then about 23 percent of the sample should also have college degrees. Similarly, in an ideal situation, the sample must match the general population in terms of age, religion, socioeconomic background, geographical location, and so on.

Another way of ensuring that experimental groups are representative of a larger population is to use **random sampling**. Random sampling requires that all members of the population have an equal chance of being selected. Given this condition, if enough representatives are drawn from the population, there is a high probability that the experimental group's characteristics will be very similar to those of the entire population. In other words, if 23 percent of a population is male and 77 percent female, a large enough sample drawn randomly from this population should be close to 23 percent male and 77 percent female. By the same token, the sample should resemble the entire population in terms of average intelligence, racial background, and other variables that might be important. In most cases, experimenters can make sure that this is the case by comparing the sample to the population on important variables.

Unfortunately, random and stratified sampling are only possible when investigators have access to the entire population to which they want to generalize. In many cases, circumstances dictate that samples will be *samples of convenience*. For example, those who do research on aging seldom have access to a random or stratified sample of the entire aging population, but are instead limited to groups such as those made up of members of clubs, religious groups, or residents of care facilities. Generalizing from these *convenient* samples requires caution. The need for comparability of experimental and control groups, and for representativeness of samples, is obvious in the toothpaste experiment. Suppose, for example, that the control group averaged 30 percent more cavities than the experimental group at the beginning of the experiment: Regardless of the effects of the new toothpaste, it would be reasonable to expect that the rate at which the children developed cavities would be higher among those who initially had more cavities. Similarly, if all children in the study were selected from a single area where dental care was exceptionally good—or exceptionally bad—the sample might be totally unrepresentative of a more general population. Deliberately or accidentally biased sampling can easily ensure that the results of an experiment will be totally invalid.

Other Problems of Psychological Research

Among other problems that face researchers, as well as those of us who look for truth among their conclusions, are those of honesty, memory distortion, and inadvertent conceptual distortion. Studies of drug use, for example, have often provided inconclusive and contradictory results, probably largely because admitting to drug use is like confessing to a crime. In studies such as this, the dishonesty of participants is a crucial factor that can do much to invalidate the results of research.

A related problem is that of having to rely on imperfect memories. Child development psychologists have had some difficulty establishing conclusively the average age at which children learn to walk, a problem related directly to the memories of their mothers. Unless the researcher is present whenever significant developmental events occur, or unless these events can be objectively recorded, reliance must be placed on the participant's memory or on that of someone else who observed the event in question. In either case, it is often wise to question the accuracy of results that are not obtained through direct observation.

And, as we saw earlier, another pitfall in psychological research relates to the correlation fallacy—the belief that if two variables are correlated, one must cause the other. There are at least two reasons why correlation cannot be used to justify cause-and-effect conclusions. One is that a correlation between A and B does not, by itself, provide evidence of the *direction* of causality. That is, even if the correlation reflected causation, we might not know whether A causes B or B causes A.

The second reason why correlation is not proof of causation is that a correlation between A and B does not answer the question of whether the reason for the correlation might be a third variable, C. For example, an investigation of people ranging in age from 2 to 22 might reveal a very high correlation between finger length and the ability to understand concepts in advanced calculus. That, of course, would not prove that having long fingers helps people understand calculus—nor that understanding calculus leads to an increase in finger length. Rather, it likely reflects the effects of a third group of variables related to changes that occur over time.

Research Ethics

The use of both human and animal participants in psychological research is an emotional and controversial topic. It raises some important ethical issues relating to how participants in experiments are treated. Many of the procedures used in earlier investigations—where, for example, animals were euthanized or human participants were deceived, coerced, or otherwise made to do things they would not ordinarily do—are no longer acceptable. Some believe that there are no circumstances under which animals should be harmed in the interests of science (Knight, 2008); others argue that when the potential benefits are sufficiently important, animals might need to be sacrificed (Brody, 2001).

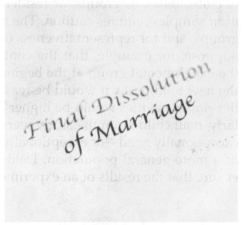

Because 100 percent of divorces begin with marriage, there is a high correlation between number of weddings and number of divorces. But it would be meaningless to say that weddings are an important cause of divorces—or vice versa. Such reasoning illustrates the correlation fallacy.

The American Psychological Association provides guidelines for the ethical treatment of animal and human participants in research (*Ethical principles . . .* , 2011; and *Guidelines for Ethical Conduct . . .* , 2011). With respect to animal research, these guidelines stipulate that the research must have a clear, scientific purpose with positive potential benefits, that animal care must comply with strict regulations, and that every effort must be made to minimize animal pain and suffering.

With respect to research with human participants, guidelines require that the ethical acceptability of the research be reviewed; that all participants be made fully aware of all aspects of the research that might affect their willingness to participate; that they be completely free *not* to take part; and that participants be protected from physical and mental danger or discomfort.

Avoiding the Pitfalls

Have you by now developed an image of psychological researchers stumbling blindly among the numerous pitfalls of scientific research, never knowing for certain what to believe? That image would be misleading: Well-trained researchers are usually acutely aware of potential pitfalls; they can guard against falling into traps that might deceive the less wary.

1.6 Philosophical Issues and Psychological Controversy

The search for explanations of human behavior is based on a number of **assumptions** that direct that search and that—in a very real sense—validate many of the beliefs resulting from the search. The most basic of these assumptions are philosophical in origin, have been subjects of controversy and debate that continue unresolved to this date, and cannot be tested or examined completely objectively. If they could, they would not be assumptions (which are, by definition, unproven) but would be laws or principles (beliefs more firmly grounded in objective observation).

Most important among these assumptions are those that deal with human nature and with the causes of behavior: Is behavior a function of free will, or is it determined by other forces? Are mind and body separate? Is behavior determined by underlying characteristics in the person (termed dispositions), or is it determined by the immediate situation?

Depending on the assumptions they make, some psychologists believe we exercise deliberate control over our behavior; others are primarily **deterministic**: They believe behavior is an inevitable consequence of identifiable causes. Some look for the causes of behavior among genetic factors; others attribute a greater role to environmental forces. And the end result of the different assumptions psychologists make is that psychology is characterized by a number of different theories.

Psychology is a science that is sometimes gray rather than always black or white. Not all the pieces of the puzzle have yet been discovered or assembled.

1.7 Psychology's Relevance

What do you want out of psychology? The question is not as simple as it might be in other fields. A bookkeeping course might teach you how to keep books; a course in dentistry, how to be a dentist; and a course in mathematics, how to do mathematics. But a course in psychology is not likely to teach you how to do psychology. Besides, what is involved in "doing" psychology is not at all clear. Clinical psychologists "do" psychology in one sense: They attempt to apply what they have learned or discovered to alleviate mental and emotional problems. Experimental psychologists also "do" psychology, but the thing they do is clearly different from the things done by clinical psychologists. A college professor "does" psychology; but that too is different. In any case, you will probably not do any of these things as a result of this single course.

What then? Is psychology going to reveal the grand mysteries of the human psyche, expanding your understanding of yourself and of humanity? Will it enable you to function better as a human being, directing you along paths of growth and happiness?

To some extent, yes. After all, psychology has enormous applications in a tremendous variety of areas. Psychology's insights can make you a better parent, a more memorable teacher, a startlingly effective salesperson. Psychology can help you understand why you feel and act as you do, how your friends and family affect your behavior, and why you are moved to do certain things and do your utmost to avoid others. Advances in our knowledge of brain structures and functions suggest new approaches for treating addictions; increased understanding of how our sensory systems work has led to more effective treatments for sensory problems. Psychology gives us insights into how memory can be improved and maintained as we age. And it suggests highly effective ways of dealing with mental and emotional disorders.

1.8 This Book

Table 1.3 An Outline of This Text as a Definition of Psychology

Chapter Outline	Definition
1. The Science of Psychology	Psychology is the science that studies behavior and mental processes.
2. The Brain and Biology	Looks at the physiological basis of behavior and at our different states of consciousness.
3. Sensation, Perception, and Consciousness	Examines our sensory and perceptual systems, which are our sources of contact with the external and internal world.
4. How We Learn	Asks how we learn.
5. Memory and Emotional Intelligence	Investigates how we remember and studies the intellectual processes that our intelligence makes possible.
6. Developmental Stages and Theories	Is concerned with the significant changes that transpire between birth and death, and with the forces that drive these changes.

Chapter Outline	Definition
7. Personality	Examines human individuality and tries to understand how each of us is different and unique—and at the same time, how we share certain characteristics that define our humanity.
8. Psychological Disorders, Problems: Struggles	Tries to understand mental and emotional disorders.
9. Therapy	Finding ways to help people.
10. Social Psychology and Beyond	Looks at relationships among individuals and at the enormous power of social influences. . . and beyond social.

It is important to note that even though our consideration of human behavior and thinking—the subject of psychology—is divided into separate topics, in the end, it is less the individual topics in which we are interested than the whole: We should not lose sight of the fact that the puzzle psychology is gnawing at involves the entire person.

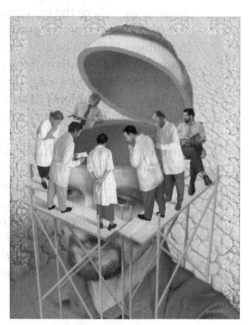

It's a complex puzzle psychology is working on. These researchers are mistaken if they think it involves only the head.

Main Points

1. **What Is Psychology?** Psychology is concerned with all that affects human behavior, thought, and emotion: It is the science that studies behavior and mental processes. About half of all psychologists are *clinical psychologists*; other divisions include *counseling, industrial/ organizational, school, educational, developmental, experimental*, and many others.

2. **The Beginnings of Psychology:** Psychology had its origins in Greek philosophy (*psyche* is Greek for "soul"; *logos*, for "study"), was profoundly affected by medical discoveries, and borrowed its scientific methodology from Newtonian physics. Its more recent origins date to Wundt's psychological laboratory (1879) and his followers who established the *structuralist* school, William James's *functionalism*, Watson and Skinner's *behaviorism*, Freud's *psychodynamics*, and the influences of *cognitivism* and *humanism*.

3. **Principles of Science:** Science is an attitude that insists on precision and replicability, as well as a collection of methods to maximize the validity of conclusions. The five steps of the scientific method are (1) ask the question; (2) develop a hypothesis; (3) collect observations; (4) test the hypothesis; and (5) reach and share a conclusion.

4. **Sources of Psychological Information:** Observation is the source of knowledge in all sciences. Psychological investigations can be *descriptive* (describe characteristics of individuals or groups) or more *experimental*. Longitudinal studies

look at the same individual(s) at different times; cross-sectional studies look at different groups at the same point in time. Descriptive research can be based on observation that occurs in natural surroundings (*naturalistic*) or in more contrived environments such as laboratories. It can be based on observations of a single individual or unit (a *case study*) or of larger groups (a *survey*). Correlational studies try to discover relationships between variables but cannot prove causation (the *correlation fallacy*). Experiments allow investigators to control *independent* variables to determine their effects on *dependent* variables. In an *ex post facto study*, investigators don't assign participants to groups and don't manipulate independent variables.

5.   **Cautions in Interpreting Psychological Research:** Single-blind and double-blind procedures (where the examiners, the subjects, or both don't know who members of the experimental group are) are used to safeguard against experimenter and subject bias. To be able to generalize findings, the experimenter must study a sample representative of the population to which generalizations are to be made (often *randomly* selected for that reason). Psychological research can also be affected by problems of subject dishonesty, memory distortions, conceptual confusion, and the tendency to assume that if two events are correlated, one must have caused the other.

6.   **Philosophical Issues and Psychological Controversy:** Psychological research is based on a number of sometimes controversial assumptions (nature vs. nurture, determinism vs. free will). The end result is a number of different theories and beliefs about human behavior.

7.   **Psychology's Relevance:** Psychology's primary goals are to explain human behavior, to make increasingly accurate predictions, and to achieve a greater degree of effectiveness in alleviating human distress and in enhancing the joyful aspects of living. Not all the pieces of the puzzle have yet been discovered or assembled.

Thoughts and Suggestions

1.   Of all the fields or specialties of psychology mentioned, which one would you pick for yourself to inter. Why?

2.   Which of the following age groups would you most like to work with Newborns; Infants; Middle School Children; Teenagers; Young Adults; Middle Age; Old Age? Why?

3.   Here are some concepts and themes we will be looking at exploring throughout this book and the class that goes with it:

All truth is God's truth. But not everything that people believe is truth is truth.

Life is made up of three things: (a) The choices you make; (b) The words you speak; (c) The people you associate with.

It's important to know the truth about myself. Am I crazy? Or am I in a crazy situation?

Study Terms

assumptions

average

behaviorism

case studies

clinical psychologists

cognitivism

control groups

correlation

correlation fallacy

correlational research

counseling psychologists

criteria

cross-sectional studies

dependent variables

descriptive research

deterministic

developmental psychologists

double-blind procedures

educational psychologists

evolutionary psychology

ex post facto study

experiment

experimental group

experimental psychologists

experimenter bias

functionalism

generalize

Hawthorne effect

humanism

humanistic psychology

hypotheses

independent variables

industrial/organizational psychologists

introspection

longitudinal studies

naturalistic observation

neuroscience

nonnaturalistic observation

philosophy

population

psychiatrists

psychoanalysis

psychodynamic

psychology

random sampling

sample

school psychologists

science

scientific method

significant

single-blind procedure

statistical procedures

stimulus

stratified sampling

structuralism

surveys

theories

third force psychology

variables

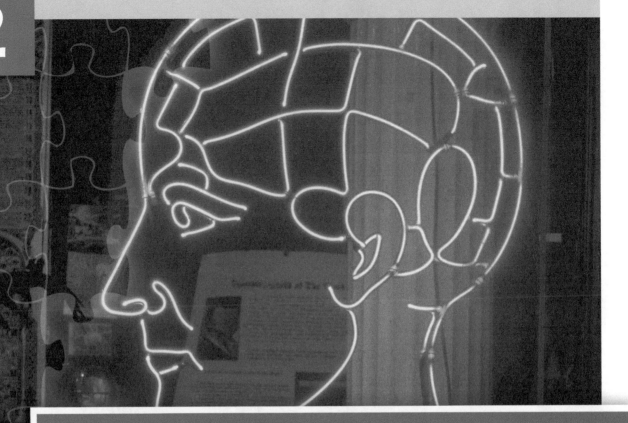

Biopsychology and the Brain

Focus Questions

By the end of the chapter, you should be able to answer the following questions:

- What are the main components and functions of nerve cells?
- How do the most important neurotransmitters relate to behavior?
- How is the human nervous system organized?
- What are the key brain structures and their functions?

Chapter Outline

. . . .

Inspirational Words

*So God **created** man in his own image, in the image of God **created** he him; male and female **created** he them. Gen. 1:27*

*And God saw everything that he had **made**, and, behold, it was very good. Gen. 1:31*

What is man, that thou art mindful of him? and the son of man, that thou visitest him? For thou hast made him a little lower than the angels, and hast crowned him with glory and honour. Psalms 8: 4,5

*For thou hast possessed my reins: thou hast covered me in my mother's womb. I will praise thee; for I am fearfully and **wonderfully made**: marvellous are thy works; and that my soul knoweth right well. Psalm 139: 13,14*

*Thus saith God the LORD, he that **created** the heavens, and stretched them out; he that spread forth the earth, and that which cometh out of it; he that giveth breath unto the people upon it, and spirit to them that walk therein. Isaiah 42:5*

*For we are his workmanship, **created** in Christ Jesus unto good works, which God hath before ordained that we should walk in them. Ephesians 2:10*

*Put on the new man, which after God is **created** in righteousness and true holiness. Ephesians 4:24*

*For by him were all things **created**, that are in heaven, and that are in earth, visible and invisible, whether they be thrones, or dominions, or principalities, or powers: all things were **created** by him, and for him. Collosians 1:16*

*And have put on the new man, which is renewed in knowledge after the image of him that **created** him. Collosians 3:10*

2.1 The Neuron – Building Block of the Nervous System

In a simple sense, our nervous system is the electrical and chemical communication system within our bodies. It is because of our nervous system that our right hand knows what our left hand is doing, that our legs alternate rather than compete when we walk, that we are sensitive to our environments. In fact, it is because of our nervous system that we can even think about such matters; hence its tremendous importance in psychology.

The human nervous system is a *communication* system; its function is to transmit messages (impulses). Many of the messages it transmits go from sensory **receptors** (such as the skin, eyes, nose, tongue, ears, muscles, joints, and tendons) to the command center (the brain). Impulses also go from the brain to what are termed **effectors** (such as muscular and glandular systems).

The cells that make up the nervous system, and whose specialized function is to transmit impulses, are called **neurons** (or *nerve cells*). Estimates vary widely, but scientists believe there are approximately 86 billion neurons in the human brain alone, with the bulk of these—some 69 billion—being in the part of the brain called the *cerebellum* (Azevedo et al., 2009). The spinal cord contains at least a billion more, and several billion more are concentrated in sensory receptors and in muscular and glandular *effector* systems. Other neurons are *connectors*: They serve as links between receptor and effector systems (Figure 2.1). Most of the connectors are located in the brain.

Like all other living cells, neurons consist of a nucleus and surrounding matter. This matter is made up of the cell body, **axons**, and **dendrites**. Neurons are surrounded by a protective coating, called a **myelin sheath** (made up of **glial cells**). The axon is the elongated part of a neuron: It may be microscopically short or as long as 2 or 3 feet, as is the case for some neurons located in the spinal cord. Dendrites are hairlike extensions emanating from the cell body of the neuron. The space between the ends of one cell's axon and another cell's dendrites is a **synapse**. Enlargements found at the terminating ends of some axons are **synaptic knobs**. Bundles of neurons make up **nerves**. The typical configuration of a neuron is shown in Figure 2.2.

Neural Transmission

The transmission of impulses from neuron to neuron involves both electrical and chemical activity. Think of each neuron as a tiny battery that can generate an electrical impulse. Electricity is the flow of negatively charged particles (called *electrons*) toward a positively charged pole. In the neuron, electrical impulses operate in exactly the same way. A neuron at rest (*resting potential*) is like a charged battery with the switch off. Stimulation brings about a series of chemical changes that effectively open the switch, causing a flow of charged particles called an **action potential**. And about 2 milliseconds later, the neuron again regains its resting potential. But for a brief period, termed a **refractory period**, it is essentially discharged and so no longer has the potential to generate an electrical impulse (Figure 2.3).

Note that the electrical impulse involves the entire neuron and is equally strong throughout the neuron: hence the expression "all-or-none" firing. What this means is that an electrical signal that is generated in your toe when you stub it will not have dwindled away to

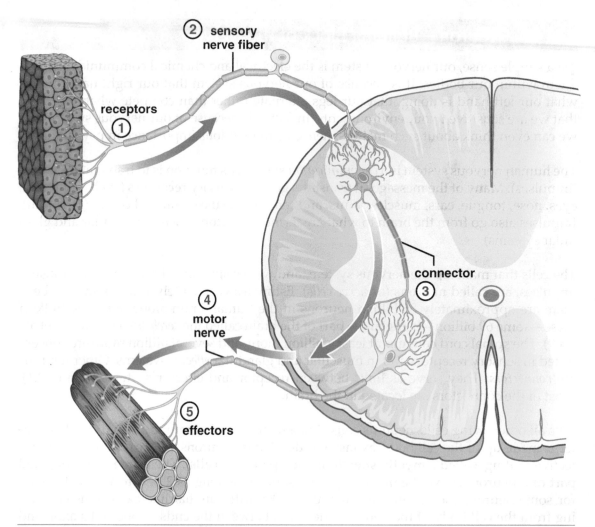

Figure 2.1

Schematic conception of the components of the sensorimotor arc. *Receptors* (1) in eyes, tactile organs, nose, ears, taste buds, and kinesthetic senses send signals (2) to *connectors* (3) in the spinal cord, brain, and other neural pathways. Signals are then sent (4) to *effectors* (5) in muscles and glands.

nothing before reaching your brain. Unfortunately, however, the "pain" sensation will not reach your brain immediately. Although electricity travels at the speed of light (186,300 feet per second), the thinnest axons transmit impulses at only around 3 feet per second. Larger axons might transmit at speeds up to 10 feet per second (Kalat, 2009).

So, less than a second after you stub your toe, you will know that you did so, unless something has happened to disrupt the flow of electrical impulses in relevant nerves. That is basically what happens when your dentist uses *novocaine* to "freeze" you. Nothing is actually frozen, but the effect of the novocaine is to block the flow of electrical impulses between neurons. No matter how desperately the receptors in your tooth yell, "It hurts," the message simply does not get to your brain.

Neurotransmission is made possible by certain chemicals, called **neurotransmitters**, which are released by neurons, changing the electrical potential of cells and thus leading to neural

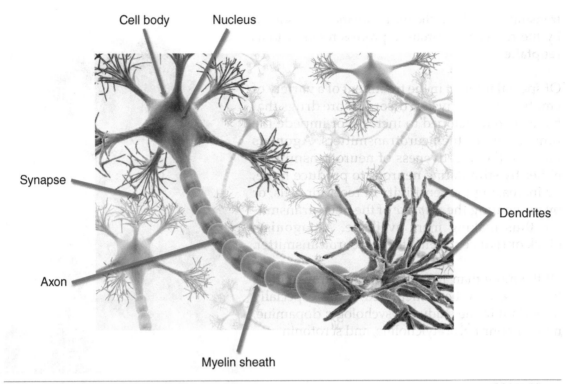

Figure 2.2

Electron micrograph photo of human nerve cells magnified many times with their principal parts identified. Neural transmission typically proceeds from the cell body, down the axon, across the synapse, and to the dendrites and cell bodies of adjacent cells. Synaptic knobs at the terminating ends of some axons facilitate transmission of electrochemical impulses.

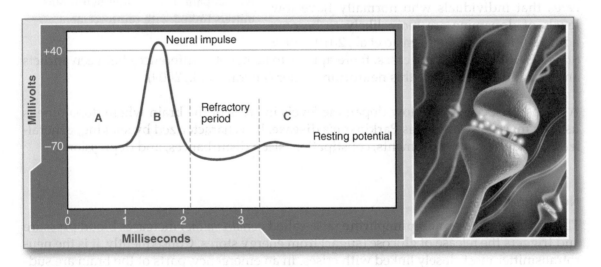

Figure 2.3

Representation of a neural impulse. At point A, there exists a state of readiness (*resting potential*). At B, a stimulus leads to an electrical impulse (*action potential*), which is followed immediately by a *refractory period* during which the cell cannot fire. A few milliseconds later, the cell is restored to its resting potential (charged) state. As shown in the photo of the synapse, certain chemical substances, neurotransmitters such as dopamine and serotonin, play an important part in the "opening" of neural membranes to allow the passage of the electrical impulse.

transmission. These chemicals are then reabsorbed by the releasing neuron—a process referred to as **reuptake**.

Of special interest in the treatment of a variety of emotional and physical disorders are drugs that have been developed to increase or impede the functioning of the neurotransmitters. **Agonists** increase the effectiveness of neurotransmitters, either by stimulating neurons to produce more, by increasing the sensitivity of receptor cells, or by preventing the *reuptake* of the neurotransmitter, thus making more available. **Antagonists** block or reduce the effects of a neurotransmitter.

Of the more than 100 different neurotransmitters that have now been identified, 4 are especially important in the study of psychology: dopamine, norepinephrine, acetylcholine, and serotonin.

Almost all abused drugs are effective because they increase the release of dopamine in the brain or prevent its reuptake. Dopamine function is a key to reinforcement and pleasure. Chocolate too, as this lad well knows, is associated with dopamine and other neurotransmitters linked with reinforcement.

Dopamine

Dopamine is key to the functioning of neurons associated with pleasure and reinforcement. In fact, almost all abused drugs are effective precisely because they increase dopamine activity in certain areas of the brain. Some research indicates that individuals who normally have low levels of dopamine are more likely to become addicted (for example, Asensio et al., 2010; Self & Staley, 2010). And in some cases, there appear to be genetic differences between addicts and nonaddicts related to this neurotransmitter (Levran et al., 2009).

A disease associated with low dopamine levels in areas of the brain where dopamine is usually most concentrated is **Parkinson's disease**. It is characterized by shaking, generalized weakness, slow movements, constipation, sleep disturbances, and depression.

Norepinephrine

The neurotransmitter **norepinephrine** (also called *noradrenaline*) increases blood pressure and triggers the release of glucose (sugar) from energy stores. Consequently, it is the neurotransmitter most closely linked with crises. In an emergency, parts of the brain are suddenly flooded with norepinephrine, a signal that prepares the body to respond, perhaps by fleeing, perhaps by fighting.

Research indicates that norepinephrine levels may be implicated in some instances of **attention-deficit hyperactivity disorder (ADHD)** (Bhaduri, Sarkar, Sionha, Chattopadhyay,

& Mukhopadhyay, 2010). One of the effects of drugs (such as Ritalin) commonly used to treat ADHD is that they act as norepinephrine/dopamine reuptake inhibitors, increasing available levels of norepinephrine and dopamine (Cohen-Yavin et al., 2009). This improves the person's ability to concentrate and to think clearly about what is being focused on, thus alleviating one of the main symptoms of ADHD.

Some manifestations of depression are also linked with norepinephrine. Many common antidepressant drugs (for example, *tricyclic antidepressants* such as Elavil, Norpramin, and Pamelor) are agonists that increase norepinephrine levels by blocking its reuptake (Craig, 2006). One of the effects of increased norepinephrine levels is a speeding up of neural activity, which counters the "slowing down" sensation that often accompanies depression. Interestingly, an overabundance of norepinephrine has been linked with *mania*, the opposite mood to depression (Narayan & Haddad, 2011).

Acetylcholine

Acetylcholine is a neurotransmitter involved in the largely unconscious functioning of the *autonomic* nervous system (concerned with functions such as heart and respiration rate). It is also importantly involved in conscious activity such as muscle movement, as well as in arousal, reinforcement, learning, and memory (Arnulf & Leu-Semenescu, 2009). It can also serve to increase the reactivity of neurons or to inhibit their responsiveness. Drugs that stimulate the acetylcholine system or that block its functioning have a variety of medical uses, including the treatment of Alzheimer's disease (Zhang et al., 2010).

Serotonin

Serotonin is involved in neural transmission in much of the brain, especially in areas having to do with emotion. Its other functions include regulating sleep, appetite, and cognitive activity related to learning and memory (Pothakos et al., 2010). Depressed levels of serotonin have been linked with depression, aggression, and even violence. Accordingly, many antidepressants and anti-anxiety drugs are *agonists* that affect serotonin levels by acting as reuptake inhibitors (Arnone, Horder, Cowen, & Harmer, 2009). Similar drugs are also sometimes used to control impulsive, violent behavior (Butler et al., 2010).

Serotonin is present in some plants and seeds, including nuts from some walnut and hickory species, many of which are toxic or at least cause pain. In fact, pain is one of the side effects of large amounts of serotonin in the blood. Interestingly, wasp, toad, and stingray venoms contain serotonin, which serves to increase the painfulness of their stings (Fevzi, Ergin, Rivers, & Gençer, 2006; Ling, Clark, Erikson, & Trestrail, 2001).

2.2 Organization of the Nervous System

The **central nervous system** consists of the brain and **spinal cord**. It is via the spinal cord that most of the major neural pathways conduct impulses between brain centers and various glandular, muscular, and sensory systems.

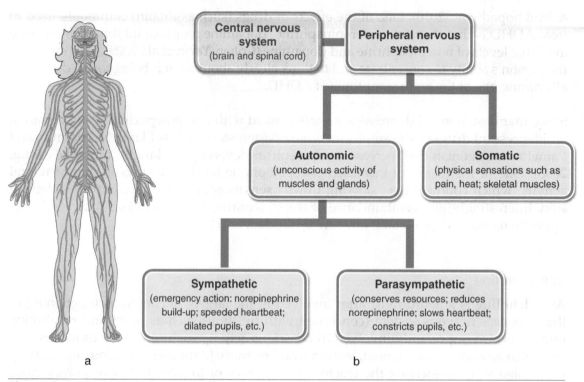

Figure 2.4

The human nervous system. Part **a** depicts the two major divisions of the nervous system: the central nervous system (bright orange) and the peripheral nervous system (darker). The organization and functions of each are described in **b**.

The system of neural networks that fan out from the central nervous system into various parts of the body is the **peripheral nervous system** (Figure 2.4). The peripheral system is linked to all sensory organs and to the muscles and glands; it is also involved in physiological activities such as respiration, heart action, sweating, and crying.

The peripheral nervous system has two divisions. The **somatic system** transmits impulses relating to sensations of heat, cold, pain, and pressure to the central nervous system. It also transmits impulses in the opposite direction, from the central nervous system to muscles involved in voluntary movement.

The **autonomic nervous system**, the other part of the peripheral nervous system, is directly involved in the action of muscles and glands that are automatic and involuntary. It includes the **sympathetic nervous system**, which is responsible for mobilizing the body's resources, particularly in emergency situations. It is your sympathetic nervous system that causes **adrenaline** to be pumped into your system. The result is that your heart beats faster, blood rushes through your blood vessels, and you might tremble in anxiety, blush in shame, or respond with any of the other physiological changes that accompany intense emotion.

Most of us have little control over our physiological reactions, a fact that led to the invention of the common lie-detector. This instrument is capable of detecting changes that result from activity of the autonomic nervous system. If you become anxious when you lie (as most people do), your sympathetic nervous system reacts accordingly. As a result, your palms perspire, your breathing changes, and your heart rate increases.

But your heart rate does not accelerate indefinitely, nor do you tremble more and more violently. The **parasympathetic nervous system**, the other part of the autonomic nervous system, slows your heart rate, steadies your trembling, increases your control over bowel and bladder functioning, and in other ways opposes some of the functions of the sympathetic nervous system. It is as though the parasympathetic nervous system serves to conserve bodily resources.

When we're anxious, as might happen when we lie to a police investigator, our sympathetic nervous system kicks up our heart rate, our palms perspire, and our breathing changes. We can't control these reactions, and the "lie-detector"—a polygraph that measures these changes—reveals our lie.

The Endocrine System

The **endocrine system** is separate from the central nervous system, but it influences most of the organs, cells, and functions of the body. It includes glands that secrete **hormones** directly into the bloodstream and are therefore known as the ductless glands. Chief among them are the **pituitary gland**, which is frequently termed the "master" gland because of its role in regulating activity of other glands. The ductless glands also include the **adrenal glands** and the **gonads**.

The adrenal glands, which sit on top of the kidneys, are mainly responsible for releasing the hormone *adrenaline* in response to stress. The gonads include the testes, which produce male sex hormones such as *testosterone*, and the ovaries, which produce *estrogen* in females. These hormones are involved in sexual maturation and in sexual motivation.

2.3 The Brain

The most important part of our central nervous systems is our brain, which is reputedly the single most complex structure in the entire known universe. We have known for some time that this unimpressive-looking lump of grayish tissue is at the very center of our ability to learn, to feel, to think—that it determines and defines our very essence. But we did not always know this. In fact, the ancient Egyptians considered the brain so unimportant that they did not bother to preserve it in their mummies, removing it instead through the left nostril (Blakemore, 1977). It is only recently that the secrets of the structures and functions of our brains have yielded new pieces for our puzzle.

Studying Brain Functions

September 13, 1848, was an unlucky day for Phineas Gage, a railway worker on a rail line in Vermont. On that day, a tamping rod measuring 3 feet, 7 inches, shot out of a blasting hole and went through the left side of his face, through his brain, and out the top of his head! The blow hurled him to the ground, but he quickly picked himself up, made his way to a cart, and went home.

Phineas's physical recovery was rapid and apparently complete. But some reports claim that he was never again the same man, that he became moody and selfish and prone to outbursts of violent temper. His physician, Dr. John Harlow, and a Harvard surgeon named Dr. Henry Bigelow concluded that the part of his brain that was affected had to do with emotions and personality (Macmillan, 2000). In fact, brain injuries provided one of the first ways of trying to discover how the brain works.

Unfortunately, as Macmillan (2008) points out, no one ever examined Phineas Gage's brain directly, so there really is no certainty about what structures were involved in his injury. Also, there seems to have been some exaggeration and contradiction in reports of his case: There is a strong likelihood that he did not change as dramatically as has sometimes been reported. And the fact that he later began to suffer seizures and eventually died as a result might indicate that his recovery was far from complete.

Brain Ablations

The problem with studying the brain using injuries such as those caused by tumors or by accidents is that these injuries don't usually have very specific effects. They often affect large parts of the brain, and investigators certainly cannot control who will have an accident—which makes for poor research.

Another approach is to deliberately cut out small portions of the brain and then see what the effects might be. Understandably, this kind of research finds very few volunteers with healthy brains. Except where surgical procedures are required in cases of brain damage, epilepsy, tumors, or for other medical reasons, most of this research has been done with animals.

A pioneer researcher in this area, Karl Lashley (1924), taught some rats how to run through a maze. He was convinced that different memories leave a trace in a tiny part of the brain, and he thought that if he cut out just the right part, the rat would no longer remember how to get through the maze. But Lashley never did find this memory trace (called an *engram*). It did not seem to matter what part of the brain he excised, or how much; the rat continued to run through the maze—although sometimes much more slowly. We now know that the kind of memories Lashley was studying were likely stored in parts of the brain he did not excise.

Brain Stimulation

Another way of studying the brain is to stimulate different parts of it with electrodes or with chemicals. For example, Olds (1956) implanted electrodes in the brains of rats and accidentally discovered that stimulating part of the *hypothalamus*—now labeled the "pleasure center"—seemed to be extremely pleasurable for the rat. When the electrodes were connected to a lever so that rats could stimulate their own brain, many would pass up food to do so. One rat stimulated himself more than 2,000 times an hour for 24 consecutive hours!

Stimulating the brain with electrodes is an invasive and difficult undertaking; chemical stimulation is much simpler. It is possible to administer different drugs (chemicals) and to observe their effects on the participant's behavior and their effects on the brain. For example, chemical stimulation of the brain reveals that the neurotransmitter dopamine is involved in neural activity associated with pleasure. Dopamine, as we saw, is a naturally occurring neurotransmitter. Normally, when it is released as a result of neural stimulation, it is quickly recaptured by affected neurons (Kalat, 2009). But certain drugs such as amphetamines and cocaine act as *agonists* by preventing the immediate reuptake of the dopamine so that *dopaminergic neurons* (those that use dopamine for neural transmission) stay active longer.

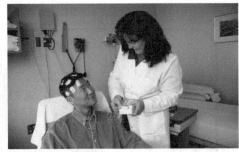

Electroencephalograms (EEGs) provide a nonintrusive way of studying brain functioning.

Because dopamine is associated with neural activity in one of the brain's "pleasure" centers, the ultimate effect of cocaine is intensely pleasurable (Morcom et al., 2010).

The prolonged use of agonists such as cocaine, however, leads the brain to synthesize less dopamine naturally as it adapts to the drug. As a result, the chronic drug user often experiences depression and other negative moods rather than pleasure when the effects of the drug begin to wear off (termed *withdrawal*). Also, dopamine receptor activity decreases with repeated drug use (termed drug *tolerance*) so that ever-increasing amounts of the drug are required (Slomski, 2006). Tolerance and the presence of withdrawal symptoms are important indicators of addiction. (Drug use is treated in more detail in Chapter 9.)

Electrical stimulation of the brain's pleasure centers, as well as natural reinforcers such as food, water, and sex and substances such as nicotine and alcohol, all lead to the release of dopamine (Lajtha & Sershen, 2010). And all of these substances and activities are potentially addictive.

Brain Imaging

The effect of chemicals on the brain is usually detected by means of one or more of the various sophisticated brain-imaging techniques researchers now have at their disposal. These include the **electroencephalogram (EEG)**, which provides recordings of brain electrical activity; **positron emission tomography (PET)**, which records changes in blood flow by responding to radioactive particles injected in the bloodstream; **functional magnetic resonance imaging (fMRI)**, which measures changes in magnetic fields related to blood oxygen level; and **magnetoencephalography (MEG)**, which detects at the scalp incredibly small changes in magnetic fields associated with neural activity. Note that these brain-imaging methods are used not only to study the effects of drugs, but also to look at brain activity during specific tasks. They are highly useful in studies of the brain's role in intellectual activities.

Structures of the Brain

Physical examination of the brain reveals a grayish mass inside the skull (Figure 2.5). Some of its various structures are identifiable through this type of examination. But determining the functions of these structures is not so simple: The structures themselves present few clues to their functions.

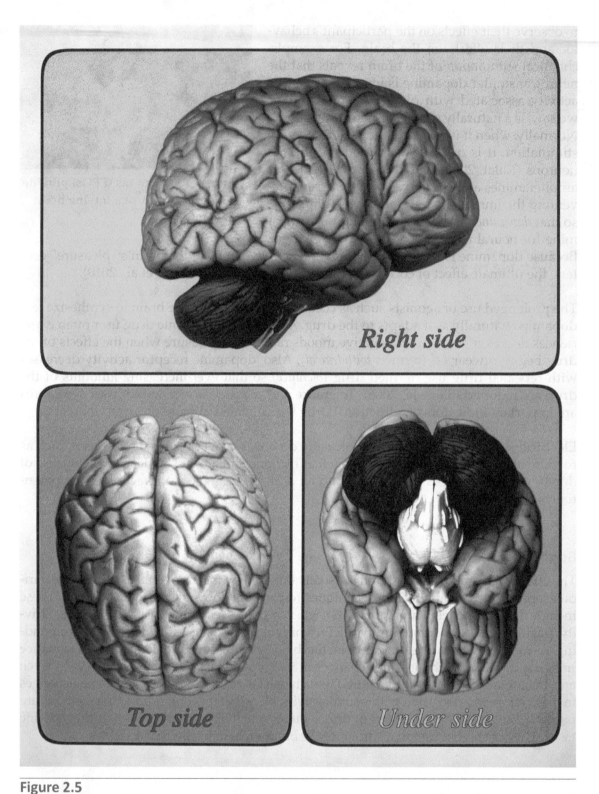

Figure 2.5

Top, right side, and under side view of the human brain. The outer covering of the brain is called the cerebral cortex.

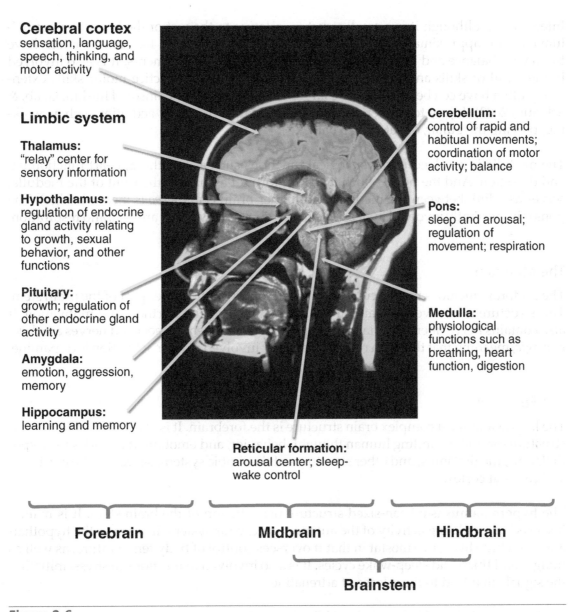

Cerebral cortex
sensation, language, speech, thinking, and motor activity

Limbic system

Thalamus:
"relay" center for sensory information

Hypothalamus:
regulation of endocrine gland activity relating to growth, sexual behavior, and other functions

Pituitary:
growth; regulation of other endocrine gland activity

Amygdala:
emotion, aggression, memory

Hippocampus:
learning and memory

Cerebellum:
control of rapid and habitual movements; coordination of motor activity; balance

Pons:
sleep and arousal; regulation of movement; respiration

Medulla:
physiological functions such as breathing, heart function, digestion

Reticular formation:
arousal center; sleep-wake control

Forebrain   **Midbrain**   **Hindbrain**

Brainstem

Figure 2.6

A sagittal (bisected front to back) view of the human brain showing major structures and some of their principal functions.

Hindbrain

As shown in Figure 2.6, the human brain is normally divided into three basic parts: hindbrain, midbrain, and forebrain. These parts are thought to have evolved in that order, with the hindbrain being the oldest structure and the forebrain the most recent. Structures of the hindbrain and of the midbrain make up the **brain stem**—that part of the central nervous system that connects the spinal cord with higher brain structures.

The hindbrain is the lowest part of the brain in an upright person. It consists mainly of the **cerebellum** (the word means *small brain*), the **medulla**, and the **pons**.

Interestingly, although it is a small structure relative to the rest of the brain, the cerebellum contains approximately 80 percent of all the brain's neurons. Its main functions have to do with balance and timing and coordination of motor movements. It is also involved in the recall of skills and habits. Musicians and others who practice motor skills extensively often have cerebellums that are larger than average (Hutchinson, Hui-Lin, Gaab, & Schlaug, 2003). Injury to the cerebellum can dramatically impair activities such as walking, playing the guitar, or catching a ball.

The medulla is involved in physiological functions such as breathing, heart functioning, and digestion. And the pons, which takes the form of a bulge at the front of the medulla, serves as a link between the medulla and higher brain centers (*pons* means bridge). The pons is importantly involved in sleep, the regulation of movement, arousal, and respiration.

The Midbrain

The midbrain includes the **reticular formation**, found on the upper part of the brain stem. This structure is involved in maintaining *arousal*, or degree of alertness and motivation. It also contains nerve fibers associated with physical movement. Associated nerves are *dopaminergic*, meaning that the main neurotransmitter involved in their activation is dopamine.

The Forebrain

The largest and most complex brain structure is the forebrain. It is also the most important structure for understanding human thought, behavior, and emotion. It includes the hypothalamus, the thalamus, and other structures of the limbic system, as well as the cerebrum and cerebral cortex.

The **hypothalamus** is a bean-sized structure near the top of the brain stem. It is mainly involved in regulating activity of the autonomic nervous system. In a sense, the hypothalamus is a little like a thermostat in that it oversees control of body temperature, as well as hunger and thirst and sleep-wake cycles. It is also involved in reactions to stress, initiating the signals that lead to the release of adrenaline.

The **thalamus** is found between the midbrain and the cerebral cortex. Its main function is to act as a relay station for transmitting sensory signals to the cerebral cortex. All sensations except those having to do with smell go through the thalamus. It is also involved in regulating sleep and consciousness.

The **limbic system** includes parts of the hypothalamus and various other structures such as the **amygdala** and the **hippocampus**. Generally speaking, these are structures involved in emotions. The hippocampus also plays an important role in long-term memory. Alzheimer's disease and amnesia are both associated with damage to the hippocampus (American Academy of Neurology, 2009).

The largest and most complex of our brain structures is the **cerebrum**, which divides naturally into two halves, the *cerebral hemispheres*. Its outer covering, the **cerebral cortex**, is centrally involved in higher mental functioning. This covering is highly convoluted and deeply fissured, the fissures resulting in four natural divisions (*lobes*) in each of the hemispheres. As a result, there is a right and a left one of each of these lobes (Figure 2.7).

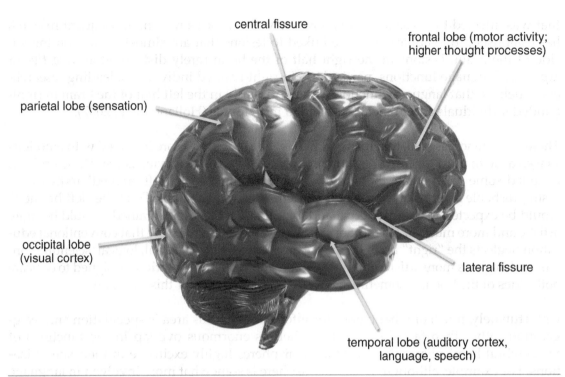

central fissure

frontal lobe (motor activity; higher thought processes)

parietal lobe (sensation)

occipital lobe (visual cortex)

lateral fissure

temporal lobe (auditory cortex, language, speech)

Figure 2.7

A right-side view of the cerebral cortex with the four right lobes labeled. Although each lobe is associated with the functions indicated, the lobes are highly integrated in terms of structure and function.

At the front of the cerebral cortex are the **frontal lobes**, which are involved in motor activity as well as in higher thought processes. On either side are the **temporal lobes**, involved in language, speech, and hearing. The *auditory* cortex is the part of the temporal lobe concerned with hearing.

Just behind the temporal lobes are the **parietal lobes**, implicated in physical movement and in sensation and physical orientation. At the very back are the **occipital lobes**, involved in vision. The part of the occipital lobes involved in vision is referred to as the *visual cortex*.

It is important to note that the main tasks and responsibilities of each of these cerebral divisions are not very simple or clear. Most functions are carried out by more than one part of the brain. Note, too, that areas of these four lobes that are not involved directly in motor activity or sensation are nevertheless involved in higher mental processes such as thinking, remembering, learning, and speaking. These are referred to as **association areas of the brain**.

The Hemispheres

Phineas Gage's accident provided some of the first crude evidence that the brain might be differentiated into separate functions. There was other historical evidence as well. Paul Broca, a neurologist, was sent a patient suffering from aphasia, a language disorder that we now know is linked to brain damage. The patient died within a few days and Broca performed an autopsy, discovering lesions in the left temporal lobe. The area of the lobe that was affected by these lesions is now known as Broca's region. Subsequent research has established that aphasia may be linked to lesions that are almost always on the left side of the brain. Lesions in the right half of the brain rarely disturb either *receptive* or *expressive* language functions, particularly in right-handed individuals, leading researchers to believe that language functions reside primarily in the left half of the brain in right-handed individuals and in most left-handed individuals (Holland et al., 2007).

There is evidence, as well, that the right hemisphere might be more involved with emotions as well as with music and art (Workman, Chilvers, Yeomans, & Taylor, 2006). These findings have led some to speculate that there are "right-brained" and "left-brained" individuals, distinguishable in terms of their major preoccupations and abilities. Thus, the "left-brained" would be expected to excel at verbal and logical tasks; the "right-brained" would be more artistic and more musical. This sort of speculation has led to the view that conventional education neglects the "right" brain because it emphasizes highly verbal, logical, scientific content and neglects more artistic and musical content. **Holistic education**, designed to educate both sides of the brain, is sometimes advocated as a remedy for this situation.

Unfortunately, much of what passes for information in this area is speculation and exaggeration rather than fact (Bruer, 2006). There is enormous overlap in the functions of the cerebral hemispheres. Nor are the hemispheres highly exclusive in their specializations. For example, although the left hemisphere is somewhat more involved in language production functions than is the right hemisphere, when the left hemisphere is injured, especially if the injury occurs early in life, the right hemisphere frequently takes over left hemisphere functions—a striking example of an important characteristic of the human brain: *plasticity*. Brain plasticity is also evident in patients who suffer motor and language problems after brain damage resulting from a stroke. These patients often recover much of their previous functioning as other parts of the brain take over (Lazar et al., 2010).

Recovery of lost brain function may also result from **neurogenesis**—the formation of new neurons. Although most neurogenesis occurs during the prenatal period, it also continues into adulthood (Reynolds & Weiss, 1992). The finding of adult neurogenesis contradicts a long-held belief to the contrary.

Thoughts and Suggestions

1. Your skin is the boundary of your personal space. Your personal kingdom if you will. You are the king or queen of this most important kingdom. Most important to you at least. As king or queen, you have the greatest power of how your kingdom functions. Your personal kingdom is your inner world that only you can experience. Your kingdom is quite vast and consists of rivers, highways, and power plants. You produce a vast array of chemicals, bioelectrical energy, and are responsible for the spiritual, emotional, and psychological atmosphere of this kingdom.

   You and I are responsible for relating to other kings and queens in the "outside world." The understanding of internal world and external reality can be a powerful paradigm in promoting health and understanding many of the individual and social problems and successes in this life on this planet.

In this chapter, we have primarily looked at the inner physical world of your kingdom. The lay of the land, or maps if you will, of your kingdom. Similar to other's maps, but vastly different in the overall make up and essence of your personal kingdom.

What are some things you do to improve the functioning of your physical kingdom?

2. If the left hemisphere is functions as the scientist part of you, and the right hemisphere is more of you the artist, are you more developed in the scientific or artistic functions? How so?
3. What do you consider to be the greatest strength and weakness of your kingdom right now. What are the top three things you could do to improve your kingdom?

Suggested readings from Hock, R. R. (1999). *Forty studies that changed psychology* (3rd ed.). Upper Saddle River, NJ: Prentice Hall. (ISBN #: 0-13-922725-3):

*   Reading 1: One Brain or Two?
*   Reading 2: More Experience = Bigger Brain
*   Reading 3: Are You a Natural?

Study Terms

action potential	dopamine
adrenal glands	effectors
adrenaline	electroencephalogram (EEG)
alpha waves	endocrine system
association areas of the brain	frontal lobes
attention-deficit hyperactivity disorder (ADHD)	functional magnetic resonance imaging (MRI)
autonomic nervous system	glial cells
axons	gonads
beta waves	hippocampus
biological constraint	hormones
brain	hypothalamus
brain stem	limbic system
central nervous system	magnetoencephalography (MEG)
cerebellum	medulla
cerebral cortex	melatonin
cerebrum	mind
delta waves	myelin sheath
dendrites	nerves

nervous system

neurons

neurotransmitters

norepinephrine

occipital lobes

parasympathetic nervous system

parietal lobes

Parkinson's disease

peripheral nervous system

pituitary gland

positron emission tomography (PET)

receptors

refractory period

reuptake

serotonin

somatic system

spinal cord

sympathetic nervous system

synapse

temporal lobes

thalamus

theta waves

3

Sensation, Perception, and Consciousness

Focus Questions

By the end of the chapter, you should be able
to answer the following questions:

- What is the difference between sensation and perception?
- What is selective attention?
- What is habituation?
- What are the primary normal states of consciousness?
- What are the primary stages of sleep?
- What is REM sleep?

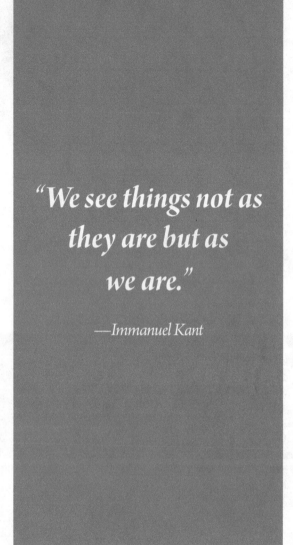

"*We see things not as they are but as we are.*"

—*Immanuel Kant*

Inspirational Words

For my thoughts are not your thoughts, neither are your ways my ways, saith the LORD. For as the heavens are higher than the earth, so are my ways higher than your ways, and my thoughts than your thoughts. Isaiah 55:8,9

As thou knowest not what is the way of the spirit, nor how the bones do grow in the womb of her that is with child: even so thou knowest not the works of God who maketh all. Ecclesiastes 11:5

That Christ may dwell in your hearts by faith; that ye, being rooted and grounded in love, may be able to comprehend with all saints what is the breadth, and length, and depth, and height;

And to know the love of Christ, which passeth knowledge, that ye might be filled with all the fulness of God. Now unto him that is able to do exceeding abundantly above all that we ask or think, according to the power that worketh in us. Unto him be glory in the church by Christ Jesus throughout all ages, world without end. Amen. Ephesians 3:17–21.

Having eyes, see ye not? And having ears, hear ye not? And do ye not remember? Jesus in Mark 8:18

What if I told you that your eyes really do not see the words you are reading right now? What if I took it a step further and told you that all your eyes see are actually rays of light? In truth, if we only had eyes and the sensory receptors located in our eyes, you would have never learned to perceive the words you are reading right now as words. It is not until the sensory impulse is passed on from the eyes to the brain that you actually perceive the light rays emitted from the page you are reading as a meaningful pattern we call words.

In this chapter, we will explore the major sensory receptor sites and the areas of the brain that help us perceive the world in a meaningful way.

3.1 Sensation and Perception

The process of *sensation* involves detecting outside stimuli via specialized sensory receptor sites located in various sense organs (i.e., eyes, ears, skin, tongue) and then sending that raw sensory information from the receptor sites to the brain. The message is sent in the form of a neural impulse. Once that message is received by the brain, perception occurs. *Perception* is the process of interpreting the raw sensory information initially processed by the sensory receptors into meaningful patterns.

Sometimes the process of sensation and perception starts from the bottom-up as we just described. That is, raw sensory data are sent up to the brain where meaning is made of the information. However, there is also a form of processing called top-down. This happens when high-level cognitive processes initiate the process.

Recall the first paragraph of this chapter in which the ability to perceive letters and words was discussed. When we first learned to read, we engaged in bottom-up processing, learning that ink on paper in certain patterns form what are called letters, which we learned are imperative to our structure of language. As we continued to become more sophisticated in our language structure over many years of schooling, we learned to perceive words as a whole, and later, words joined together in meaningful patterns within a sentence rather than perceiving each single letter. It is simply more efficient when reading. This is a more sophisticated process and is referred to as top-down processing.

A Closer Look at Sensation

In this section we will cover the sensory receptor sites for each of our major sense organs. Before we do this, though, we need to understand in a little more detail how our sensory receptors gather data from the outside world and how those data are sent on to the brain.

The first step in the process involves *detection,* meaning our sensory receptors must detect the external stimulus. Once the stimulus is detected, it needs to be sent to the brain where meaning can be made of it. This process is called *transduction* and is jump-started by the energy from the stimulus converted by the receptor into a neural impulse. Finally, *coding* takes place that allows the brain to know what kind of sensory information is being sent (e.g., visual, auditory, touch). Coding helps determine what pathway to use to assure the information arrives in the correct area of the brain (specific areas of the brain important for perception will be described later in the chapter).

Sensory Adaptation

Sensory adaptation occurs when our sensitivity to a stimulus decreases after prolonged and constant exposure. Our receptors actually get fatigued and stop firing as quickly as they once did. Since I lived around the smell every day, the sensory receptors in my nose adapted to the smell. As for my friend, the smell was new to her and thus much more intense.

Some senses adapt faster than others, with touch and smell being the quickest to adapt. The receptors for our eyes, for example, never completely adapt. If they did, we could not stare at a stimulus that remains constant without it eventually disappearing from our line of sight. From an evolutionary perspective, there are also some senses that we do not adapt to as well because doing so could compromise our survival. Heat and pain are just two examples.

THINK ABOUT IT – As you prepare to get dressed and come to class, you place shoes on your feet. When you first put on your shoes, you feel their presence since just moments earlier they were not touching your skin. However, you do not feel your shoes all day the same way you feel them when you first put them on. In fact, if your shoes are comfortable, you rarely notice you have them on the rest of the day. Why is this?

After class, you hop in your car to drive home. You hook your MP3 player up to your car and begin jamming to some of your favorite music. As you hit the open road, you crank up the volume on your radio even higher to make sure you can hear it over the increased road noise. As you pull into your neighborhood, you continue to jam at

the same decibel level until you pull into your driveway. You turn the car off and go inside without turning the radio off or giving the decibel level of the MP3 player in your car a second thought. The next day when you start your car for the first time the music is playing at the same level you left it at the previous evening. However, it is so loud in the morning that you jump out of your seat before quickly reaching to

© Vlue, 2011. Used under license of Shutterstock, Inc.

turn it down. You wonder to yourself why it seemed so loud this morning after it was so perfect the previous evening. Explain how this is possible.

A Tour of Our Major Sensory Receptors and Perception in the Brain

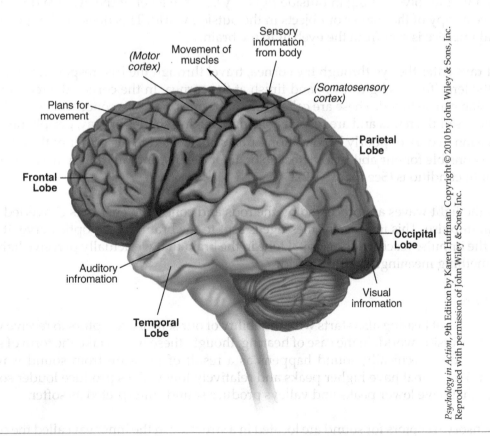

Psychology in Action, 9th Edition by Karen Huffman. Copyright © 2010 by John Wiley & Sons, Inc. Reproduced with permission of John Wiley & Sons, Inc.

Figure 3.1

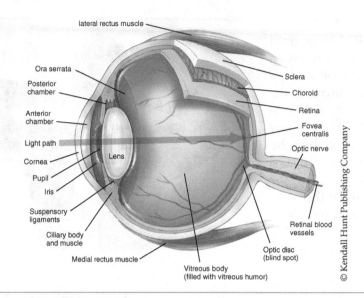

Figure 3.2

Vision

As mentioned at the start of the chapter, the process of making meaning out of visual stimuli first involves taking in outside light rays. At the level of the eye, we do not actually see a copy of the shapes or objects in the outside world. This does not happen until a neural impulse is sent from the eyeball to the brain.

Light rays enter the eye through the cornea, travel through the iris (responsible for color) and the lens (focuses light rays), and finish at the cornea. In the cornea the receptor sites for vision can be found. These are called rods and cones. *Rods* are concentrated on the outside edges of the retina and are responsible for detecting shades of gray, peripheral vision, and vision in dark or poorly lit conditions. *Cones* are located in the center of the retina and are responsible for our ability to detect color, finer details, and our ability to see in well lit or bright conditions (See Figure 3.2).

After the light waves are processed by the rods and cones, the energy is converted into a neural impulse. This impulse or message is sent to the brain via the optic nerve. It is not until the impulse reaches the occipital lobe in the brain that we actually perceive light rays as something meaningful in our world.

Audition

The process of hearing also starts with the ability of our sensory receptors to receive waves from the outside world. In the case of hearing, though, these waves take the form of sound waves. More specifically, sound happens as a result of pressure from sound waves in the ear. Waves that have higher peaks and relatively low valleys produce louder sounds. Waves that have lower peaks and valleys produce sounds interpreted as softer.

The sensory receptors for sound are located in a structure in the inner ear called the *cochlea*. Within the cochlea (See Figure 3.3) lie many tiny hair cells on the basilar membrane. These hair cells move in different ways as a result of sound waves and serve as the sensory receptors for audition. After the sound waves are received by the hair cells in the cochlea, a neural impulse is sent to the auditory cortex of the temporal lobe in the brain. Here, sound is perceived and assembled into meaningful patterns.

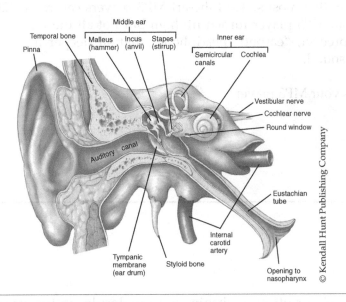

© Kendall Hunt Publishing Company

Figure 3.3

THINK ABOUT IT – Take a look around campus and you will likely notice many people with headphones on. This has become more and more common in the last decade with the creation of the MP3 player, giving us the ability to take an entire music library with us on one device. While this piece of technology certainly has its advantages, what do you suppose might be some of the disadvantages in terms of potential damage it might cause our sensory receptor sites for hearing?

Sound is measured in decibels. As the decibel level increases, so does the chance prolonged exposure will do damage to our hearing. As a general rule, prolonged exposure to any sound over

Jose AS Reyes, 2011. Used under license of Shutterstock, Inc.

(continued)

85 decibels can cause permanent hearing damage. Exposure to a sound over 120 decibels can do damage much more quickly.

Do you know that most state-of-the-art MP3 players can reach 120 decibels? This means that an MP3 player turned up high but not all the way can still exceed 85 decibels. Moreover, "earbud" headphones that sit deeper in the ear can further amplify the sound.

How loud is your MP3 player?

Olfaction

Our sense of smell, or olfaction, begins with molecules in the air reaching the olfactory epithelium in the nose. The *olfactory epithelium* is where our sensory receptors for smell are located. When air molecules make contact and bind with these tiny receptors, a neural impulse is generated. The impulse moves through the olfactory bulb where specific smells are coded and on through the temporal lobe and then the limbic system. The temporal lobe is responsible for most of the smells we perceive on a day-to-day basis. The limbic system is the emotional center of our brain and is also responsible for important aspects of memory, which explains why smells can trigger very intense memories.

Our ability to smell is a more important sense than some people realize. For example, do you notice how you often smell something you are not sure about eating before you put it in your mouth? While not a perfect solution, smelling something before consuming it can serve as a protective mechanism to avoid eating something that might be potentially dangerous to the body.

Gustation

Taste, or gustation, involves five major taste sensations: salty, sweet, bitter, sour, and umami (which means delicious). Umami involves a separate taste receptor than the first four taste sensations designed to detect glutamate, which is often found in meat. Receptors for taste are located on the tongue, where they receive information from food and liquid molecules. Most of these receptors reside inside of the little bumps on the tongue called papillae (See Figure 3.4), but there are a limited number of receptors located in the back of the mouth in the palate.

ACTIVITY

A man is standing in the line at the grocery story looking at the tabloids, candy, and other impulse buys as he waits to checkout. After standing in line for about 30 seconds, a woman walks up behind him in line. She is wearing a particular perfume that the man's "first love" used to wear over a decade ago in high school. All of a sudden, the man experiences a flood of internal emotions and memories about his first love. He's euphoric, jealous, and angry all at the same time.

Using what you've learned about the process of olfaction, explain what in the brain is likely causing this man's strong reaction to the perfume of the woman standing behind him in line.

vectorfaces_com, 2011. Used under license of Shutterstock, Inc.

HUMAN TONGUE
the organ of taste

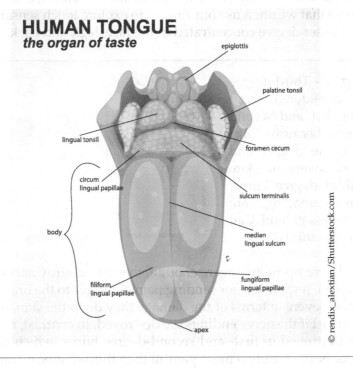

© rendix_alextian/Shutterstock.com

Figure 3.4

THINK ABOUT IT – Have you ever noticed how some people are pickier about foods than others and wondered why? Perhaps you have also noticed that there are certain foods you did not like as a child that you were surprised to learn you now enjoy. In short, children have more taste buds than adults. Moreover, the taste buds of children die more quickly and are replaced approximately once a week. When the tastes buds of adults die, they regenerate at a much slower pace. Due to the fact children have more taste buds, they are often more sensitive to foods with intense tastes. In addition to our taste buds, some taste preferences are learned as a result of the culture we are a part of.

Taste was once one of our most crucial senses in that if something tasted bad it was a sign that we might not want to eat it, thus serving as a protective mechanism necessary for survival. In the Western world today, taste is more of a luxury.

Touch

Our skin serves as one of the most important and also most complex sensory systems. Not only does it register touch, or pressure, but it also registers temperature and pain. Our skin has many layers and our receptors for touch, temperature, and pain can be found at various depths. For touch, many of the receptors are concentrated on the fingers, which makes sense given that we often use our fingers to explore touch sensations. Touch receptors are also to a lesser degree concentrated in the face, legs, and back.

THINK ABOUT IT – Third-degree burns are considered more serious than first and second degree burns because third degree burns are deeper and destroy more layers of skin. However, third degree burns, while more damaging, are almost always less painful. Can you explain why this is?

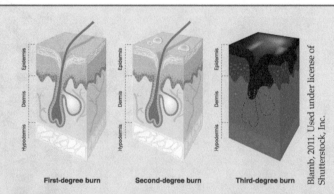

First-degree burn   Second-degree burn   Third-degree burn

When third-degree burns are severe enough, they can destroy nerve endings. These nerve endings are responsible for sending pain messages to the brain. So while these burns are more severe in terms of the damage they do to the skin, the ability to feel pain will not exist if the nerve endings are destroyed. In contrast, crucial nerve endings are not destroyed in first- and second-degree burns, which can explain why second-degree burns are often more painful than third-degree burns.

Vestibular Sense

Have you ever experienced sea or motion sickness? You might be surprised to learn that the origin of this uncomfortable state of being is actually the inner ear. Semicircular canals in the inner ear give the brain important information about balance. Near the end of the canals reside the vestibular sacs. Inside of these sacs there are tiny hair cells that bend and move in accordance with the movement of the head. In other words, as our head moves and turns, so do the hair receptors and fluid inside the vestibular sacs. A neural impulse is carried from the semicircular canals and vestibular sacs to the brain, which communicates important information about balance and body orientation, especially with regard to the position of the head. Unexpected or random movement (like the movement one might experience on a boat) can cause the vestibular sense to become disrupted, causing symptoms often associated with motion sickness such as nausea, light-headedness, and dizziness.

wavebreakmedia ltd, 2011. Used under license of Shutterstock, Inc.

Kinesthesia

When we think of the major senses, kinesthesia is not a word that is often mentioned. However, the information provided by our kinesthetic receptors is truly invaluable. While our vestibular sense provides information about balance, our kinesthetic receptors provide equally important information about out bodily position and movement. The specific receptors are found inside of tendons, muscles, and joints. Important information such as where our limbs are with respect to the rest of our body and whether muscles are contracted or relaxed is registered with every movement and a neural impulse is sent to the brain.

ACTIVITY

Imagine that you have just finished working out and all of a sudden your kinesthetic receptors stopped functioning. As you begin stretching, now without functioning kinesthetic receptors, what potential risks do you now face when stretching that you would not have had your kinesthetic receptors remained in working order?

Anthony Maragou, 2011. Used under license of Shutterstock, Inc.

A Closer Look at Perception

ACTIVITY

What do your perceive?

Look at the above figure for the next two minutes and write down as many meaningful figures within the picture as you can find:

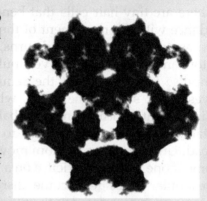

Kheng Guan Toh, 2011. Used under license of Shutterstock, Inc.

Now that you have finished, compare the list of what you saw to the list of the people near you. What similarities and differences are there?

Chances are, in the previous activity your list of what you saw in the figure did not completely match the list of the people sitting around you. Why is this? Shouldn't everyone *perceive* the figure the same way since everyone in the class was looking at the same figure? While there is some consistency in the general strategies our brains use to organize sensory information, there are differences in the ways people organize or perceive ambiguous (or random) stimuli.

Most people who were reared in a more Western culture perceive the vertical line as being longer due to the fact that we are regularly exposed to long, straight lines in the world around us (think of roads and skyscrapers as just two examples). In reality, both lines are actually the same size. Note: If you don't believe this, get out a ruler and measure for yourself.

Some of you have undoubtedly been exposed to this illusion previously. While you may have learned the correct answer is that both lines are the same size, this doesn't mean you actually perceive this to be the case. In other words, just because you learned to answer the question correctly doesn't mean you've changed the way your brain actually perceives the length of the lines.

Illusions like the one we have just played with, while fun, are actually much more. They provide us with the opportunity to study how perception occurs in the brain. Furthermore, they raise the important question: Is what we perceive always reality? As the line illusion shows, the answer to the aforementioned question is no.

ACTIVITY

More fun with perception.....

Look at Figure 3.5 and indicate whether you believe the vertical or horizontal line is longer.

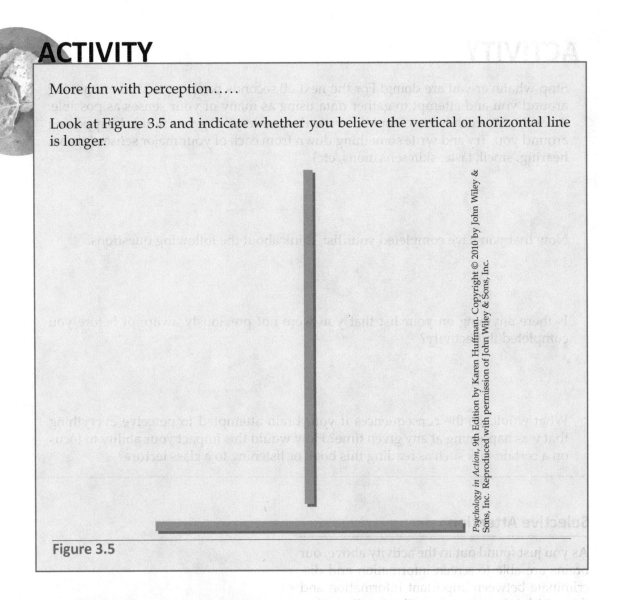

Figure 3.5

3.2 How Our Brain Selects What Information to Perceive?

Just as our sensory systems are bombarded with external stimuli and must decide what messages to attend to or prioritize, our brain must do the same with perception. There are a number of tools our brain uses to help simplify this process.

Feature Detectors

Our brain has highly specialized neurons concentrated in certain areas that are designed to select and respond to specific sensory information. We have feature detectors that respond to certain angles, shapes, and even specific kinds of movement. For example, we have feature detectors in our occipital and temporal lobes that are responsible for helping us perceive and recognize the faces of others.

ACTIVITY

Stop whatever you are doing! For the next 60 seconds pay attention to everything around you and attempt to gather data using as many of your senses as possible. After the 60 seconds are complete, write down everything you noticed happening around you. Try and write something down from each of your major senses (vision, hearing, smell, taste, skin sensations, etc).

Now that you have completed your list, think about the following questions:

Is there anything on your list that you were not previously aware of before you completed this activity?

What would be the consequences if your brain attempted to perceive everything that was happening at any given time? How would this impact your ability to focus on a certain task such as reading this book or listening to a class lecture?

Selective Attention

As you just found out in the activity above, our brains are able to screen information and discriminate between important information and that which is less important. This is called selective attention. If our brains did not possess the ability to do this, our lives would be chaotic, and it would be very hard to focus on any one important activity.

Habituation

Have you ever purchased a new videogame or perhaps a new smart phone and noticed how much fun it is at first? Right from the moment you open it and smell the packaging, your brain registers the fact that this is a new experience. There is an excitement to learning the new controls and features. Of course, anyone who has experienced the feeling of tinkering with a new

iQoncept, 2011. Used under license of Shutterstock, Inc.

gadget also understands this feeling does not last forever. Over time, we become used to the new technology and it loses its sense of novelty. This process is called habituation. *Habituation* can be defined as the brain's tendency to ignore stimuli in the environment that remain relatively constant. In other words, our brains like new experiences and attempt to avoid boredom.

Diego Cervo, 2011. Used under license of Shutterstock, Inc.

3.3 Gestalt Principles of Grouping and Organization

After the process of selecting what stimuli to attend to, our brains then attempt to organize the information into meaningful patterns. One of the primary ways our brains accomplish this is through a method known as the Gestalt principles of grouping. Without these principles for organization, our perceptual worlds would be chaotic and confusing. What follows is a look at some of the basic Gestalt principles.

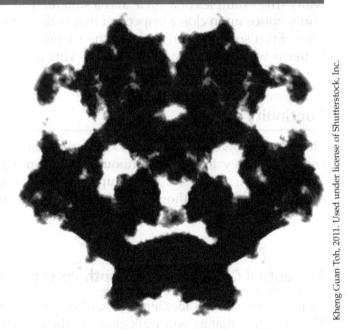

Kheng Guan Toh, 2011. Used under license of Shutterstock, Inc.

Figure Ground

Remember this card from earlier in the chapter? Chances are that most of you see this as a white card with black ink on it. Why is this? Why don't you see it as a black card with white ink? The answer is the Gestalt principle of figure-ground. The figure (black ink) is always seen as being closer than the ground (white background).

Similarity

Look at Figure 3.6. How do you group the dots together? Most people group the first horizontal line together because all of the dots are gray. They do the same thing for the third line with the gray dots and the second and fourth lines with the black dots. We group similar objects together, in this case by color. This concept is called similarity.

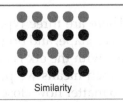

Similarity

Figure 3.6

Proximity

How do you group the vertical lines together in Figure 3.7? Most people have a tendency to see three pairs of vertical lines. But why don't we just see six vertical lines? The answer is because of how close the lines are to one another. We tend to group the first two lines together because of their proximity to one another. We do the same thing with the third and fourth lines and also the fifth and sixth lines. This is the Gestalt concept of proximity.

Proximity

Figure 3.7

Closure

What shapes do you see in Figure 3.8? If you grew up in a Western culture, you probably answered circle and square without even giving it a second thought. Take a closer look, though? Are those really true examples of a circle and a square? You will almost certainly notice upon closer inspection that both shapes are not complete. Even so, our brain closes in the shapes to form meaningful patterns we are already familiar with. This is an example of the Gestalt principle of closure.

Closure

Figure 3.8

Continuity

Our brains have a tendency to perceive things as belonging together if they form a continuous and meaningful pattern. In Figure 3.9, we see an "X" and group each line of the "X" as a continuous pattern even though geometrically they are not continuous. This is the Gestalt concept of continuity.

Continuity

Figure 3.9

Perceptual Constancy and Depth Perception

Imagine that you are looking at a herd of elk on a hillside. You focus in on a single elk. Now imagine that as you walk closer to the animal, you perceive it as getting bigger. In order to avoid this, you would literally have to re-evaluate the size of the elk relative to your position with each step. Fortunately, this is not a perceptual exercise we have to engage in. Instead, our brain perceives the environment as constant despite changes in sensory input. This is called perceptual constancy.

There are three types of perceptual constancy: size, shape, and brightness. The previous example with the elk is an example of *size constancy*, which means we perceive the size as constant no matter how close or far away we move from the object.

Shape constancy refers to our ability to perceive the shape of an object as unchanging regardless of what angle we see it from. Imagine that you have a penny in front of you and you start out looking at the front of coin. If you move it a quarter turn, you still perceive it as a penny. If you move it another quarter turn and see just the edge of the penny, you still see it as a penny thanks to shape constancy.

Imagine that you have purchased a nice pair of light brown shoes. You admire them as you walk throughout campus on a sunny day. As you walk inside for your class, all of a sudden you notice these once light brown shoes become darker. Obviously, you under-stand that your shoes do not actually change colors. Instead, you know the light around the shoes changes. This happens as a result of *brightness constancy.* Without brightness constancy we would constantly be reinterpreting colors in different lights and would believe our clothes were actually changing colors.

Along with size constancy, *depth perception* provides us with important information that allows us to see the world around us in three dimensions. While we can also estimate the distance of objects from using senses such as hearing and even smell, we rely on sight more than any other sense for estimating how far away a stimulus is from us.

THINK ABOUT IT – Is depth perception inborn or learned?

In research, often referred to as the *visual cliff,* done by Gibson and Walk (1960) and Witherington et al. (2005), it was demonstrated that babies would hesitate when they reached a perceived cliff. For the safety of the babies, the cliff was actually an illusion created by a mirror. Nevertheless, the babies hesitated. What information does this give us with regard to the ability of infants to perceive depth and whether it is a learned behavior?

3.4 Consciousness

If a neurosurgeon were to crack open the thick bony casing that protects your brain, would he uncover your mind? Perhaps, although he would not really *see* it; all he would see is a grayish lump of matter. But he might well presume that your *mind,* your *self-awareness,* resides in complex patterns of billions of interconnections that have formed among the neurons in your brain. And he might speculate, as he looks at this chunk of tissue, that at this very moment chemical and electrical changes and impulses swarm through many of the intricate patterns of neural networks. And some of these impulses will be associated with thoughts and feelings that you are now having: They will define your own private state of **consciousness**.

Consciousness, like *mind,* is a term with many meanings. The two terms are very closely related. *Mind* refers primarily to activities of the brain such as thinking and feeling that result in a sense of self; *consciousness* refers to an awareness of self.

Psychology: The Human Puzzle by Guy R. LeFrancois © 2013 Bridgepoint Education. Reprinted by permission.

In effect, there are two broad states of consciousness: sleeping and waking. In addition, there are *altered* states of consciousness such as might result from certain drugs or perhaps from hypnosis.

3.5 Sleep

Sleep, as you well know, is the state that ensues when you close your eyes and eventually lose immediate contact with your environment. It ends when you regain awareness of external events. But that does not mean you are completely unaware of your physical environment as you sleep. As you lie precariously on your narrow bed, a dangerous height above your stone floor, you have little fear of falling. You casually assume that your body has some control over its movements during sleep and that it is responsive to signals indicating dangerous proximity to the edge of your sleeping platform. And if your baby cries in the middle of the night, you instantly awaken—strong evidence that you are not totally unconscious while you sleep, that part of your brain remains alert.

Circadian Rhythms

We seem to be biologically prepared to sleep at night and to be active during the day—a phenomenon labeled a **circadian rhythm**. Circadian rhythms are daily cycles in biological and behavioral processes such as sleeping, temperature change, and the production of **melatonin**. Melatonin is a hormone closely tied to the regulation of sleep. It increases in the evening and during the night and decreases during the day. Melatonin is sometimes used to treat sleep disorders (Zee, 2010).

Although our sleep-wake cycles seem to be closely tied to the rising and setting of the sun, that we generate our own cycles becomes clear when we find ourselves in latitudes that have more or fewer hours of daylight. Other things being equal, we continue to sleep for approximately the same length of time and at about the same time each day. Even when participants are kept in surroundings that provide no clues about day and night, circadian rhythms tend to adjust to periods very close to 24 hours (Gronfier, Wright, Kronauer, & Czeisler, 2007).

Stages of Sleep

When early sleep researchers observed sleeping subjects, they saw that sleep involves eye closure, reduction of muscle tension, reduction of heart rate, lowering of blood pressure, slowing of respiration rate, and a marked decrease in body temperature. They also noticed that people, and animals, don't seem to sleep uniformly and consistently. Sometimes sleepers breathe rapidly, moving and fidgeting as they sleep; at other times, breathing is regular and there is little twitching and jerking. Dogs, too, jerk and fidget and moan and even bark as they sleep. Based on these changes, researchers concluded that there are distinct stages in depth of sleep (Neubauer, 2009).

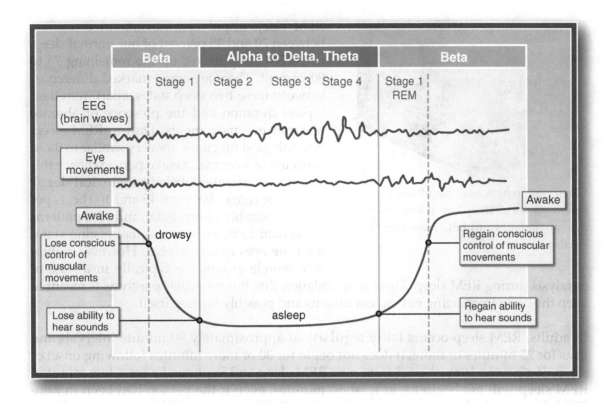

Figure 3.10

Physiological changes during sleep. Stage 1 REM sleep is sometimes labeled Stage 5 sleep, although brain waves during this stage are identical to those of Stage 1 sleep. The difference is that during this stage the rapid eye movements that typically accompany periods of dreaming are observed.

More recently, EEG recordings and observations of eye movements below closed eyelids have led researchers to describe four stages of sleep based on changes in brain activity. These four stages are followed by a period of rapid eye movements (Figure 3.10).

EEG recordings indicate that when awake, the brain typically produces small, fast waves called **beta waves** (13 to 30 per second), but these become slower, changing to **alpha waves** (8 to 12 waves per second) as the individual relaxes. During Stage 1 sleep, different waves called **theta waves** (4 to 7 per minute) become evident, interspersed with spikes of rapid brain activity. Perhaps 10 minutes later, if not awakened first, the sleeper enters Stage 2 sleep, also marked by bursts of rapid brain activity called *sleep spindles*. Note that Stages 1 and 2 are very brief.

In Stage 3, body temperature and heart rate continue to decrease and **delta waves** (up to 4 per minute) begin to appear. These slow, deep waves are characteristic of Stage 4 sleep, often described as the *deepest* stage of sleep.

Now, interestingly, brain activity shows the sleeper regressing through stages 3, 2, and 1 *before* entering the stage of **rapid-eye-movement sleep (REM sleep)**. It is during this stage that most of our dreaming takes place.

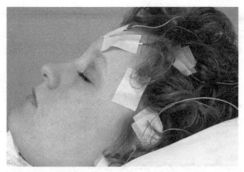

Sleep researchers have identified different stages of sleep based largely on eye movements and EEG recordings of brain activity.

REM sleep (rapid eye movement) comprises between 20 and 25 percent of our normal sleep; non-REM sleep makes up the remaining 75 to 80 percent. There are some marked differences between these two sleep states, apart from their typical duration and the presence or absence of rapid eye movements. During REM sleep, physiological functions are very similar to those expected in a normal, awake person (hence this stage of sleep is often labeled **paradoxical sleep**): Heart rate ranges between 45 and 100 beats per minute, breathing is irregular, and EEG patterns are similar to those seen in quiet resting states with the eyes closed (alpha). However, voluntary muscle groups are typically in a state of paralysis during REM sleep. There is speculation that this muscular paralysis is meant to keep the body from acting out violent dreams and possibly hurting itself.

In adults, REM sleep occurs fairly regularly at approximately 90-minute intervals and lasts for 25 minutes or more. It does not begin for 30 or more minutes following onset of sleep. If a person is awakened from non-REM sleep and kept awake for a few minutes, REM sleep will not begin for at least 30 minutes, even if the person had been in non-REM sleep for the last hour or more (Figure 3.11). Thus it is possible to deprive subjects

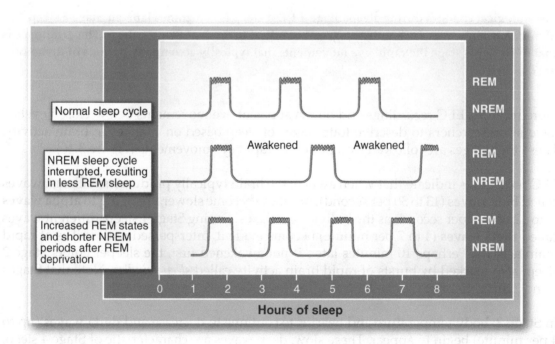

Figure 3.11

Cycles of REM/non-REM sleep. During a normal sleep cycle, REM sleep occurs fairly regularly at about 90-minute intervals and lasts for 25 minutes or more. If we are awakened from non-REM sleep, REM sleep will not begin for 30 minutes or more after the onset of sleep. If we are awakened during REM sleep (as in a dream-recording experiment), the result is shorter non-REM periods between REM states during the subsequent night.

of REM sleep simply by waking them whenever rapid eye movements begin. Similarly, it is possible to deprive subjects of non-REM sleep. One of the results of this procedure is that subjects who are deprived of one type of sleep tend to make up for it during subsequent nights. A second effect of REM or non-REM deprivation is that subjects who are allowed only one type of sleep frequently feel and function as if they had not slept at all. It seems clear that we have a need for both types of sleep and that neither is more restful than the other in spite of the apparently greater reduction in rate of physiological functioning during non-REM sleep.

3.6 Why We Sleep

We still don't know for sure why we must sleep (*The Science of Sleep*, 2010). What we do know is that following prolonged periods of sleep deprivation our behavior becomes very bizarre, we suffer from hallucinations, our ability to respond appropriately to the environment is severely impeded, and we might eventually die (Buysse, Strollo, Black, Zee, & Winkelman, 2008). No experiments have been conducted with human subjects that directly substantiate this last bit of speculation, although sleep deprivation of animals sometimes leads to their deaths (Newman, Paletz, Obermeyer, & Benca, 2009).

There are a number of theoretical explanations for sleep. One theory maintains that it is necessary to repair physiological damage and maintain the body and mind in good working order. Evolutionary theory speculates that sleep is an evolved mechanism whose usefulness lies in the fact that hidden sleeping animals are less likely to be preyed upon, particularly if their sleep cycles correspond with predation cycles. It also appears reasonable to suppose that sleep might have evolved as a system for conserving energy. Some researchers suggest that some stages of sleep, especially REM sleep, are important for consolidating memories and perhaps for resting important neural systems.

None of these explanations is necessarily exclusive; that is, sleep might result from a combination of factors. But, as Siegel (2003) notes, we still don't know exactly what is repaired or improved during sleep. And the fact is that none of these explanations has been clearly substantiated. There is no physiological evidence that sleep involves unconsciousness due to oxygen deprivation; the theory of cell damage remains unsupported; and no toxins or other harmful substances have been discovered to accumulate in the body's cells that must be destroyed through sleep. Nor is there any significant change in the body's consumption of energy during sleep, so that the commonly held belief that the body needs to sleep in order to conserve and restore its energy levels does not appear to be substantiated either. Despite marked declines in physiological functioning during sleep, the level of energy consumption increases dramatically during the first hour of sleep, although it falls off rapidly after that.

So the question of why we sleep remains unanswered. It is a missing piece of the puzzle, although we have a pretty clear notion of what the implications of not sleeping are. Nor do we know why we dream: another missing piece.

3.7 Dreams

Contrary to some beliefs, everybody dreams: But not everyone remembers dreams with equal clarity. In fact, most people remember only a small portion of what they dream, with women remembering their dreams more often than men (Schredl, 2010). Nor, as is popularly believed, is a dream a condensed version of real-time events. Indications are that the amount of time that might have elapsed had dream events been real is very similar to the amount of time during which the dream occurred. Evidence that this is so is derived from tracings of eye movements, from verbalizations, or from movements corresponding to an event in a dream. Interestingly, in many cases, eye movements during dreams appear to actually scan dream objects. It is as though dreamers were actually looking at the dream scene or at the object for which they're reaching (Leclair-Visonneau, Oudiette, Gaymard, Leu-Semenescu, & Arnulf, 2010).

Why We Dream

Psychologists are not certain why we dream. Nor can we easily investigate the effects of not dreaming because doing so requires the interruption of sleep and any observed effect could as well be due to sleep deprivation as to dream deprivation. Still, we have a number of dream theories.

1. *Dreams as symbols for disguised impulses.* Perhaps the best-known dream theory is that proposed by Sigmund Freud—sadly, a theory that is generally unsupported by any scientific research. Freud believed that dreams represent disguised manifestations of unconscious impulses. He thought that most of these impulses are linked to sexual desires, aggression, or other socially taboo inclinations. Hence they're disguised, even in dreams, as a form of self-protection or, more precisely, as a form of sleep protection. Were they not disguised, we would continually awaken horrified at our vile and base cravings. If the father we want to murder appears in a dream as a spider, we can step on that creature with no fear of self-reprisal. Only Freud and other gifted psychoanalysts would be expected to recognize the spider.

2. *The threat-simulation theory of dreams.* Another dream theory suggests that our dreams provide us with an opportunity to practice responding to threats. This might be why, as Revonsuo (2000) suggests, so many of our dreams and nightmares have to do with chasing or being chased. Revonsuo's *Threat Simulation Theory* argues that even though our legs and arms might not be moving while we dream, we might still be practicing a variety of "fight and flight" responses. In support of this theory, there is evidence that when we dream our brains often fire in ways highly similar to the way they might fire if we were awake and actually threatened.

3. *Dreams as cognitive tools.* There is also the possibility that dreaming may have a beneficial effect on cognitive functioning and attention (Cartwright, 2010). This is suggested by studies of partial and temporary dream deprivation, accomplished by waking individuals at the onset of REM periods. In the absence of dreams, explains Cartwright, the individual finds it difficult to attend to reality upon awakening.

    Additional evidence that dreams might provide a cognitive benefit is found in the observation that when rats are placed in mazes during the day, their patterns of brain activity that night closely parallel their brain activity while they were in the maze (Ego-Stengel & Wilson, 2010). These authors suggest that dreams provide us with an opportunity to sort our memories into those worth remembering and those we can afford to forget.

4. *Dreams as therapy.* Another current dream theory, somewhat reminiscent of Freud's, suggests that dreams are a form of therapy. Hartmann (2007) notes that dreams are often laden with emotion. As such, they provide an opportunity to confront difficult and surprising emotions and perhaps learn how to deal with them. Dreams allow us to think through our emotions.

In this connection, Cartwright (2010) notes that the various dreams collected from a single individual on the same night typically present such a coherent pattern that it is impossible to believe that dreams represent random happenings. She argues that dreams may well have a therapeutic purpose, since they often appear to be directed toward the resolution of conflict-laden situations.

Throughout history people have claimed to have prophetic or clairvoyant dreams. People receiving and/or claiming to have received communication from the spirit world or God have been written in most of the major religious texts throughout history. Both the Old Testament and New Testament give examples of God communicating to some in dreams. These spiritual and/or paranormal claims are obviously controversial, but still important to discuss and be aware of. What are your views on this matter?

And, of course, there are those who believe that dreams serve none of these functions—that they are simply the result of random brain activity.

Relatively few dreams are nightmares. These tend to occur near the end of non-REM sleep rather than during REM sleep (which is when most other dreams occur).

Many misconceptions surround hypnosis, partly owing to years of demonstrations of bizarre activity onstage. Only within the past few decades has it become a serious focus of psychological research.

3.8 Hypnosis

Sleep—and the dreams that might then come—are one state of consciousness; being awake is the other. Does hypnosis represent a third, altered type of consciousness?

Perhaps, although the final verdict is not yet in. We are not quite certain about **hypnosis**—not even certain whether or not we should investigate it: There has long been a faint odor of mysticism and of magic about the subject. We often fear and distrust the mysterious.

Some Facts

Contrary to some popular misconceptions, hypnosis does not involve some powerful personality putting subjects into a state where, zombie-like, they have to obey. As defined by the American Psychological Association, hypnosis is a procedure where subjects are given suggestions for "imaginative experiences" and where "one person (the subject) is guided by another (the hypnotist) to respond to suggestions for changes in subjective experience, alterations in perception, sensation, emotion, thought or behavior" (*The Official Division 30 Definition and Description of Hypnosis*, 2010).

Basically, what happens in hypnosis is this: The hypnotist uses some form of what is termed *hypnotic induction* to heighten the **suggestibility** of the subject (Gafner, 2010). A common hypnotic induction technique, the *eye-fixation method*, uses an object to focus the subject's attention while the hypnotist speaks. Pocket watches were used extensively in 19th-century France and Germany and are often shown in graphic portrayals of hypnotists plying their trades. Of course, it is not an object that induces hypnosis, but the hypnotist's words. A very common induction technique does not ask subjects to fix their gaze on an object; it simply uses verbal directions to increase the subject's relaxation and suggestibility.

A rather surprising discovery is that, in terms of physiological functioning, a hypnotic state is much closer to a waking state than to a sleep state. EEG waves are typically alpha, and respiration and heart rate may range from deep relaxation to strenuous physical activity. The single most striking feature of a hypnotic state is the willingness of subjects to do what is asked and the matter-of-factness that accompanies even the most bizarre behaviors requested of them.

Is Hypnosis a Different State of Consciousness?

Whether hypnosis is a different mental state or whether it simply involves imaginative role-playing remains uncertain and controversial (Revonsuo, Kallio, & Sikka, 2009). Much of the research that has looked at this question has compared the performance of hypnotized subjects with that of others pretending to be hypnotized. Those who believe that hypnosis represents a different state of consciousness try to find differences between the psychological processes of hypnotized and nonhypnotized persons; those who think hypnosis involves imaginative role-playing look for similarities.

Among other things, this research has sometimes found that *simulators* are often capable of many of the same impressive feats and deceptions as are hypnotized subjects, including total-body catalepsy (rigidity), apparent amnesia, age regression, hallucinations, and the ability to tolerate pain (anesthesia) (Orne, 2009). These findings would seem to support the notion that hypnosis does not represent an altered state of consciousness.

However, there are studies indicating that brain activity changes during hypnosis (Naish, 2010); simulators are not ordinarily able to alter their brain activity deliberately to please an investigator. For example, when hypnotized subjects are instructed to imagine that black-and-white objects are brilliantly colored, activity in the part of the brain associated with color vision increases; this is not the case for nonhypnotized participants asked to imagine the same thing (Oakley & Halligan, 2010).

Applications of Hypnosis

There is evidence that the use of hypnosis can be effective for a variety of medical procedures, including childbirth and even surgery. It has also been used successfully in dentistry (Brown, 2009).

A variety of psychotherapies also make use of hypnosis (Barber & Westland, 2011). For example, Almas and Landmark (2010) reviewed a large number of studies where the use of hypnosis was effective in treating sexual problems.

Hypnosis has also been used in courtrooms in an attempt to help witnesses, and sometimes victims, recall details of a crime. However, because it is difficult to establish the veracity of what hypnotized individuals appear to remember, the use of hypnosis in court remains highly controversial (Lynn, Boycheva, Deming, Lilienfeld, & Hallquist, 2009).

The results of research that has attempted to determine whether hypnosis can be beneficial in the teaching-learning process remain somewhat uncertain. Some studies claim to have demonstrated that learning, motivation, and retention can sometimes be improved as a result of posthypnotic suggestion (Vernon, 2009). But other studies have failed to find differences between experimental groups and control groups, particularly when control groups are highly motivated. The most valid conclusion to be derived from a large number of related studies appears to be that hypnosis can be very effective in increasing motivation, but that it does not increase intelligence or memory. There is virtually no evidence that it has any harmful effects.

3.9 Drugs and Consciousness

Consciousness refers to our personal conceptions of the realities that surround us and of who we are. Sleeping and waking are natural states of consciousness, regularly and predictably manifested in humans; hypnosis may represent an altered state of consciousness, the alteration seldom being very dramatic or violent. Various recreational and addictive drugs, which we look at in Chapter 9, can provide yet another way of shaping reality. Or is it fantasy that drugs shape?

Main Points

1. Sensation is in part the process of taking in information from the world around us. Reality comes to us primarily through all the holes in our head and our skin. Our interpretation of that communication makes up our personal experience or perception of reality. One reality. Many personal interpretations, view, and perceptions of that reality.

2. Consciousness has various stages and levels. Our consciousness, or awareness, can be altered and influenced by many variables. The sleep cycle, meditation, and drugs to name a few.

3. **Sleep:** Sleep, of which there are two states, REM sleep (during which we do most of our dreaming) and non-REM sleep, is not a completely unconscious state. Stages of sleep are distinguishable by the nature of accompanying brain waves, ranging from small fast beta waves when awake, through alpha, theta, and delta waves (progressively slower and deeper). We don't know clearly why we sleep or why we dream, but we do know that deprivation has negative consequences.

4. **Hypnosis:** Hypnosis is a procedure where subjects are given suggestions for "imaginative experiences" that lead to "alterations in perception, sensation, emotion, thought, or behavior." Its hallmark is the desire of participants to obey the hypnotist's instructions. It is not clear whether it represents a different state of consciousness, but it has important implications in medicine and psychotherapy.

Thoughts and Suggestions

Many times our current beliefs and past experiences cloud or distort how we perceive or interpret reality. Can you give any examples of how you have needed to change your inner view-beliefs-biases in order to see reality more clearly and accurately?

Sometimes we are so focused on one thing, we don't see other important things in our daily experiences and lives. This can be true for both spiritual and psychological matters as well as very concrete and practical matters. Can you give any examples of this.

Altered states of consciousness can come about in many forms: dream states; meditation and prayer states; use of drugs and alcohol. Just to name a few. Some people even say that some people are in an altered state of consciousness when they "fall in love" or are "head over heels for someone." Can you give some examples of how you have been impacted in either positive or negative ways by experiencing altered states of consciousness? Have you witnessed this phenomenon in others so that it has resulted in your own growth?

Suggested readings from Hock, R. R. (1999). *Forty studies that changed psychology* (3rd ed.). Upper Saddle River, NJ: Prentice Hall. (ISBN #: 0-13-922725-3):

- Reading 6: To Sleep, No Doubt To Dream
- Reading 7: Unromancing The Dream
- Reading 8: Acting As If You Are Hypnotized

4

How We Learn

Focus Questions

By the end of the chapter, you should be able
to answer the following questions:

- How is learning defined?
- What is behaviorism?
- How do classical and operant conditioning differ?
- How do the various schedules of reinforcement affect behavior?
- What experimental findings present significant problems for behavioristic explanations?
- What are the main beliefs of cognitive psychology?
- What is reciprocal determinism?
- How can learning principles be applied to real life?

Chapter Outline

- -

Inspirational Words

And if it seem evil unto you to serve the LORD, choose you this day whom ye will serve; whether the gods which your fathers served that were *on the other side of the flood, or the gods of the Amorites, in whose land ye dwell: but as for me and my house, we will serve the LORD. Joshua 24:15*

And be not conformed to this world: but be ye transformed by the renewing of your mind, that ye may prove what is that good, and acceptable, and perfect, will of God. Romans 12:2

Thus saith the LORD, thy Redeemer, the Holy One of Israel; I am the LORD thy God which teacheth thee to profit, which leadeth thee by the way that thou shouldest go. Isaiah 48:17

All scripture is given by inspiration of God, and is profitable for doctrine, for reproof, for correction, for instruction in righteousness: That the man of God may be perfect, throughly furnished unto all good works. 2 Timothy 3: 16,17

Give instruction to a wise man, and he will be yet wiser: teach a just man, and he will increase in learning. The fear of the LORD is the beginning of wisdom: and the knowledge of the holy is understanding. Proverbs 9: 9,10

4.1 What Is Learning?

Learning, consists of changes in behavior—changes like no longer grabbing a bull by the tail. But not all changes in behavior are examples of learning. Some changes are temporary; they might result from fatigue or from the use of drugs. Other changes appear to be mainly due to physical maturation; still others might result from injury or disease of the brain or other parts of the nervous system.

Learning is defined as relatively permanent changes in behavior that result from experience but are not caused by fatigue, maturation, drugs, injury, or disease (Figure 4.1). Strictly speaking, however, it is not the changes in behavior themselves that define learning; the changes are simply evidence that learning has occurred. Learning is what happens to the organism as a result of experience.

Although we look at behavior—at actual performance—for evidence that learning has occurred, changes in behavior are not always apparent following experiences that might be presumed to have led to learning. In many cases there will be no evidence of learning until an opportunity to display a behavior is presented; and in some cases, that opportunity may never occur. For example, you might have learned a particularly clever way of blowing your nose after seeing someone else blow theirs. But that does not mean that you will ever perform the trick. It might forever remain *latent* (meaning *potential* but not apparent).

Approaches to Learning

Learning is not easily separated from other major topics in psychology. Changes in behavior are centrally involved in many aspects of psychology, including motivation, personality, perception, development, and even mental disorders. We are not simple, highly predictable organisms with static and unchanging patterns of behavior. It is only fools who don't profit from experience, and we are not fools; we are *Homo sapiens*, the wise one. We profit from experience—and that defines learning.

Not surprisingly, most of the first psychologists to look for pieces of the human puzzle devoted considerable effort to discovering the laws and principles of learning. These early efforts, especially in the United States, rejected the more philosophical and intuitive approach of an earlier age. Instead, they embraced a scientific approach—an approach concerned mainly with the objective and observable aspects of human functioning. The most important pieces of the puzzle, they thought, would have to do with the rules that govern relationships between stimuli (observable conditions that can give rise to behavior) and responses (actual, observable behavior).

Learning is a change in behavior (or in potential for behavior) as a result of experience. Like learning not to grab a bull by the tail.

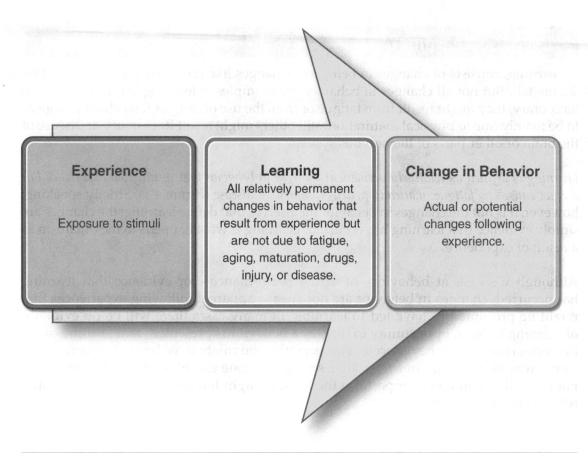

Experience

Exposure to stimuli

Learning
All relatively permanent changes in behavior that result from experience but are not due to fatigue, aging, maturation, drugs, injury, or disease.

Change in Behavior

Actual or potential changes following experience.

Figure 4.1

Evidence of learning is found in actual or potential changes in behavior as a result of experience. But learning itself is an invisible, internal neurological process.

Because they deal with observable *behaviors*, the theories that resulted are labeled **behavioristic theories**. Sometimes they're also referred to as *S-R* or *associationistic* theories because they deal mainly with associations between **stimuli** and **responses**. And although they have sometimes been accused of leading to a mechanistic and incomplete description of human learning, they have contributed a great deal to our understanding that continues to be both valid and valuable.

A second major group of learning theories are **cognitive theories**. They're concerned less with the objective aspects of behavior than with more *mental* processes such as thinking, imagining, anticipating, problem solving, decision making, and perceiving.

4.2 Behavioristic Approaches

Classical Conditioning

In the early 1900s, a Russian by the name of Ivan Pavlov presented his theory of Learning.

Ironically, the discovery that made Pavlov so famous came about almost by accident. Pavlov was a physiologist, not a psychologist, and at the time of his lucky discovery, he was busily investigating and measuring secretions related to digestion. That's when he noticed that some of his more experienced dogs began to salivate whenever they saw their handlers. The less experienced dogs also salivated, but only when given food.

Pavlov rightly guessed that his older dogs had learned something that the more naive dogs had yet to learn: They had learned to associate the sight of a handler (stimulus) with food (Figure 4.2). But only one of these stimuli, food, would normally lead to salivation. So, in a sense, what the dogs had learned was to substitute one stimulus (handler) for another (food). Not surprisingly, this kind of learning is sometimes called *learning through stimulus substitution*; its more common label is **classical conditioning**.

That the dog has *learned* something is clear: there has been a change in behavior (specifically, in the response to the handler) as a result of experience (repeated pairing of the handler and food). That is, a previously neutral stimulus (sight of handler) now leads to a response ordinarily associated with another stimulus (food). This defines *classical conditioning*.

Pavlov's Experiments

To clarify the laws of classical conditioning, Pavlov devised a series of experiments (Pavlov, 1927). In the best known of these, a dog is placed in a harness-like contraption similar to the one shown in Figure 4.3. The apparatus allows food powder to be inserted directly

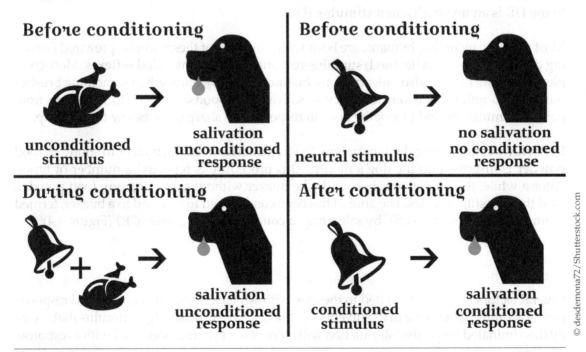

Before conditioning

unconditioned stimulus → salivation unconditioned response

Before conditioning

neutral stimulus → no salivation no conditioned response

During conditioning

→ salivation unconditioned response

After conditioning

conditioned stimulus → salivation conditioned response

© desdemona72/Shutterstock.com

Figure 4.2

What Pavlov first noticed was that the sight of the handler was enough to cause experienced dogs to salivate. He later paired other stimuli, such as bells and buzzers, with the presentation of food to study the details of classical conditioning.

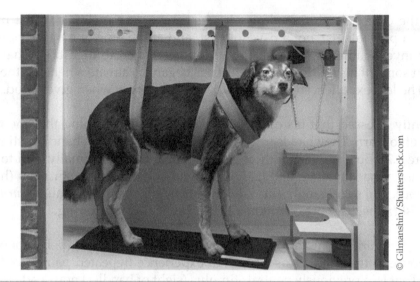

© Gilmanshin/Shutterstock.com

Figure 4.3

Pavlov's dogs were placed in harnesses. Saliva dropping through the tube activates the balancing mechanism so that the amount of salivation is recorded on the revolving drum. In this demonstration, presentation of food is paired with a light that shines through the window.

into the dog's mouth or to be dropped into a dish in front of the dog. The salivation that occurs when food powder is placed in the dog's mouth is an unlearned response and is therefore an **unconditioned response (UR)**. The stimulus of food powder that gives rise to the UR is an **unconditioned stimulus (US)**.

Most animals, including humans, are born with a number of these simple, prewired (meaning they don't have to be learned) stimulus-response associations called **reflexes**. More complex behaviors that are also unlearned are **instincts**. That we blink when something brushes our eye is a reflex—as is our tendency to salivate in response to food, to withdraw from painful stimulation, and to jerk the knee in response to a sharp blow below the kneecap.

In Pavlov's conditioning demonstration, the trainer arranges for a buzzer to sound as food powder is inserted into the dog's mouth. This procedure is repeated a number of times. After a while, the trainer simply sounds the buzzer without providing any food powder. And the dog still salivates. The animal has been conditioned to respond to a buzzer, termed a **conditioned stimulus (CS)**, by salivating, a **conditioned response (CR)** (Figure 4.4).

Acquisition

Several factors are directly related to the ease with which a classically conditioned response can be acquired. One is the distinctiveness of the CS. Not surprisingly, a stimulus that is easily discriminated from other stimulation will more easily become associated with a response.

A second critically important factor is the temporal relationship between the conditioned and the unconditioned stimulus. The ideal situation, *delayed* (or *forward-order*) *conditioning*, presents the conditioned stimulus before the unconditioned stimulus, with the CS continuing during the presentation of the US (Hussaini, Komischke, Menzel, & Lachnit,

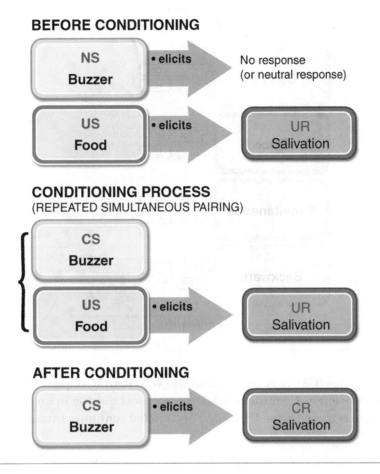

BEFORE CONDITIONING

NS Buzzer • elicits → No response (or neutral response)

US Food • elicits → UR Salivation

CONDITIONING PROCESS
(REPEATED SIMULTANEOUS PAIRING)

CS Buzzer

US Food • elicits → UR Salivation

AFTER CONDITIONING

CS Buzzer • elicits → CR Salivation

Figure 4.4

Classical conditioning. Initially, the stimulus (buzzer) does not elicit salivation. After repeated pairings of this stimulus with the unconditioned stimulus (food), the buzzer has become a conditioned stimulus that now elicits a conditioned response (salivation).

2007). In the classical Pavlovian experiment, for example, fastest learning occurs when the buzzer sounds just before the presentation of food powder and continues while the food powder is injected into the dog's mouth. Other alternatives are to have the CS begin and end before the US, termed *trace conditioning*; to present the US and the CS simultaneously (*simultaneous conditioning*); or to present the US prior to the CS (*backward conditioning*). Figure 4.5 summarizes the relationship of these temporal factors to classical conditioning.

As noted, fastest learning typically occurs when the conditioned stimulus precedes the unconditioned stimulus (forward-order conditioning). The opposite situation, backward conditioning, in which the conditioned stimulus follows the unconditioned stimulus, has generally not resulted in learning except under very specific circumstances. For example, presenting a dog with food and then later ringing a bell does not normally lead the dog to salivate in response to the bell.

Backward conditioning can sometimes be effective, however. For example, Minnier, Misanin, and Hinderliter (2007) successfully conditioned taste aversions in rats by injecting them with lithium chloride (which makes them sick—a US) either 15 or 45 minutes *before*

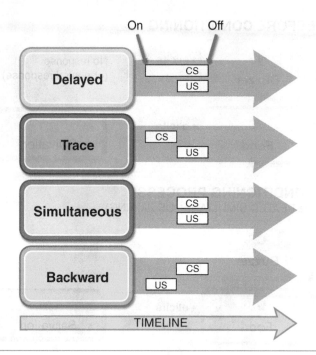

Figure 4.5

Unconditioned stimulus (US)–conditioned stimulus (CS) pairing sequences are shown here in the order of effectiveness. Conditioning takes place most quickly in the delayed sequence where the CS (buzzer) precedes the US (food powder) and continues throughout the time the US is presented.

they were allowed to drink sweetened water (the CS). Most rats who experienced the 15-minute delay later avoided the sweetened water.

Keith-Lucas and Guttman (1975) conditioned rats to avoid a plastic toy by shocking them electrically and then placing a plastic hedgehog-like toy in their cages. A significant number of rats exposed to the hedgehog 1, 5, or 10 seconds after receiving an electric shock displayed avoidance behavior the following day. Backward conditioning had been established after a single trial—unlike Pavlov's dog, who required many trials before learning.

The significance of these results is not simply that they illustrate that backward conditioning can be accomplished. More important, they illustrate that many organisms have biological predispositions to learn behaviors that have survival value. Rats are prepared to learn to avoid strange objects such as plastic hedgehogs. And many preyed-upon animals, as Griffin and Galef (2005) point out, are highly prepared to learn about predators. That a warbler flies like the devil when a dark shadow sweeps by may well be because the shadow has previously been preceded by signs of alarm among other warblers, one of whom might have succumbed to a swift-flying merlin or a sharp-shinned hawk. And, as we saw in Chapter 2, humans seem to be prepared to learn strong taste aversions—which is useful when the tastes you learn to avoid belong to objects that might kill you if you ate them. Similarly, many people acquire fear of snakes, insects, and other potentially dangerous creatures relatively easily (Öhman et al., 2007).

Generalization and Discrimination

A dog trained to salivate in response to a buzzer may also salivate in response to a bell, a gong, or a human imitation of a buzzer. This phenomenon is called **stimulus generalization**. It involves making the same responses to different but related stimuli. An opposite phenomenon, **stimulus discrimination**, involves making different responses to highly similar stimuli.

Watanabe (2010) conditioned a group of pigeons by reinforcing them when they pecked at paintings that human judges had labeled "good" and not reinforcing them when they pecked at others judged "bad." When these pigeons were later shown new paintings, they *generalized* what they had learned, pecking the "good" paintings far more often than the "bad." As Watanabe puts it, "the results showed that pigeons could discriminate novel 'good' and 'bad' paintings" (2010, p. 75).

Extinction and Recovery

Many classically conditioned responses are remarkably durable. A dog conditioned to salivate in response to a tone and then left to do nothing but dog things for many months will immediately salivate when he is brought back into the laboratory and he hears the bell.

But classically conditioned responses can be eliminated—a process called **extinction**. Extinction requires that the experimenter present the conditioned stimulus repeatedly without the unconditioned stimulus. For example, if Pavlov's well-conditioned dog heard the tone repeatedly but it was never again paired with food, it would soon stop salivating in response to the tone.

Once a classically conditioned response has been extinguished, it can be reacquired much more easily than was initially the case. A dog who has learned to salivate in response to a tone and whose conditioned response is later extinguished will learn to salivate again after only one or two pairings of tone and food powder. In fact, an extinguished response sometimes recurs in the absence of any training. This phenomenon, termed *spontaneous recovery*, illustrates that behaviors that are apparently extinguished are not necessarily completely forgotten.

Contiguity

When I was 5 years old, my grandfather's dog bit me. I remember it as a vicious attack, although I suspect it really wasn't that bad. I haven't been bitten by a dog since, and I have raised and loved various dogs.

But last week my truck broke down on the way to the lake and I had to walk into a farmyard for assistance. When the farm dog came bounding across the field, barking, I tasted fear, as I have on

Classical conditioning is sometimes a good explanation for unconscious emotional learning—like acquiring a fear (or a love) of dogs.

many other occasions since I was 5. I'm conditioned to fear strange dogs. I have no control over my physiological reactions when I meet one.

Why does an emotional (or other) response such as fear become conditioned to a particular stimulus (or class of stimuli)? Pavlov's explanation is that the simultaneous or near-simultaneous presentation of a stimulus and a response leads to the formation of a neural link between the two. In this view, what is most important in the conditioning situation is the **contiguity** (closeness in time) of the stimulus and response. A contiguity explanation of classical conditioning maintains that the stimuli associated with "dog" (appearance, smell, sound, movement) were also associated with my initial fear response. Thus the sight, sound, or smell of a dog continues to plague me in my otherwise peaceful adult life.

Blocking

Although contiguity might appear to be an adequate explanation for what happened to Pavlov's dogs, and perhaps for my fear of strange dogs, there are some relatively simple experimental situations that it does not explain. For example, Kamin (1969) paired a noise and a light (two unconditioned stimuli) with electric shock (a conditioned stimulus) administered to the feet of a group of rats (we'll call them the A group). In this study, the light and noise were turned on, and immediately afterwards the rats were shocked. Classical conditioning theory would clearly predict that after the light and noise are paired often enough with the shock, either the light or the noise alone would cause an avoidance reaction in the rat. The prediction is correct.

But now Kamin threw a twist into the procedure. First he conditioned a group of rats by pairing only noise and electric shock (this is the B group). Then, once these rats showed a well-conditioned fear response to the noise, he conditioned them exactly as he had the A group, this time pairing both light and noise.

Recall that the A-group rats responded with fear to both the light and the noise. The B group rats also responded with fear to the noise. Strikingly, however, they showed no fear in response to the light in spite of the fact that they were conditioned in exactly the same way as the A group—but only after they had already been conditioned to the noise alone. It seems that for the B-group rats, learning that noise means shock *blocked* them from learning that light might also mean shock—a phenomenon appropriately labeled **blocking**.

Contiguity does not explain blocking. Clearly, if conditioning depends only on the simultaneous presentation of stimulus and response, there is no reason why both groups of animals should not have learned the same things.

One explanation for blocking is this: Whenever something new happens to an animal, it immediately searches its memory to see what events could have been used to predict it. When a lynx leaps at a rabbit and narrowly misses, the terrified rabbit scans its memory banks for immediately preceding events. Maybe it remembers a looming shadow, the thudding of padded footfalls, the stink of hungry lynx. And forever after, it flees from footfalls and shadows and hot stenches.

So when a rat receives a mild foot shock, it scans its memory to see what just preceded the event. The A-group rat notes that both light and noise always come before the shock, and so it freezes whenever it hears the noise or sees the light. But the B-group rat, who already knows that noise means shock, learns absolutely nothing new when later exposed to both noise and light followed by shock. Once the rat has learned that noise means shock, it no longer needs to pay attention to other stimuli.

Consequences

Learning is a fundamentally adaptive process: Changes in behavior are what allow organisms to survive. Clearly, we, like any other animal, need to remember what is edible and where to find it; we need to recognize potential enemies; we need to stay away from electric shocks. Put another way, we have to learn what goes with what—what the most likely outcomes of our behavior are.

One explanation for classical conditioning says, in effect, that what is learned is not a simple pairing of stimulus and response as a function of contiguity, but the establishment of relationships between stimuli. This explanation holds that what is important in a conditioning situation is the information a stimulus provides about the probability of other events. When a dog salivates in response to a tone, it is because the tone now predicts food. In the blocking experiments, animals who have learned that stimulus A means shock find it difficult to learn that B also means shock. That's because when A and B are subsequently paired, there is no new information provided by stimulus B.

Operant Conditioning

Classical conditioning theorists were not especially concerned with consequences; they studied relationships among stimuli and responses. But a second form of conditioning, **operant conditioning**, is built around the importance of behavior's consequences. Operant conditioning is closely associated with B. F. Skinner (1953, 1969, 1971, 1989), one of the most influential psychologists of this age. He dealt with a large and important piece of the puzzle.

Skinner noted that although classical conditioning explains some simple forms of learning where responses are associated with observable stimuli (termed **respondent** behavior), most of our behaviors are of a different kind. Behaviors such as walking, jumping, listening to music, writing a letter, and so on are more deliberate; they are seldom associated with a specific stimulus the way salivation might be. These behaviors appear more voluntary. Skinner calls them **operants** because they are operations that are performed on the environment rather than in response to it. Classical conditioning does not provide an easy explanation for behaviors such as deciding to go for a walk or, at a simpler level, a dog learning to sit or roll over.

The Skinner Box

In his investigations, Skinner used a highly innovative piece of equipment now known as a **Skinner box**. Typically, this *experimental chamber* is a small, cagelike structure with a metal grid for a floor. At one end is a lever; above it, a light; below it, a small tray. Outside the structure are various mechanical or electronic devices designed so that if the lever inside the cage is pushed down, the light will go on, a click will be heard (if someone is listening), and a food pellet will drop into the tray.

When a naive rat is placed in this box, it does not respond as predictably as a dog in Pavlov's harness. Its behaviors are more deliberate, perhaps more accidental. It does not know about Skinner boxes and food trays. It needs to be *magazine trained*. In a typical magazine training session, the experimenter depresses a button that releases a food pellet into the tray. At the same time, there is an audible clicking sound. Eventually the rat is drawn to the tray, perhaps by the smell of the pellet, perhaps only out of curiosity. Now the experimenter releases another food pellet, the rat hears the click, eats the pellet, hears another click, runs over to eat another pellet . . . In a very short period of time, the rat has been magazine trained.

Now the experimenter stops rewarding the rat unless it depresses the lever near the food tray. Most rats will eventually do so in the course of sniffing around and exploring. And when they do, they hear the telltale click and immediately rush over to the food tray. Very shortly, the rat will have learned to depress the lever. And if a light is paired with the presentation of food, the rat may eventually learn to depress the lever simply to see the light go on (Figure 4.6).

The Basic Operant Conditioning Model

All of the basic elements of Skinner's theory of operant conditioning are found in the rat-in-Skinner-box demonstration. The bar pressing is an operant—an emitted behavior. The food is a **reinforcer; reinforcement** is its effect. Any stimulus (condition or consequence) that increases the probability of a response is said to be reinforcing. In the Skinner box the light, too, may be a reinforcer.

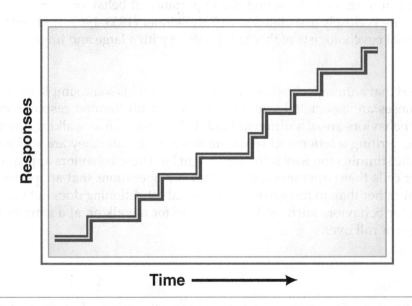

Figure 4.6

The graph is a typical learning curve recorded on a revolving drum. The drum revolves at a constant speed, and each depression of the lever causes the recording pen to move up a notch. Steepness of the curve reveals response rate.

What happens to a rat in the Skinner box may be described simply: A naive rat placed in this situation eventually emits a specific operant (bar pressing); the operant is reinforced; the probability of the operant occurring again increases with each reinforced repetition. When placed in the same situation on another occasion, the rat may begin to emit the operant immediately. The rat has learned associations not only between the operant and reinforcement, but also between the operant and specific aspects of the situation—called **discriminative stimuli (S^D)**. These discriminative stimuli might include things such as the sight and smell of the inside of the cage. They are stimuli that allow the rat to discriminate between this situation and others where the operant is impossible or will not be reinforced. To some extent, the operant is now controlled by discriminative stimuli as well as by its consequences.

In brief, Skinner's explanation of learning is based not on associations that might be formed between stimuli as a function of their co-occurrence (classical conditioning), but on associations that are established between a behavior and its consequences. Any other distinctive stimulus that happens to be present at the time of those consequences may also come to be associated with the operant.

The basic law of operant conditioning is the **law of effect**, first proposed by Edward Thorndike (1898). This law states that behaviors that are followed by reinforcement (Thorndike called them "satisfying states of affairs") are more likely to be repeated. Conversely, behaviors that are not followed by reinforcement (that lead to "annoyers," in Thorndike's words) are less likely to reoccur.

Shaping

If you wanted to train a rat to depress a lever, you might not have to do much more than sit by the Skinner box and watch while the rat sniffs around, eventually depresses the lever, eats, depresses the lever again, eats, and on and on. In short order, your rat will rush over and begin working the lever as soon as you put it in the cage.

But what if someone asked you to train a cow to sit on a chair? Do you think, if you put a chair in the cow's pen, she might eventually sit on it and you could then reward her with a nice bale of timothy hay?

Not too likely. But operant conditioning does suggest a way of teaching animals very complex behaviors. This is done by reinforcing small sequential steps in a chain of behaviors that will ultimately lead to the desired final behavior—a process called **shaping**. The animal (or person) does not learn a complete final response at once, but is reinforced instead for behaviors that come progressively closer to that response—hence the phrase *differential reinforcement of successive approximations*. Using shaping techniques, pigeons have been taught to bowl, chickens to play baseball, mules to dive into shallow waters from precarious heights, and pigs to point pheasants.

Shaping can be a useful technique for toilet-training infants. For example, in the first phase of a potty-training study described by Smeets, Lancioni, Ball, and Oliva (1985), whenever infants "strained" as though they were about to soil their diapers, mothers or research assistants tapped on a nearby potty and called or touched the infant. This first

Nope, you can't get me to fetch a stick or read a book. Those aren't things we cows do! It seems that organisms are biologically "prepared" to learn certain things and not others.

phase of the *shaping* procedure was designed to draw the child's attention to the potty and to reinforce the infant for paying attention to it—after which the infant was placed on that piece of equipment.

In the second phase, the potty was kept within reach of the child so that when signs of imminent defecation or urination appeared, the infant could be guided to grab the potty before being placed on it. And in the third phase, the potty was placed further away so that self-initiated movement toward the potty could be reinforced. By then, many of the infants had learned to crawl toward the potty.

Throughout all three phases, mothers and attendants reinforced the infants, primarily through smiling, verbal praise, and other gestures of approval. And all were toilet trained before they had learned to walk.

Schedules of Reinforcement

Skinner's primary interest had been with discovering the relationships between behavior and its consequences. His investigations with rats and pigeons quickly revealed that the way in which reinforcement is given (the *schedule of reinforcement*) is an important factor in determining responses.

The experimenter has several alternatives: Every correct response (called a "trial") might be reinforced (*continuous reinforcement*) or only some responses might be (*partial* or *intermittent reinforcement*). In turn, partial reinforcement can be based on a proportion of trials (*ratio reinforcement*) or on the passage of time (*interval reinforcement*). Furthermore, reinforcement can be regular (fixed), or irregular (random or variable) (Figure 4.7).

Effects of Different Schedules

The effects of different schedules of reinforcement are evident in three different *dependent* variables: rate of learning (*acquisition rate*); rate of responding; and rate of forgetting (*extinction rate*). The

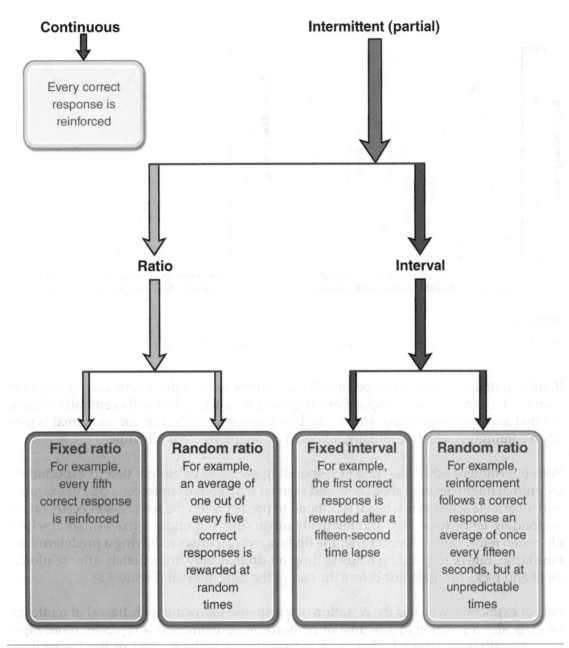

Figure 4.7

Schedules of reinforcement. Each type of schedule tends to generate a predictable pattern of responding.

independent variable in studies of operant conditioning is the experimenter's control of reinforcement (the schedule of reinforcement).

Initial learning—that is, rate of acquisition—is usually more rapid when every correct response is reinforced (a continuous schedule). If only some responses are reinforced (intermittent schedule), learning tends to be slower and more haphazard.

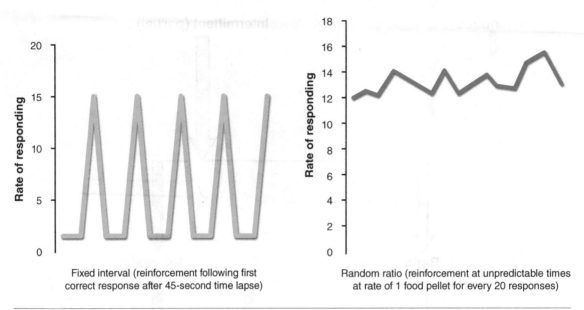

Figure 4.8

Idealized graphs showing the effects of two reinforcement schedules on rate of responding.

If, after initial learning, the experimenter continues to reinforce every correct response with food, the animal may respond at a high rate for a while, but will eventually become satiated and stop responding. Hence, the best training combination for an animal is usually a continuous schedule initially, followed by an intermittent schedule.

With intermittent schedules, rate of responding seems to be closely tied to expectations the animal might develop about how and when it will receive reinforcement. For example, under variable schedules, when it is difficult to predict when the reward will occur, rate of responding tends to be high and relatively unvarying. But under a fixed-interval schedule, when reinforcement occurs after the first correct responses following a predetermined time lapse, rate of responding tends to drop off dramatically immediately after reinforcement and picks up again just before the end of the time interval (Figure 4.8).

Rate of extinction, which is the cessation of a response following withdrawal of reinforcement, is also a function of schedule of reinforcement. Extinction is typically more rapid with a continuous schedule than with intermittent schedules. And of the intermittent schedules, variable ratio schedules typically result in the longest extinction times—a fact that has not escaped the attention of slot-machine programmers. Skinner reports the case of one pigeon that, after complete withdrawal of reinforcement, emitted more than 10,000 pecks before extinction was complete.

Types of Reinforcement

The fact that a pigeon would wear its beak to a frazzle before giving up an apparently unreinforced behavior may be evidence that reinforcement is not nearly as simple or as obvious as these few pages might suggest. We really have no basis for concluding that pecking itself is not a rewarding activity for the pigeon and that it requires no extrinsic reinforcement to be maintained. As we saw in Chapter 2, pigeons are biologically programmed to peck—as pigs are to root and humans are to explore. These activities don't necessarily require **extrinsic reinforcement**.

Extrinsic reinforcement includes the variety of external stimuli that might increase the probability of a behavior. In contrast, **intrinsic reinforcement** may be loosely defined as satisfaction, pleasure, or reward that is inherent in a behavior and that is therefore independent of external rewards. The satisfaction that people sometimes derive from their work is a form of intrinsic reinforcement; the money and the praise that might also result are forms of extrinsic reinforcement.

Skinner distinguishes between two broad classes of reinforcers. **Primary reinforcers** are stimuli that are rewarding for most people, most of the time, without anybody having had to learn that they are rewarding. They include food, drink, sleep, comfort, and sex.

Secondary reinforcers include the wide range of stimuli that may not be reinforcing initially but that eventually become reinforcing as a function of having been associated with other reinforcers. Thus, secondary reinforcers are learned; primary reinforcers are not. Social prestige, praise, money, and applause are very powerful secondary reinforcers.

In general, reinforcement is any stimulus (situation) that increases the probability of a response occurring. If the stimulus increases the probability of a behavior it follows, it is a **positive reinforcer**. Food pellets in the rat's cage are examples of positive reinforcers. So is the applause a performer receives, the money a worker gets paid, and the satisfaction a student gets from learning.

But some reinforcers are effective not when they are *added to* a situation, but rather when they are *removed*. For example, if a mild electric current is turned on in the rat's cage and then is turned off when the rat depresses the lever, the result might be an increase in the probability that the rat will subsequently press the lever. In this case, turning off the electric current is an example of a **negative reinforcer**. In much the same way, the removal of pain might be a negative reinforcer for taking some medication, even as the alleviation of withdrawal symptoms might be a negative reinforcer for continued drug use.

The important point is that reinforcement is defined in terms of its *effects* rather than in terms of the characteristics of the reinforcing stimuli used. And the effect of reinforcement, by definition, is to *increase* the probability of a behavior. A positive reinforcer does so when it *follows* a behavior; a negative reinforcer does so when it is *removed* following a behavior.

Operant conditioning is based on the consequences of behavior. They can be positive and reinforcing, as when this young lad is given his medal. Or they can be negative, as this driver is discovering.

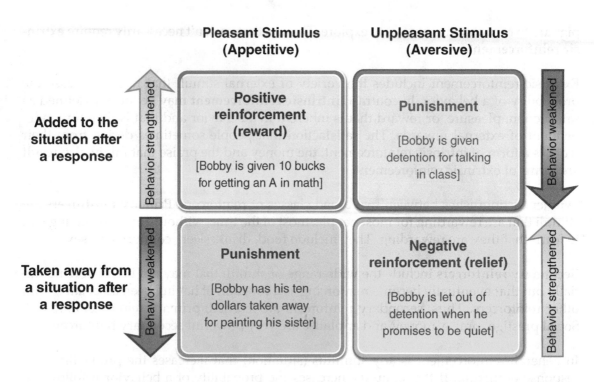

	Pleasant Stimulus (Appetitive)	Unpleasant Stimulus (Aversive)
Added to the situation after a response	**Positive reinforcement (reward)** [Bobby is given 10 bucks for getting an A in math]	**Punishment** [Bobby is given detention for talking in class]
Taken away from a situation after a response	**Punishment** [Bobby has his ten dollars taken away for painting his sister]	**Negative reinforcement (relief)** [Bobby is let out of detention when he promises to be quiet]

Figure 4.9

Reinforcement and punishment.

Punishment

Negative reinforcement is often confused with punishment, although the two are quite different. Negative reinforcement increases the probability of a response; the intended effect of punishment is precisely the opposite.

In essence, the consequences of behavior can involve the removal or presentation of stimuli that are pleasant or unpleasant (noxious). This presents the four distinct possibilities that are relevant to operant learning: positive reinforcement, negative reinforcement, and two types of punishment (Figure 4.9). There are countless illustrations of each of these possibilities in human behavior: Josephine is complimented on a new hairstyle (the addition of a pleasant stimulus; positive reinforcement); a pill relieves Norbert's headache (removal of an unpleasant stimulus: negative reinforcement); Arnaldo is reprimanded for losing his homework (addition of an unpleasant stimulus: punishment); Ronald has his jelly beans confiscated for throwing one in the goldfish bowl (removal of a pleasant stimulus; punishment).

The Ethics of Punishment

Is punishment ethical? Is it even effective? Or does it just teach us to be sneakier? Psychology offers some tentative answers.

First, punishment is not always effective in eliminating undesirable behavior. Certainly, it is not nearly as effective as reinforcement is in bringing about more desirable behavior.

Second, punishment often leads to undesirable emotional side effects sometimes associated with the punisher rather than with the punished behavior. For example, punishment might lead a child to dislike and fear the punisher, and might result in efforts to avoid punishment rather than efforts to avoid the transgressions for which the punishment was administered.

Third, punishment does not present a guide for desirable behavior; instead, it emphasizes undesirable behavior.

Finally, some research indicates that punishment sometimes has effects opposite to those intended. For example, Mulvaney and Mebert (2007) found that physical punishment of young children actually increased maladjustment and misbehavior later in life.

Verbal reprimands and loss of privileges are legitimate and effective forms of punishment not subject to the same objections as physical punishment.

Note that most of these objections apply mainly to physical punishment and not to other forms of punishment. These other forms of punishment (verbal reprimands, loss of privileges) have long been considered legitimate and effective means of controlling behavior. There are instances when punishment appears to be effective in suppressing destructive, aggressive, and dangerous behavior in children (and sometimes in adults as well).

Operant Conditioning and Human Behavior

Human behavior is seldom as simple as the key pecking of a pigeon or bar pressing of a rat. Still, many of the results of investigations with these animals generalize easily to our behavior. There is no denying the effectiveness of rewards and punishments in our lives. The persistence with which people play slot machines, where reinforcement is on a random ratio schedule, is one example.

But in some ways, we are quite unlike the caged rat or pigeon. Neither of these animals has much choice: to peck or not to peck; to press or not to press. You, on the other hand, have a stunning array of choices: to study or not to study, to go to a movie, to go to the gym, to text a friend, to listen to music, and on and on. And each of these behaviors might be associated with a very different type and schedule of reinforcement. In short, our lives illustrate what are called **concurrent schedules of reinforcement**—a variety of options, each linked with different kinds and schedules of possible reinforcement.

Studies of the effects of concurrent schedules on animal behavior typically present the animal with the choice of two behaviors (two levers to press; two keys to peck), each of which is linked to a different type or schedule of reinforcement. In a study of a new drug treatment for cocaine addiction, for example, rats had a choice of lever A, which would lead to a small dose of intravenously administered cocaine, or lever B, which would provide a highly palatable food as a reinforcer (Thomsen et al., 2008). The rat preferred the drug.

Other studies indicate that, when given choices, rats and pigeons typically match their responses to maximize the likelihood of reward (Herrnstein, 1997). Not surprisingly, studies with humans lead to much the same conclusion. In experimental situations where participants can choose between different behaviors with different probabilities of reward, they try to maximize the payout (Borrero, Frank, & Hausman, 2009).

4.3 A Transition to Cognitivism

Historically, behavioristic theory has recognized two general classes of behaviors, respondent and operant (elicited or emitted) and two general sets of rules and principles to account for each of these. One set relates to classical conditioning; the other, to operant conditioning.

Classical conditioning theory has been found most useful for explaining learning involving autonomic and reflexive reactions, such as those associated with emotional responses, over which we ordinarily have no conscious control.

Operant conditioning had generally been thought to apply to all behaviors that were not respondent—that is, to all behaviors that were not elicited by specific, identifiable stimuli but that simply occurred and could then presumably be brought under the control of reinforcement. Whereas classical conditioning appealed to principles of contiguity, operant conditioning invoked the law of effect: The consequences of behavior determine the probability of future occurrence or of change.

Problems for Traditional Behaviorism

Early behaviorists had hoped to discover laws of learning that would prove sufficiently general to explain most human behaviors. Unfortunately, behavior did not prove to be as simple as behavioristic theory might have indicated. Even animals sometimes behave in ways that are troublesome for traditional conceptions of behaviorism. In Chapter 2, for example, we described how the Brelands, two of Skinner's students, trained some 6,000 animals to perform a bunch of stunning animal tricks. But then many of these animals began to "misbehave," reverting to their more natural inclinations—a phenomenon called *instinctive drift*.

Instinctive drift presents a problem for traditional operant theory. It is now apparent that not all behaviors can be conditioned and maintained by schedules of reinforcement, that there is some degree of competition between unlearned, biologically based tendencies and the conditioning of related behaviors.

There are other examples of what are labeled *biological constraints* that have a clear effect on what an organism learns. Behaviors that are highly probable and relatively easy are typically those that have high adaptive value. Among humans, these might include behaviors such as avoiding bitter-tasting substances so that we don't poison ourselves, or learning a language so we can communicate. Among animals, behaviors such as pecking in birds and nosing around levers in rats are examples of highly probable, biologically based learning.

As we noted in Chapter 2, organisms are *prepared* to learn certain things and *contraprepared* to learn others. Thus, it is almost impossible to teach a rat to depress a lever to escape an electric shock (Bolles, 1970). A rat's natural response to danger is to fight, flee, freeze, or become frantic; it is not to approach a lever and depress it. Therefore, a rat can be trained to jump to escape shock. The ease with which this is accomplished demonstrates preparedness. That the rat cannot be trained to depress a lever to escape a shock illustrates contrapreparedness. As Guthrie (1935) put it, "We cannot teach cows to retrieve a stick because this is one of the things that cows do not do" (p. 45).

Insight

Bertrand Russell (1927) made the interesting observation that U.S. and German rats must be quite different. "Animals studied by Americans rush about frantically, with an incredible display of hustle and pep, and at last achieve the desired result by chance," he wrote, adding, "Animals observed by Germans sit still and think, and at last evolve the solution out of their inner consciousness" (p. 33).

He was referring to the fact that U.S. psychology was then largely dominated by the behavioristic notion that responses are learned as a result of the reinforcement of a "correct" response that occurs through trial and error (that is, by chance). At the same time, some German psychologists were working on different parts of the human puzzle.

One of these psychologists, Wolfgang Köhler, spent four years in the Canary Islands during World War I trying to frustrate apes with a pair of problems: the "stick" problem and the "box" problem. Both problems are essentially the same; only the solutions differ. In both, an ape finds itself unable to reach a tantalizing piece of fruit, either because it is too high or because it is outside the cage beyond reach. In the "stick" problem, the solution involves inserting a small stick inside a larger one to reach the fruit. In the "box" problem, the ape has to place boxes one on top of the other.

The solution, insists Köhler (1927), does not involve trial and error, although some of that type of behavior might be displayed in the early stages. When the ape realizes that none of its customary behaviors is likely to obtain the bananas, it may sit for a while, apparently pondering the problem. And then, bingo, it leaps up, quickly joins the sticks or piles the boxes, and reaches for the prize.

That, according to Köhler, is **insight**, the sudden recognition of relationships among elements of a problem. It is a complex, largely unconscious process, not easily amenable to scientific examination.

The behaviorists were hard-pressed to explain the behavior of Köhler's apes. Many were tempted to assume that the apes simply tried a number of apelike actions, eventually resorting to combinations of these when none of the simple behaviors was rewarded. Staunch behaviorists would assume that the ape's recognition of the solution would not occur until the fruit was in hand.

Many psychologists, however, were reluctant to accept behavioristic explanations for insight, a phenomenon that is common enough among our species that its existence is difficult to deny. And in time, the lowly rat was allowed to contribute in a small way to the study of insight.

In a pioneering study, Tolman and Honzik (1930) allowed a rat to become totally familiar with a maze in which there were several routes to the goal. Once the rat has learned the maze, barriers were placed so that the rat had to choose one of the alternatives. Typically, a rat will always select the shortest route—and the next shortest if that one is later blocked. The behaviorist assumption is that the rats developed a preference for the shortest routes as a result of receiving reinforcement more quickly when they follow these routes than when they stupidly meander through lengthy detours.

The maze, shown in Figure 4.10, has three alternatives. Path 1 is the most direct and is almost invariably chosen when there are no barriers. When there is a barrier at A, the rat would be expected to choose alternative 2. This is, in fact, the case some 93 percent of the time. When the barrier is at B, rats might again be expected to select path 2 since its opening is not blocked. They don't. These clever rats now run all the way around path 3, despite the fact that they should still have a higher preference for path 2. One explanation

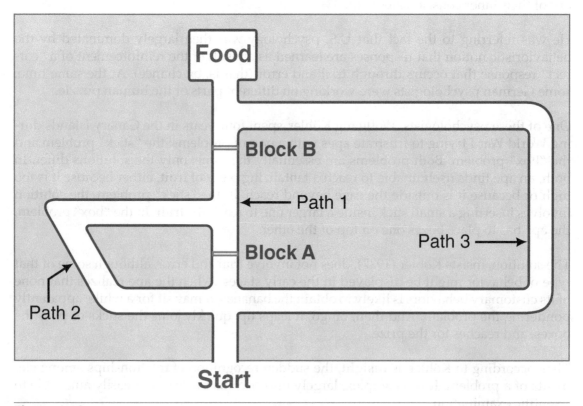

Figure 4.10

In the Tolman and Honzik (1930) blocked-path study, rats that had learned this maze almost invariably selected path 3 when path 1 was blocked at B. It seemed they somehow knew that the barrier at B also blocked the much shorter path 2.

is simply that they have developed a *cognitive map*—a mental representation—of the entire maze, and that they understand that a barrier at B also blocks route 2.

Other studies have shown that a rat will learn a maze even without any tangible reinforcement. Rats who are allowed to explore a maze without food learn the maze considerably more quickly than naive rats when food is later introduced. Such observations indicate that rats, too, have some understanding of their environments that goes beyond the formation of simple associations among stimuli, responses, and rewards.

And we humans, too, form cognitive maps that allow us to navigate in our environment. In doing so, report Foo, Warren, Duchon, and Tarr (2005), we tend to rely heavily on our recollection of landmarks and their positions relative to each other and to our preferred paths. Forming mental representations of our worlds is a uniquely *cognitive* activity.

4.4 Cognitive Approaches

Instinctive drift, delayed taste aversion, cognitive maps, and insightful learning present serious problems for traditional behavioristic theories. And if behaviorism does not explain the simpler behaviors of animals, then the presumably more complex behaviors of humans might be even less well explained. If even animals have concepts and apparent thought processes, psychology should perhaps concern itself with these as well as with more easily observed and described behaviors.

Enter **cognitivism**, an approach concerned mainly with intellectual events such as problem solving, information processing, thinking, and imagining. It is an approach that has sometimes rejected behaviorism as overly mechanistic and incomplete. Behaviorism does not deal well with thinking—with *cognition*. For that, we need other approaches.

The Main Beliefs of Cognitive Psychology

The dominant metaphor in cognitive psychology, notes Garnham (2009), is a computer-based, *information processing (IP)* metaphor. The emphasis is on the processes that allow the perceiver to perceive, that determine how the actor acts, and that underlie thinking, remembering, solving problems, and so on. Not surprisingly, experimental participants in cognitive research tend to be human rather than nonhuman.

Learning Involves Mental Representation

Cognitive approaches to learning presuppose mental representation and information processing. The behaviorist view, as we saw, tends to describe learning as a largely unconscious process where factors such as repetition, contiguity, and reinforcement push the organism this way and that. In contrast, the cognitive view describes an organism that is more *thoughtful*, that can mentally imagine and anticipate the consequences of behavior. In this view, the learner is not a passive receiver of information, pushed and prodded by stimuli and their consequences. Instead, the learner actively participates in the learning process, discovering, organizing, and using strategies to maximize learning and reward.

Learners Are Not Identical

Behaviorism sees all learners as relatively equal in terms of their susceptibility to the effects of reward and punishment. In contrast, cognitivism emphasizes that learners are different. Individuals come with different background information, different inclinations and motives, different genetic characteristics, and different cultural origins. As a result, even in the same situation, they often learn very different things.

New Learning Builds on Previous Learning

The importance of individual difference among learners rests partly on the fact that new learning is often highly dependent upon previously acquired knowledge and skills. Take a hundred naive rats, and most of them can easily be conditioned to depress a small lever. But take a hundred 15-year-olds, and perhaps only a handful will be ready to understand the mysteries of quantum theory.

As we see in later chapters, for most important topics in human psychology (such as memory, motivation, and social learning), the continuing search for pieces of the puzzle has taken a largely cognitive turn.

Bandura's Social Cognitive Theory

Imitation is a powerful teacher among children. And sometimes among animals too.

You cannot, in any simple sense, *condition* someone to learn quantum physics. Still, explains Albert Bandura (1997), we learn many things through conditioning. It is clear that we are highly responsive to reinforcement—and perhaps to punishment as well. What is not so clear in most accounts of human learning through operant conditioning is just how operants come about in the first place.

Bar pressing and key pecking are simple behaviors that are highly likely to occur in a given situation. A complex human behavior such as driving a car is not likely to appear fully formed, ready to be reinforced. And *shaping* such a complex behavior by reinforcing behaviors that slowly approximate the complete sequence of required behaviors would be a highly ineffective way of learning.

Nor do we learn complex behaviors such as how to drive a car through trial and error. We learn many of these complex behaviors, explains Bandura, through **observational learning**—that is, by observing and imitating **models**. And, in a sense, learning through **imitation** is a form of operant learning in that the imitative behavior is like an operant that is learned as a result of being reinforced.

A large number of studies indicate that social imitation is a powerful teacher among humans: Even children as young as 2 or 3 imitate and learn from each other. Moreover, a number of investigations show that monkeys, dogs, birds, and dolphins can learn a variety of relatively complex behaviors by observing their trained fellow-animals (Ferrari et al., 2009; Miller, Rayburn-Reeves, & Zentall, 2009).

Models

In Bandura's **social cognitive theory**, models are not limited to people who might be imitated by others; they include **symbolic models** as well. Symbolic models are any representation or pattern that can copied, such as oral or written instructions, pictures, book characters, mental images, cartoon or film characters, and television actors.

Models provide the imitator with two kinds of information: how to perform an act, and what the likely consequences of doing so are. And if the observer now imitates the behavior, there is a possibility of two different kinds of reinforcement. One, **direct reinforcement**, results from the consequences of the act itself. If 10-month-old Norbert is given a glass of milk when, in trying to imitate his sister, he says, "mwuff," he may soon learn to say "mwuff" whenever he is thirsty.

The other source of reinforcement is *secondhand*, labeled **vicarious reinforcement.** When you see someone doing something repeatedly, you unconsciously assume that the behavior must be reinforcing for that person. You might now imitate this behavior and continue to produce it even in the absence of any direct reinforcement.

Reciprocal Determinism

There is little doubt that we engage in many behaviors because of the reinforcing consequences of so doing. But reinforcement does not control us blindly, explains Bandura (1997); its effects depend largely on our *awareness* of the relationship between our behavior and its outcomes. What is fundamentally important is our ability to figure out cause-and-effect relationships and to anticipate the outcomes of our behaviors.

Not only can we anticipate and imagine the consequences of our behavior and therefore govern ourselves accordingly, but we can also deliberately select and arrange our environments. That we are both products and producers of our environment is the basis of Bandura's concept of **triadic reciprocal determinism**.

In this view, there are three principal features of our social cognitive realities: our personal factors (our personalities; our intentions; what we know and feel); our actions (our actual behaviors), and our environments (both the social and physical aspects of our world). These three factors affect each other reciprocally. For example, a harsh, demanding environment might alter Joe's personality, making him bitter and cynical. This might change his behavior, driving him to more selfish acts. These actions might destroy friendships, thus changing important aspects of his social environment. And the changing social environment, in turn, might further affect his personality and his behavior.

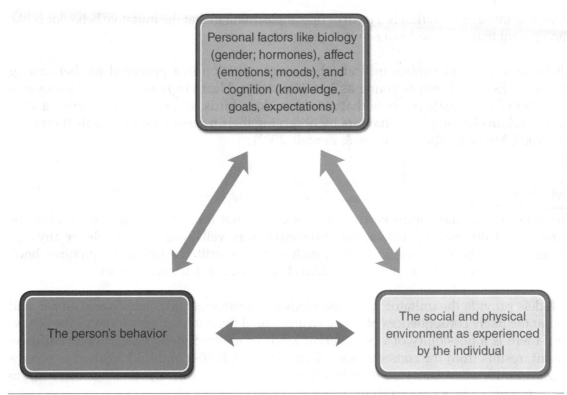

Figure 4.11

Bandura's notion of triadic reciprocal determinism. Behavior, the person, and the environment all mutually influence and change each other.

On the other hand, instead of making him bitter and cynical, a tough environment might lead Joe to rally his friends that they might struggle together to ease their lot. The reciprocal influence of person, action, and environment might be no less in this case, but the outcomes might be vastly different (Figure 4.11).

Effects of Imitation

Through observational learning, we learn three different classes of behaviors, explain Bandura and Walters (1963): We learn brand new behaviors (**modeling effect**); we learn to suppress or stop suppressing deviant behaviors (**inhibitory/disinhibitory effect**); and we learn to engage in behaviors similar but not identical to the model's behavior (**eliciting effect**) (Table 4.1).

Humans as Agents of Their Own Behaviors

Some of our behaviors, such as our classically conditioned fears, are under the control of stimuli. Others, like our highly reinforced imitations, are controlled more by their consequences. And a third group of behaviors are controlled by cognitive activities such as thinking and imagining. Bandura labels these three behavior control systems *stimulus control*, *outcome control*, and *symbolic control*.

Table 4.1 Three Effects of Imitation: Bandura's Theory

Type of Effect	Description	Illustration
Modeling Effect	Acquiring a new behavior as a result of observing a model.	After watching a mixed martial arts program, Jenna tries out a few novel moves on her young brother, Liam.
Inhibitory-Disinhibitory Effect	Stopping or starting some deviant behavior after seeing a model punished or rewarded for similar behavior.	After watching Jenna, Nora, who already knew all of Jenna's moves but hadn't used them in a long time, now tries a few of them on her sister (disinhibitory effect). Nora abandons her pummeling of her sister when Liam's mother responds to his wailing and takes Jenna's smartphone away (inhibitory effect).
Eliciting Effect	Engaging in behavior related to that of a model.	Robin tries to learn to play the guitar after her cousin is applauded for singing at the family reunion.

In the end, although stimuli and outcomes might affect our behaviors, it is the symbolic control system that is most important in Bandura's description. We are not simply pawns pushed hither and yon by rewards and punishments and classically conditioned reflexes. We are in charge, Bandura (2001) insists: We are agents of our own actions.

Being agents of our own actions requires three things: First, it requires *intentionality*. If someone bumps into you, causing you to spill your latte on your friend, you would not be considered an agent of that action. But if you deliberately threw your coffee at said friend, you would be the agent of *that* action.

Second, intentionality implies *forethought*. It is the ability to symbolize that allows you to foresee the consequences of the actions you intend. You could not intend to amuse your friend with your behavior unless you could foresee the effects of tossing your coffee.

Finally, being agents of our actions implies being able to reflect on them and to reflect on ourselves and especially on our own effectiveness—on our **self-efficacy**. Self-efficacy, as we see in Chapter 6, is a very important concept in human motivation. Our estimates of our personal effectiveness, of our likelihood of success, have a lot to do with what we choose to do and how much effort we are willing to expend doing it.

4.5 Practical Applications of Learning Principles

There are countless, everyday, intuitive applications of classical and operant conditioning principles and of Bandura's social-cognitive theory. People are controlled and manipulated by organizations and by other people, sometimes quite unconsciously—although often consciously as well. Performers' behaviors are shaped by the responses of their audience; the behavior of teachers is shaped by the responses of their students; consumers' behaviors are affected by advertising media; models are used to influence consumers; drug addicts are reinforced by the effects of the drugs they take. Even criminals are reinforced by the outcomes of their behaviors.

Applications of Behaviorism

Findings in behaviorism have led to the development of a variety of practical applications in fields such as education and psychotherapy. For example, many teachers use systematic reinforcement programs to foster learning or to prevent or correct deviant behavior.

General instructional recommendations that derive from conditioning principles suggest that teachers should:

- Try to maximize pleasant unconditioned stimuli in their classrooms. This might involve making sure learners are comfortable, that surroundings are colorful and upbeat, and that no individual is faced with overwhelming demands. At the same time, teachers need to minimize the unpleasant aspects of being a student to reduce the number and potency of negative unconditioned stimuli in the classroom.
- Use punishment—especially corporal punishment—sparingly as it is not very effective for eliminating undesirable behavior and even less effective for teaching desirable behavior.
- Be aware of what is being paired with what in the classroom, so as not to inadvertently condition undesirable behaviors. If the teacher smiles when Johnny does something outrageous—or if his classmates all laugh—doing outrageous things may well be what Johnny learns.
- Limit the use of repetition without reinforcement; it does little to improve learning.
- Emphasize positive rather than aversive methods of control.

The systematic application of learning principles to change behavior is labeled **behavior modification**. Behavior modification is widely used in schools and institutions for children with behavioral and emotional problems, as well as in the treatment of mental disorders. Essentially, it involves the deliberate and systematic use of reinforcement, and sometimes punishment, to modify behavior.

Two behavior modification techniques are described in Chapter 9. One, *systematic desensitization*, is widely used to treat phobias (intense, debilitating fears). Basically, it involves conditioning a relaxation response that conflicts with the fear responses characteristic of phobias. The other, *aversive conditioning*, is sometimes used to treat drug or alcohol addiction. It attempts to attach negative, avoidance, responses to the use of these substances, perhaps by using stimuli such as electric shock or nausea-inducing drugs.

Applications of Cognitivism

Cognitivism typically views the learner as an active, information processing being, capable of imagining and anticipating the consequences of behavior, and essentially responsible for its own actions as well as for constructing its own view of the world. This orientation lends itself especially well to **discovery learning**. This is a learner-centered approach where content is not organized by the teacher and presented in a relatively final form.

Instead, learners are expected to investigate and discover for themselves, and to *construct* their own mental representations—hence the current expression for discovery and other related approaches, widely used in educational circles: **constructivism**.

A cognitive view of the learner also supports approaches designed not so much to teach students specific content, but more to teach them *how* to learn—to make self-regulated learners of them. To this end, cognitively oriented educational psychologists suggest that teachers should develop problem-solving skills in students—for example, by giving them practice with the five-step strategy for general problem solving suggested by Bransford and Stein (1993). The five steps are easily remembered with the acronym IDEAL:

Identify problems and opportunities

Define goals and represent the problem

Explore possible strategies

Anticipate outcomes and act

Look back and learn

There are a wide variety of specific cognitively based approaches to teaching, including **reciprocal teaching**, a method designed to improve reading comprehension, and **cognitive apprenticeship**, where novice learners are paired with older learners, teachers, or parents who serve as mentors and guides. There are also various programs designed to develop cognitive strategies, as well as to help learners become aware of their own use of cognitive strategies, to reflect on them, to evaluate their effectiveness, and to change them as needed.

We are all players of what Flavell (1985) calls *the game of cognition*. It is a strategic game—a game for which we need to have mastered the strategies that allow us to understand and make sense of information, to organize it and process it, to recall it when we need it, and to use it in the best way possible. Most of us learn cognitive strategies incidentally in the course of learning other things. Now cognitive psychology suggests there should be concerted attempts to make sure all learners develop the best cognitive strategies possible.

Some people play the game of cognition very badly.

Some play it extraordinarily well.

Main Points

1. **What Is Learning?** Learning is a relatively permanent change in behavior resulting from experience but not including the effects of fatigue, maturation, drugs, injury, or disease.
2. **Behavioristic Approaches:** Classical conditioning (Pavlov) describes learning through stimulus substitution as a result of repeated pairings of an unconditioned with a conditioned stimulus. Operant conditioning (Skinner) describes changes in the probability of a response as a function of its consequences.

3. **A Transition to Cognitivism:** Phenomena such as *blocking*, *instinctive drift*, *delayed taste-aversion*, and *insightful learning* present problems for behavioristic explanations, but less for cognitive explanations.

4. **Cognitive Approaches:** Cognitive psychology describes a self-aware individual, able to anticipate the consequences of behavior and guide actions accordingly. Bandura's social cognitive theory explains how we learn by imitating (observational learning), how we shape our environments even as they shape us (triadic reciprocal determinism), and how we are agents of our own actions.

5. **Practical Applications of Learning Principles:** Behavioristic approaches to learning underscore the importance of maximizing positive stimuli and minimizing the more negative. They suggest ways of using reinforcement and punishment for instruction as well as in behavior modification programs. Cognitive approaches encourage learner-centered approaches to instruction (discovery learning, reciprocal teaching, teaching problem solving, and helping learners develop cognitive strategies).

Thoughts and Suggestions

1. Everyone has be influenced and taught by families, communities, tribes, and cultures from the day we were born. We didn't really have a say about what year we were born or who are parents would be, or what culture we grew up in. Everyone has been shaped and conditioned by things outside of our control. You were raised by Jewish parents, it is unlikely you were taught about the virtues of the Hindu religion and vice versa. If your parents were strong democrats, it is unlikely you were told about the republican party. And on and on it goes. Can you think of any beliefs, views, or behaviors, you have had to unlearn and then relearn from your experiences of growing up acculturalization?

2. Can you think of any mental or lifestyle habits that you personally have that you would like to unlearn? How would you go about shaping and conditioning a new thought life and/or lifestyle to improve your spiritual, psychological, social, and/or daily lifestyle?

Suggested readings from Hock, R. R. (1999). *Forty studies that changed psychology* (3rd ed.). Upper Saddle River, NJ: Prentice Hall. (ISBN #: 0-13-922725-3):

- Reading 9: It's Not Just About Salivating Dogs?
- Reading 10: Little Emotional Albert
- Reading 11: Knock Wood
- Reading 12: See Aggression . . . Do Aggression!

Study Terms

behavior modification	cognitive apprenticeship
behavioristic theories	cognitive theories
blocking	cognitivism
classical conditioning	concurrent schedules of reinforcement

conditioned response (CR)

conditioned stimulus (CS)

constructivism

contiguity

direct reinforcement

discovery learning

discriminative stimuli (S^D)

eliciting effect

extinction

extrinsic reinforcement

imitation

inhibitory/disinhibitory effect

insight

instincts

intrinsic reinforcement

law of effect

learning

modeling effect

models

negative reinforcer

observational learning

operant conditioning

operants

positive reinforcer

primary reinforcers

reciprocal teaching

reflexes

reinforcement

reinforcer

respondent

responses

secondary reinforcers

self-efficacy

shaping

Skinner box

social cognitive theory

stimuli

stimulus discrimination

stimulus generalization

symbolic models

triadic reciprocal determinism

unconditioned response (UR)

unconditioned stimulus (US)

vicarious reinforcement

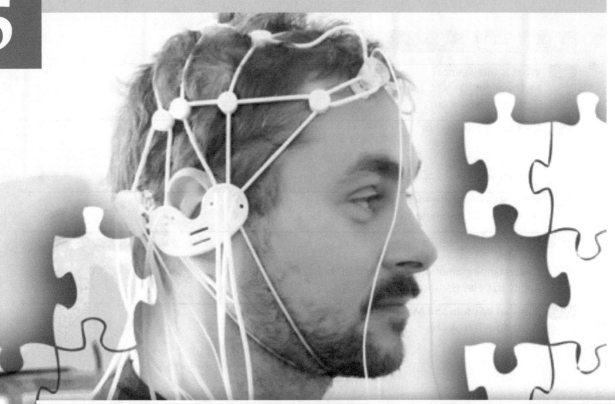

5

Mental and Emotional Intelligence

Focus Questions

By the end of the chapter, you should be able to answer the following questions:

- What are some important techniques for improving memory?
- Which common beliefs about IQ are mythical?
- How can intelligence be defined and measured?
- What determines intelligence?
- What is emotional intelligence?
- What is spiritual intelligence?

Chapter Outline

· ·

Inspirational Words

Then shalt thou understand righteousness, and judgment, and equity; yea, every good path. When wisdom entereth into thine heart, and knowledge is pleasant unto thy soul; Discretion shall preserve thee, understanding shall keep thee: To deliver thee from the way of the evil man, *from the man that speaketh froward things; Who leave the paths of uprightness, to walk in the ways of darkness; Who rejoice to do evil,* and *delight in the frowardness of the wicked; Whose ways* are *crooked, and* they *froward in their paths. Proverbs 2: 9–15.*

The wise in heart shall be called prudent: and the sweetness of the lips increaseth learning. Understanding is a wellspring of life unto him that hath it: but the instruction of fools is folly. The heart of the wise teacheth his mouth, and addeth learning to his lips. Pleasant words are as *an honeycomb, sweet to the soul, and health to the bones. There is a way that seemeth right unto a man, but the end thereof are the ways of death. Proverbs 16: 21–25.*

Because the foolishness of God is wiser than men; and the weakness of God is stronger than men. 1 Corinthians 1:25.

The fool hath said in his heart, There is *no God. They are corrupt, they have done abominable works,* there is *none that doeth good. Psalm 14:1.*

5.1 What Is Intelligence?

But you do have to be reasonably intelligent to learn the phonetic system. Does that mean you have to have a high **intelligence quotient (IQ)**? Just what is intelligence? Is IQ the best measure of intelligence?

Myths about IQ

Or, just as important, what is *not* intelligence? What beliefs are mythical? Which ones might be puzzle pieces that mislead us and that should be discarded?

Myth 1

IQ is synonymous with intelligence. Not true. IQ is just a score on an "intelligence" test. These tests do not always measure very accurately, and they do not always measure what they are intended to measure. Although they reflect some of the characteristics of what we think of as intelligence, they may also be influenced by factors such as mood, fatigue, and motivation. Hence IQ and intelligence are not synonymous.

Myth 2

IQ tests measure everything that is important for intelligent behavior. Unfortunately, intelligence tests seldom tap abilities such as creativity, perseverance, motivation, and emotional or social skills—all fundamentally important components of what Sternberg (2005) describes as *practical* or *successful* intelligence.

Myth 3

IQ tests are fair and impartial. They should be, but, sadly, many are culturally biased. That's because they have usually been developed and standardized with white middle-class children, and therefore tend to favor them. Note, however, that more recent revisions of the most widely used intelligence tests often include a variety of minority groups in their standardization samples to increase their fairness.

Myth 4

IQ is more or less fixed. What we have is what we have. It is dangerous to believe this myth because, as Dweck (2006) points out, if we believe this, we will make no efforts to increase our intelligence. And if we find a task difficult, we are likely to give up rather than try to master it. That is, if we think intelligence is fixed, we need to believe we have more than an average amount if we are to have the confidence to undertake challenging tasks.

That IQ is not fixed is apparent not only in the fact that people's measured IQs can change dramatically, but also in the observation that measured IQ throughout the world has been increasing at the rate of about 3 IQ points a decade, a phenomenon known as the **Flynn effect** (Flynn, 1994; Flynn & Weiss, 2007) (Figure 5.1). The reasons for this phenomenon are not clear. Better school programs, improved nutrition, increasing familiarity with tests, and stimulation from technology and media may all contribute.

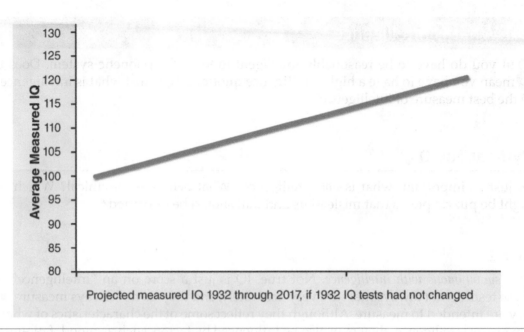

Figure 5.1

The Flynn effect: Measured intelligence has been increasing at about 3 IQ points per decade. If our 1932 measures of IQ had not been revised and renormed, our average measured IQ would now be over 120!

It is not a myth that measured IQ predicts success; witness this Columbia doctoral graduate with a high IQ. But it is a myth that it is a fixed quality that cannot be improved.

Not a Myth

IQ predicts success, both in life and in school. While considerable research supports this conclusion (for example, Deary, Strand, Smith, & Fernandes, 2007), this does not mean that IQ is the only, or even the most important, predictor of future success. Motivation, personality characteristics, and previous achievement may be even more important (Thorndike & Hagen, 1977).

Views of Intelligence

When psychologists and related "experts" were asked, way back in 1921, what they thought intelligence was, most agreed that it had to do with the ability to learn and to adapt. And when another group was asked the same question 65 years later, they responded in much the same way, although many now added that the individuals' awareness of their own cognitive processes and their ability to monitor and control these processes were also important (Sternberg & Kaufman, 1998).

In spite of this apparent agreement, there have been a wide range of different definitions and views of intelligence.

Successful Intelligence: Sternberg

The best approach, suggests Sternberg (2006), is to look at people who are most successful in adapting to the world. If we do that, we find that these people are those who not only learn well, but who are adept at selecting and even at shaping the world to maximize their success. What they have is *successful intelligence* as opposed to *psychometric*, or *measured*, intelligence. Note how this view emphasizes *adaptation*. What it says, in effect, is that the most intelligent people are those who are most successful in choosing or changing their environments or their goals to match their abilities. It would not be intelligent for someone with an uninspiring and uncontrollable voice to strive for a career as a singer, although it might be quite intelligent for the same person to become a pianist.

Successful intelligence requires that the individual be able to evaluate options, devise strategies for attaining goals, and assess the extent to which goals are being met. In other words, it requires *analytical* abilities, and it also requires *creative* abilities. These make it possible to invent strategies, to uncover new options, to find ways of selecting and shaping the environment.

Finally, successful intelligence requires the sorts of *practical* abilities that are involved in carrying out options, in putting into practice the behaviors and skills that are required for selecting, shaping, and adapting to environments.

These three groups of abilities—*analytical*, *creative*, and *practical*—make up the three components of what Sternberg labels the **triarchic theory of successful intelligence**. It is a theory that highlights the importance of adaptation; it also emphasizes creative and practical abilities, features that conventional intelligence tests typically do not take into consideration (Figure 5.2).

This view of intelligence has the advantage of making the concept less abstract and theoretical. It brings it to a more concrete, more easily understood level. It also has the

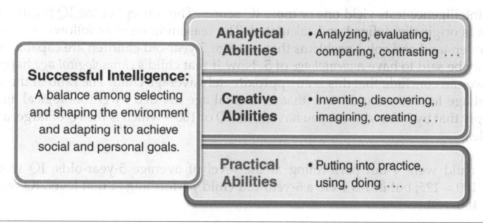

Figure 5.2

The three arches of Sternberg's triarchic view of successful intelligence.

advantage of emphasizing that intelligence is not a fixed, unchanging quality about which we can do nothing. In this view, intelligence is a little like a box of tools that we use to play the game of cognition. We might each have very different tools in our boxes, but we can certainly learn to take advantage of the ones we do have. And we might also learn from how others use their tools.

Multiple Intelligences: Gardner

Gardner points out that if you ask people how smart they are, many will hesitate. Why? Because it depends on what they think you mean. If, instead, you ask not "How smart are you?" but rather, "How are you smart?" the answer might be more immediate and more revealing. Now the person can say, "Hey, I'm really good at math." Or, "I'm smart when it comes to remembering names." Or, "Well, compared to my brother, I'm pretty smart."

We don't have just one kind of "smarts," explains Gardner (2006). We have at least eight largely unrelated kinds of intelligence: logical-mathematical, linguistic, musical, spatial, bodily kinesthetic, naturalistic, interpersonal, and intrapersonal. Their characteristics are summarized in Figure 5.3.

Sadly, our schools tend to ignore many of these abilities. And when we try to measure intelligence, we overlook most of them as well, says Gardner. Mostly, we concentrate on logical and linguistic abilities; most of the other abilities cannot easily be measured with our paper-and-pencil tests.

5.2 Measuring Intelligence

Intelligence tests are used mainly for prediction. In a sense, an intelligence test score is a prediction that an individual will do well or less well on tasks requiring intelligence.

The IQ

Most intelligence tests yield one or more IQ scores. The concept of the IQ is quite simple as it was originally defined and calculated. The reasoning went as follows: A child who can understand and solve problems that average 5-year-old children are capable of solving may be said to have a *mental age* of 5. Now if that child's *chronological age* happens to be 5, we can conclude that this is an approximately average child. The ratio of this child's mental age to chronological age (that is, mental age divided by chronological age) is 1. Multiply that by 100 and there you have it, an IQ of 100—which is the IQ of large, average samples.

If the child were 4 but performing at the level of average 5-year-olds, IQ would be $5/4 \times 100 = 125$; but if this were a 6-year-old child performing at that level, IQ would be $4/5 \times 100 = 80$.

The earliest recognized measure of intelligence was based on this reasoning and calculation. Alfred Binet and Théodore Simon, two French psychologists, developed the first

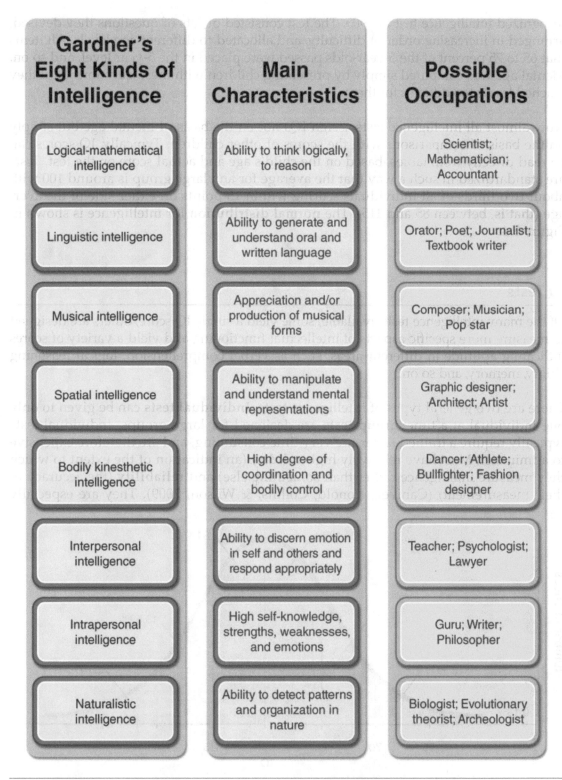

Figure 5.3

Gardner's eight kinds of intelligence, their characteristics, and possible occupations. Gardner also explored the possibility that there might be an additional type of intelligence dealing with existential questions (relating to spirituality and the purpose of life), but he concluded that it did not meet the criteria for inclusion among the eight intelligences.

recognized intelligence test in 1905. The test consisted of sets of questions they devised, arranged in increasing order of difficulty, and allocated to different age levels. All items that 65 to 75 percent of the 5-year-olds passed were placed in the 5-year level, and so on. Mental age was computed simply by presenting children with these questions until they reached levels too difficult for them.

Now almost all intelligence tests assign IQs not on the basis of mental age but simply on the basis of comparisons with the scores of other children. Typically, IQ scores can be read directly from tables, based on the child's age and actual score on the test. Tests are standardized in such a way that the average for any large group is around 100 with about two thirds of all individuals scoring within 15 points on either side of the average (that is, between 85 and 115). The **normal distribution** for intelligence is shown in Figure 5.4.

IQ Tests

Of the many intelligence tests available, some yield a single IQ score; others are designed to measure more specific aspects of intellectual functioning and yield a variety of scores indicating aptitude in different areas, such as verbal comprehension, logical reasoning ability, memory, and so on.

There are two general types of intelligence tests. **Individual tests** can be given to only one individual at a time; **group tests** are designed for large groups. Individual tests typically require a trained tester, are very time consuming, and are therefore expensive to administer. Most have relatively high **validity** (an indication of the extent to which they measure intelligence rather than something else) and **reliability** (the accuracy of their measurement) (Canivez, Konold, Collins, & Wilson, 2009). They are especially

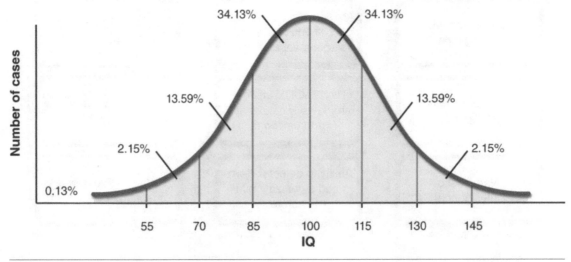

Figure 5.4

A normal curve depicting the theoretical distribution of IQ scores in an unselected group. Average score is 100; 68.26 percent of the population score between 85 and 115; only 2.29 percent score either above 130 or below 70.

useful for identifying exceptional talent and for diagnosing learning problems (Shavinina, 2009). The best-known individual intelligence tests are the Stanford-Binet, currently in its fifth revision, and the Wechsler Intelligence Scale for Children (4th ed.) (versions are available for preschoolers and for adults). Both can be administered only by trained professionals.

Group tests, which are typically paper-and-pencil or computer administered, can usually be administered by anyone. As is the case for individual tests, the scores they yield can then be interpreted using tables provided by test makers. The Cognitive Abilities Test (CogAT) is one of dozens of widely used group intelligence tests. Another is the Goodenough-Harris Drawing Test (Harris, 1963), which provides a measure of intelligence based on the child's drawings of a person. Drawings are judged in terms of factors such as detail, proportion, and presence or absence of specific body parts, all of which reveal the child's conceptual sophistication. It has the advantage of being nonthreatening and nonverbal, and can therefore be used with children from different cultures or those who might have language problems. Research indicates that it correlates reasonably well with other measures of intelligence and with school achievement (Oakland & Dowling, 1983). Some studies suggest that it might also be useful in identifying mental retardation (Naglieri, 1988) (Figure 5.5).

4 years, 7 months   4 years, 9 months   5 years, 9 months

Figure 5.5

The Goodenough-Harris Draw-A-Person test is a nonthreatening way of assessing the child's conceptual sophistication. It provides a quick estimate of IQ. Note how this boy's drawing of himself changed in the 14 months represented by these three drawings.

Misuses and Abuses of Tests

Intelligence tests are among the best tools we have for predicting academic success (Kuncel, Ones, & Sackett, 2010). Unfortunately, however, they are less than perfectly valid and reliable, they are often misunderstood and misused, and their use is sometimes highly controversial. Some of the reasons for the controversy are apparent in the very strong reaction to books such as *The Bell Curve* (Herrnstein & Murray, 1994) and *The Global Bell Curve* (Lynn, 2008). The main idea in these books is that IQ is a clear and important predictor of success in a wide variety of endeavors, including school, parenting, and business, that it is highly related to poverty and low socioeconomic status, that it predicts things such as the probability of being on welfare and of having unwanted children, and that it is inherited and reflects important racial differences in intelligence.

For many, these are inflammatory, inaccurate, and socially dangerous notions. Critics have been quick to reject the notion that IQ tests identify those who will fail and that they separate people on the basis of race.

But there is agreement with some of the less politically dangerous conclusions. IQ tests properly developed, used, and interpreted need not be biased against any group. And they can be very useful for important decisions such as school placement, college admission, job placement, and scholastic awards. In one sense, IQ tests are impeccably objective and impartial. The tests do not know whether the testee is rich or poor, brown or yellow, male or female. And they really do not care.

5.3 Influences on Intelligence

There are two great forces that shape what we become: heredity and environment. Untangling and sorting out the contributions of each to the development of intelligence has been difficult and controversial, and it has occupied a great deal of the time and effort of those dedicated to finding pieces of the human puzzle.

Unfortunately, it is not possible to devise an experiment where an investigator can sort out sequences of DNA and combinations of genes and then give each subject a different assortment so as to observe the effect of so doing on intelligence. Nor is it possible to assign subjects to different environments, say, group A to an impoverished situation and group B to a wealthy and privileged environment.

Heredity and Environment

But we do have a naturally occurring phenomenon that has proven invaluable for separating genetic from environmental influences: twins. That is because **monozygotic twins** are genetically identical, a condition that is not true for any other pair of humans including **dizygotic twins**, which are *fraternal* rather than identical. So, if intelligence is caused mainly by heredity, monozygotic twins should have almost identical IQs (except for errors of measurement). But if environment is more important, then fraternal twins should be as similar as identical twins.

Furthermore, when identical twins are raised together, both their environments and their genes are highly similar. But when they are raised apart, genes remain identical but environments differ.

There have been a very large number of twin studies designed to unravel the contributions of heredity and environment. Several of these are summarized in Figure 5.6. Note that in that summary, correlation coefficients are consistently higher for monozygotic than for dizygotic twins—strong evidence that intelligence is influenced by genes.

But note, too, that twins resemble each other more when younger than when older—strong evidence that the environment exercises increasing influence with the passage of time.

Physically, monozygotic twins are often nearly identical—right down to the hair and the facial expressions in this instance. They're also remarkably similar in measured intelligence and on various personality traits—strong evidence of the power of genetics in determining human characteristics.

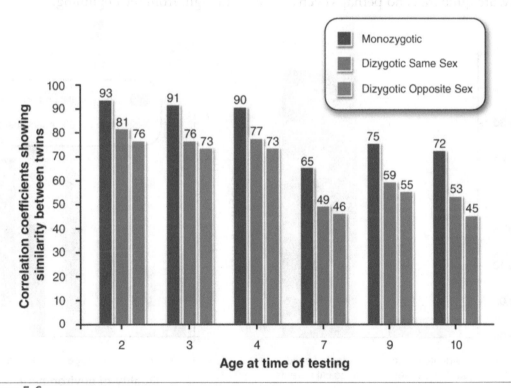

Figure 5.6

Similarity coefficients for intelligence test scores for more than 6,900 twin pairs. Based on data reported in F. M. Spinath, A. Ronald, N. Harlaar, T. S. Price, & R. Plomin (2003). Phenotypic *g* early in life: On the etiology of general cognitive ability in a large population sample of twin children aged 2–4 years. *Intelligence, 31,* 195–210; and in O. S. P. Davis, R. Arden, & R. Plomin (2008). *g* in middle childhood: Moderate genetic and shared environmental influence using diverse measures of general cognitive ability at 7, 9, and 10 years in a large population sample of twins. *Intelligence, 36,* 68–80.

A second group of studies provides additional clarification. These studies look at the correlation between intelligence test scores of adopted children with both their adoptive parents, with whom they share an environment, and their biological parents, with whom they share genes but not an environment. These studies typically find a higher correlation between adopted children and biological parents than between adopted children and adoptive parents—again strong evidence of the importance of heredity (Figure 5.7).

The Rubber-Band Hypothesis

While studies such as these show clearly that genes are important determiners of characteristics such as intelligence, they also provide clear evidence that experiences also contribute. A good analogy to describe the relationship between the two is Stern's (1956) rubber-band hypothesis. It compares our inherited potential to a rubber band whose final length represents our manifested intelligence. A very good environment can stretch the band a long ways; a poorer one, not so much (Figure 5.8).

Of course, some bands stretch more easily than others (better genetic endowment); others, sadly, are quite frail and perhaps even a little brittle right from the beginning.

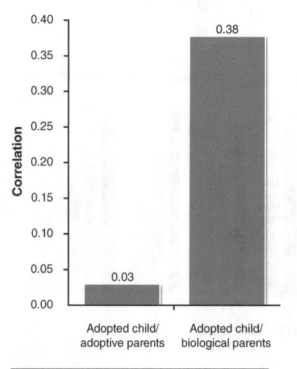

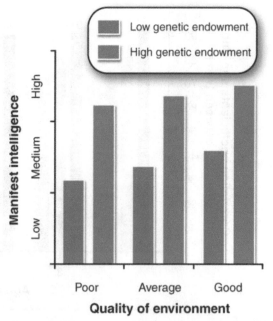

Figure 5.7

Correlations in late adolescence for general cognitive ability. Based on R. Plomin, D. W. Fulker, R. W. Corley, & J. C. DeFries (1997). Nature, nurture, and cognitive development from 1 to 16 years; A parent-offspring study. *Psychological Science, 8,* 442–447.

Figure 5.8

The Stern rubber-band hypothesis. People with different inherited potentials can develop below-average, average, or above-average intelligence depending on environmental forces.

5.4 Emotional Intelligence

Emotional Intelligence (EI)

Daniel Goleman (1995, 2000) proposed an additional type of intelligence he called emotional intelligence (EI). He believes that people with high EI are able to recognize and label their own emotions as well as having a generally accurate sense for the emotions others are feeling along with ability to demonstrate empathy for another's plight. High EI lends itself well to forming successful and meaningful relationships with others. Goleman has suggested that people with a modest IQ but a high EI often have more successful all-around lives when compared to people with high IQs. Skills such as self-regulation, empathy, recognizing and behaving appropriately in various social contexts, appropriate charisma and humor, and self-awareness are crucial in finding success in not just school and the workplace but also in interactions with others. Goleman believes these skills are often ignored or neglected in traditional intelligence tests. Furthermore, he believes that EI can be developed in people by encouraging them to be able to identify and label emotions as well as learning how those emotions are related to actions they may be taking in the world. Goleman indicates that EI training programs should coincide with elementary education and could help decrease future violent and criminal acts such as assault and domestic violence.

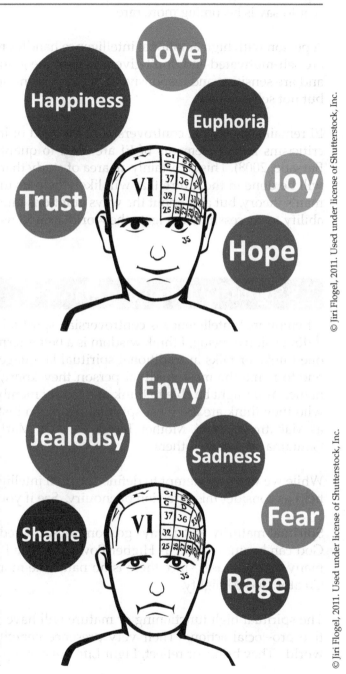

© Jiri Flogel, 2011. Used under license of Shutterstock, Inc.

© Jiri Flogel, 2011. Used under license of Shutterstock, Inc.

A person can have a high IQ, but a low EQ. You can have a low IQ and a high EQ. IQ points are handy to have. EQ points are nicer to have and more important when it comes to interpersonal relationships. And just think of how much of life is about relationships and emotional matters.

Emotional intelligence is perhaps more closely related to what many people would call character. Think about it. A person with a high IQ but poor character can do some very bad and even evil things. There are such things as criminal geniuses. A person who is caring and willing to work hard and go the extra mile for others is highly valued. And some would say is becoming more rare.

A person with high emotional intelligence handles relationships and emotions well. They are self-motivated and don't give up when the going gets tough. They are not impulsive and are sensitive and responsive to the needs and feelings of others. They are self-aware but not self-centered.

EI remains somewhat controversial in the field of intelligence. One of the most common criticisms is that elements of EI are hard to quantify and measure (Mayer, Roberts, & Barsade, 2008). This is certainly an area of study that is still in progress, and more research will be done in the future that will likely help us understand more about not only Goleman's theory, but also about the ways emotions interact with intelligence and predict our ability to successfully navigate the world around us.

5.5 Spiritual Wisdom and Maturity

If emotional intelligence is controversial, spiritual wisdom is even more so. (With this dimension of being, I think wisdom is a better term than intelligence.) While not everyone thinks or talks in traditional spiritual language, many people do. If you ask someone to name the most spiritual person they know, they will probably come up with a name. You might be able to think of a family member. If you ask people to name people who they think are the most spiritual people in history, you will likely hear names such as Mahatma Gandhi, Mother Teresa, Rev. Dr. Martin Luther King Jr., Jesus, Siddhartha Gautama, and many others.

While we will not attempt to define spiritual intelligence, let's look at some concepts that help us consider this direction of enquiry. See if you agree with the following:

Spiritual maturity will always go from self-centered focus, to a focus on others and God. God can be understood as Higher Power, Devine Presence, Holy Spirit, Divine One and many other phrases since there is no name the mortal tongue can name the can contain Creator God Almighty.

The spiritual high functioning or mature will have values and beliefs that result in positive pro-social action. Their very presence benefits those around them and the entire world. They bring, or reflect, Light Life Love in highest of forms.

High functioning spiritual beings will give to the poor and needy and those less fortunate. There will be a degree of self-sacrifice given willingly and with joy. They are peace keepers and peace makers to the best of their ability.

Since most would agree that a truly spiritual person would not only be enlightened but also highly moral, perhaps a test or questionnaire could be constructed to tap into:

How important is honesty and integrity to me? How much is this a part of my daily life. Do I do what I say I will do? Do I think of others above myself? If I could get away with it, would I (or do I) lie, steal, or gossip? What is my personal relationship with God? Am I quick to judge? Do I judge too harshly, or do I give people the benefit of the doubt. Am I quick to forgive?

I have often shared what I believe to be four portraits of Jesus. Written portraits of Jesus found in the Old and New Testaments that only Jesus Christ fully embodied. Those portraits are:

- The 10 Commandments found in Exodus 20.
- The Beatitudes found in Mathew 5.
- The Fruit of the Spirit found in Galatians 5
- LOVE found in I Corinthians 13.

What would you add or take away from the list. How do you and I stack up to these moral and spiritual descriptions? There is room for improvement for all of us. Asking for God's help to be men and women of God. Men and women of high integrity and great reflections of Life Light and Love seems to me to be wise advice. Part of a never ending journey.

Main Points

1. **What Is Intelligence?** It is not synonymous with IQ, IQ tests do not measure all that is important, they are not always fair, and IQ is malleable. It does predict academic achievement. Successful intelligence (Sternberg) is an adaptive quality that requires analytical, creative, and practical abilities. We may have as many as eight distinct kinds of intelligence (Gardner).
2. **Measuring Intelligence:** Average IQ is 100 as measured by group and intelligence tests, all of which have less than perfect validity and reliability. They have sometimes been misused and misinterpreted.
3. **Influences on Intelligence:** Heredity and environment are the two great forces that shape intelligence.
4. **Emotional Intelligence:** Being high in emotional intelligence is found in mature and psychologically healthy people. Characteristics of such people include: being empathic; in touch with feelings in self and others; able to delay gratification; caring for the needs of others.
5. **Spiritual Wisdom:** Is found in the highest of spiritual human beings. Characteristics of such people include: Being enlightened and walking in light and truth; loving God and others; living a life of high morals and integrity. Several example of such people were noted with hopes that each of us would grow in Light, Life, Love Eternal.

Thoughts and Suggestions

1. If you had to place yourself into one of Gardner's 8 types of mind frames, what would it be. Is this consistent with your current major in school and/or future career plans?
2. In this chapter we have primarily looked and intellectual and emotional intelligence. Do you think considering Spiritual Intelligence could be as helpful and the other two classifications? How would you personally define Spiritual Intelligence? Perhaps thinking of maturity or wisdom could be helpful.
3. What would you personally say is the difference between wisdom and intelligence? How about education and wisdom and intelligence. Can you think of examples from your own experience that would reflect these differences?

Suggested readings from Hock, R. R. (1999). *Forty studies that changed psychology* (3rd ed.). Upper Saddle River, NJ: Prentice Hall. (ISBN #: 0-13-922725-3):

- Reading 13: What You Expect Is What You Get.
- Reading 14: Just How Are You Intelligent?
- Reading 15: Maps In Your Mind.
- Reading 16: Thanks For The Memories.

Study Terms

intelligence quotient (IQ)   triarchic theory of successful intelligence

reliability   validity

6

Developmental Stages and Theories

Focus Questions

By the end of the chapter, you should be able to answer the following questions:

- What is the nature-nurture controversy?
- What are the principal developmental characteristics of infancy?
- How does Piaget describe development during childhood?
- What are Marcia's four possibilities with regard to identity formation in adolescence?
- How does Erikson's psychosocial theory describe the adult years?
- What are the key parenting styles?
- How does kohlberg explain moral development?
- How is death and dying understood?

Psychology: The Human Puzzle by Guy R. LeFrancois © 2013 Bridgepoint Education. Reprinted by permission.

- -

Inspirational Words

And when they had fulfilled the days, as they returned, the child Jesus tarried behind in Jerusalem; and Joseph and his mother knew not of it. But they, supposing him to have been in the company, went a day's journey; and they sought him among their kinsfolk and acquaintance. And when they found him not, they turned back again to Jerusalem, seeking him. And it came to pass, that after three days they found him in the temple, sitting in the midst of the doctors, both hearing them, and asking them questions. And all that heard him were astonished at his understanding and answers. And when they saw him, they were amazed: and his mother said unto him, Son, why hast thou thus dealt with us? behold, thy father and I have sought thee sorrowing. And he said unto them, How is it that ye sought me? Wist ye not that I must be about my Father's business? And they understood not the saying which he spake unto them. And he went down with them, and came to Nazareth, and was subject unto them: but his mother kept all these sayings in her heart. And Jesus increased in wisdom and stature, and in favour with God and man. Luke 2:43–52.

And I, brethren, could not speak unto you as unto spiritual, but as unto carnal, even as unto babes in Christ. I have fed you with milk, and not with meat: for hitherto ye were not able to bear it, neither yet now are ye able. For ye are yet carnal: for whereas there is among you envying, and strife, and divisions, are ye not carnal, and walk as men? For while one saith, I am of Paul; and another, I am of Apollos; are ye not carnal? Who then is Paul, and who is Apollos, but ministers by whom ye believed, even as the Lord gave to every man? I have planted, Apollos watered; but God gave the increase. 1 Corinthians 3:1–6

When I was a child, I spake as a child, I understood as a child, I thought as a child: but when I became a man, I put away childish things. For now we see through a glass, darkly; but then face to face: now I know in part; but then shall I know even as also I am known. And now abideth faith, hope, charity, these three; but the greatest of these is charity. 1 Corinthians 13:11–13

To every thing there is a season, and a time to every purpose under the heaven: A time to be born, and a time to die; a time to plant, and a time to pluck up that which is planted; A time to kill, and a time to heal; a time to break down, and a time to build up; A time to weep, and a time to laugh; a time to mourn, and a time to dance; A time to cast away stones, and a time to gather stones together; a time to embrace, and a time to refrain from embracing; A time to get, and a time to lose; a time to keep, and a time to cast away; A time to rend, and a time to sew; a time to keep silence, and a time to speak; A time to love, and a time to hate; a time of war, and a time of peace. Ecclesiastes 3:1–8

And it shall come to pass afterward, that I will pour out my spirit upon all flesh; and your sons and your daughters shall prophesy, your old men shall dream dreams, your young men shall see visions. Joel 2:28

But speak thou the things which become sound doctrine: That the aged men be sober, grave, temperate, sound in faith, in charity, in patience. The aged women likewise, that they be in behaviour as becometh holiness, not false accusers, not given to much wine, teachers of good things; That they may teach the young women to be sober, to love their husbands, to love their children, To be discreet, chaste, keepers at home, good, obedient to their own husbands, that the word of God be not blasphemed. Young men likewise exhort to be sober minded. In all things shewing thyself a pattern of good works: in doctrine shewing uncorruptness, gravity, sincerity. Sound speech, that cannot be condemned; that he that is of the contrary part may be ashamed, having no evil thing to say of you. Titus 2:1–8

6.1 The Beginning: Prenatal Development

Things have changed drastically in North America in recent decades: Now fathers are often present at the births of their children. But George H. Davies may still be at least partly right because with today's medical technology, the dad does not necessarily have to be there at the beginning. His role can be taken over by **artificial insemination**, in which a physician introduces sperm into the uterus, or by **in vitro fertilization**, where a previously fertilized egg is used.

But no matter the procedure, in the very beginning, we are a **zygote**—a fertilized egg. Most mature human females produce a single **ovum** (egg cell) once every 28 days. Some women occasionally produce more than one egg at a time, making multiple births possible. Multiple births also occur if a single egg separates after fertilization. Where two eggs are involved, the resulting twins will be fraternal, or **dizygotic**, since they come from two zygotes. Where a single egg is involved, the twins will be identical or **monozygotic**.

A mature human male normally produces several billion **sperm cells** every month. These are among the smallest cells in the human body, but they have an extraordinarily long tail. In contrast, the ovum is the largest cell in the human body at about 0.15 millimeter in diameter, which is about half the diameter of the period that ends this sentence. Under the right circumstances, an egg cell can be seen with the naked eye.

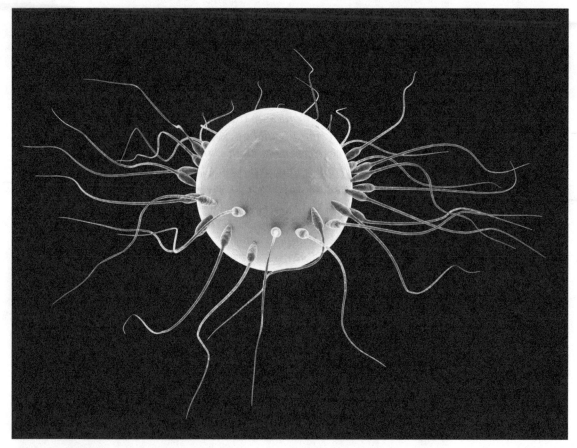

Figure 6.1

The odds of these sperm cells making it this far are about one in a million. And in the end, only one, if any at all, will succeed in penetrating the ovum's tough outer shell and fertilizing it.

The egg and sperm cell are the immediate origins of life. After activities beyond the scope of this book, the sperm, competing against 300 or 400 million other sperm, undertakes an immense journey across the colossal expanse of the **uterus** and up a gigantic **fallopian tube**. It uses its whiplike tail to swim against horrendous currents, determined to be the first to reach the ovum. And if it gets that far, it will be one of only 300 or 400 that have done so. (Figure the odds! About one in a million of ever reaching the ovum; and about half the surviving sperm have gone up the wrong tube! See Figure 6.1.)

But the game is not yet won, even if there happens to be an egg here, roughly halfway up one of the fallopian tubes (remember that only one is released about every 28 days). The battered and exhausted sperm must now butt its head against the egg's tough outer shell to penetrate it. And if it succeeds, it will be the only one to do so because the egg will immediately release an enzyme that hardens the shell and makes it virtually impenetrable. All the other sperm that have survived the journey are now doomed.

In the next stage of this incredible drama, the very matter of which the sperm is composed fuses with matter inside the egg and we have **conception** (the formation of a *zygote*, a fertilized egg). Now slow-moving currents carry the zygote back down the fallopian tube into the uterus, where it attaches itself to the uterine wall. All of this takes place within 7 days. During the next short while, the **placenta** and **umbilical cord** form, the placenta being a flat membrane that links mother and **embryo**. The umbilical cord is a tubular affair perhaps 18 inches in length, containing two veins and an artery and linked to the placenta at one end and to what will eventually be the child's navel at the other. There are no nerves in the umbilical cord, and the child's developing nervous system is never linked with the mother's (Figure 6.2).

Some 266 days after conception (280 days following the onset of the last menstrual period, which is roughly 9 *calendar* or 10 *lunar* months, each lunar month consisting of 28 days), barring accident or design to the contrary, a child will be born. And this child will be different from any other that might have been born instead. Why?

Heredity and Environment

Genetics alone does not complete this part of the human puzzle. Take yourself as a case in point. Blue or yellow eyes; straight, kinky, or curly hair; peach, alabaster, copper, or ebony skin; straight, hooked, curved, flat, small, or large nose; tall or short; thin or wide; freckled, speckled, mottled, striped, or plain: Your physical systems, we assume, correspond relatively closely to your genetic code.

Lunar Month	Weight	Length	Characteristics
1	Negligible	Negligible	Cell differentation into those that will be bones, nerves, or other cells
2	2/3 oz. (19 g)	1½–2 in. (3.75–5 cm)	Leg buds and external genitalia appearing
3	7/8 oz. (24.5 g)	3 in. (7.5 cm)	Bones forming, organs differentiated. If aborted, will make primitive breathing movements.
4	4 oz. (112 g)	6 in. (15 cm)	
5	11 oz. (308 g)	10 in. (25 cm)	Fetal movement (*quickening*) appears
6	20 oz. (560 g)	12 in. (30 cm)	Heartbeat clearly discernible; eyelids present
7	2.6 lb. (1.2 kg)	15 in. (37.5 cm)	
8	4 lb. (1.8 kg)	16 in. (40 cm)	Development is now largely a matter of increasing weight and length
9	4.7 lb. (2.1 kg)	17.5 in. (44 cm)	
10	7.5 lb. (3.4 kg)	20 in. (50 cm)	

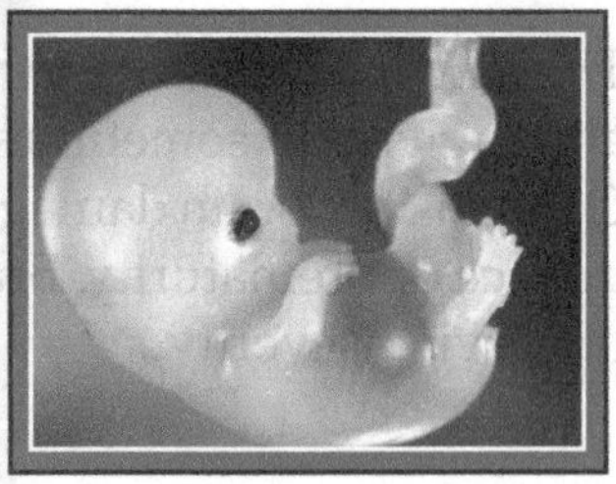

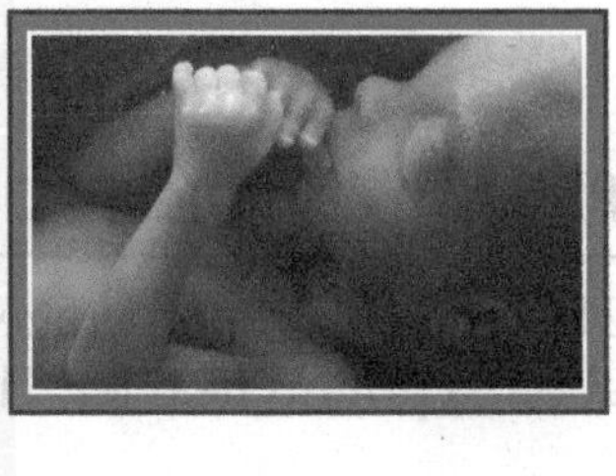

Figure 6.2

Prenatal development by lunar month (weight and length are approximate).

Look at yourself again. Your language: French, English, German, Swahili, Barnbuti, or Texan; your talents: musical, poetic, manual, verbal, athletic, numerical, or hidden; your values; your political beliefs; your *self*. Clearly, what you have become is inextricably bound with the experiences you have had.

Psychology has long debated the relative contributions of heredity and environment—the **nature-nurture controversy**. Is intelligence inherited? Mental disorders? Personality traits?

Extremists have often adopted one point of view or the other. But it is clear that both are involved in determining developmental outcomes. Even physical characteristics such as height and weight are susceptible to environment influences such as nutrition and exercise. The important question is no longer whether heredity is the most potent force in development, or whether the honor should go to the environment; rather, the question is how they interact in the course of human development.

Prenatal Development

Human development, begins with the zygote, the fertilized egg. And for the next 266 days, the course of prenatal development is more predictable than it is for any other stage of development. Thus, the average newborn infant will more closely resemble all other newborn infants than the average 12-year-old will resemble other 12-year-olds.

The actual process of birth presents more of a medical than a psychological phenomenon, although it can sometimes have pronounced effects on the later development of the child. On occasion, brain damage can result from oxygen deprivation during birth, or as a consequence of prematurity. Brain damage may be evident in intellectual or motor impairment of varying severity.

6.2 Infants

It is sometimes disquieting to learn about all the defects and diseases to which we are potential heirs. The truth is that in spite of all that can go wrong, most often nothing does and in the end another normal, happy infant is born.

Physical and Motor Development in Infancy

This infant, if an average male, will be perhaps one-quarter to one-half inch taller, and about a pound heavier. There are, of course, many individual exceptions.

Human development is typically divided into various stages (Table 6.1): **Infancy**, which lasts until age 2, is the first of these.

Table 6.1 Major Stages in Human Development	
Stages and Substages	**Time Span**
Prenatal	Conception to birth
Neonatal	Approximately first 2 to 4 week of life
Infancy	Until age 2
Childhood	2 to 11–12 years
Early Childhood	2 to 6–7 years
Middle Childhood	6–7 to 11–12 years
Adolescence	11–12 to 19–20 years
Adulthood	20 to the end
Early Adulthood	20 to 40–45
Middle Adulthood	40–45 to 65–70
Late Adulthood	65–70 to the end

One of the important developmental outcomes of infancy involves changes in motor abilities. Although newborn infants are almost unique among the earth's animal species in their inability to locomote within a short time of birth, they are among the few that eventually learn to walk on two legs. Other nonhuman primates who are capable of this same feat are usually more at home on all fours than on two; and the kangaroo, which does move on two legs, cannot run or even walk very well on those two legs, but must instead resort to hopping.

But the newborn does not hop, does not even crawl. In fact, the newborn's first movements are largely uncoordinated and purposeless. But these movements are a way of exercising and developing control over muscle systems. Gradually, they become more purposeful. At first the infant can only stare at an interesting object, waving hands and arms wildly, clearly excited but incapable of coordinating action with intention. Learning to reach and grasp, like learning to walk, is not an easy matter.

In time, infants do learn to walk—and eventually, like the kangaroo, to hop. But first they go through a relatively predictable sequence of motor achievements: learn to lift the head, to turn over on the back, to direct hand movements, to sit, to crawl, to stand, to walk, and finally, to hop.

Perception in the Newborn

For a long time, psychologists believed William James's (1890/1950) claim that the infant's world is "one great blooming, buzzing, confusion," that, in particular, vision and hearing are so poorly developed as to be virtually useless. We now know that is not quite true. Infants are sensitive to light almost immediately after birth and are capable of visually following moving objects within a few days. When shown blurred or clear images of human faces, they show preference for the clear face (Berger, Donnadieu, Meary, Kandel, & Mazens, 2010). With respect to hearing, evidence suggests that, unlike the young of many species that are deaf at birth (dogs and cats, for example), the neonate is sensitive to a wide range of sounds and can also locate the direction of sounds (Volpe, 2008).

The smell system, too, is functional in newborns. When presented with unpleasant odors, newborns turn away (Porter & Rieser, 2005). In contrast, the smell of their own mother's milk, but not that of other mothers, has a calming effect on them (Nishitani et al., 2009).

The taste, system, too, seems to be relatively well developed in newborns. In fact, it seems that they can learn about different tastes even before they're born. Mennella, Jagnow, and Beauchamp (2001) had a group of pregnant mothers drink carrot juice during pregnancy. Their infants later showed stronger preference for carrot-flavored cereal than did other infants whose mothers had not drunk carrot juice while pregnant.

Cognitive Development in Infancy

So even before birth, newborns begin to learn, as is evident in their recognition of flavors to which their mothers have been exposed. But the fact is, they aren't born with a great store of knowledge and ideas and opinions. For the first three months of their infants' lives, Super and Harkness (1998) tell us, Kipsigis mothers in rural Kenya refer to them as *monkeys*; only later do they call them *children*.

Why? One plausible answer is that the newborn is much like a little monkey: It can respond to a small range of stimuli, it can cry and vomit, and it is heir to a handful of survival-related reflexes such as sucking and rooting. But it would surely die if its environment did not include adults devoted to its survival. There is much that the infant needs to learn, much with which it must become familiar, before it can stand on its own two feet—not only physically, but also cognitively.

We know that infants are born with an impressive array of cognitive tools—tools that will eventually allow them to know and understand things of which they cannot yet even dream. They can look and see; they can hear; they can smell and taste. And more impressive than anything else, they have an astonishing brain. In fact, they are remarkably ready to become familiar with all there is out there.

Infants are born with an impressive array of cognitive tools. This tyke is learning more than just one thing at a time.

That infants begin to learn before and immediately after birth seems clear. As an example, Lipsitt (1971) conditioned infants' rooting reflex by stroking their cheeks when a tone sounded. (Rooting is the infant's reflexive head turning when the cheek or corner of the mouth is stimulated—an important reflex for finding nipples.) If they turned in the appropriate direction, they were reinforced by being allowed to suck briefly on a nipple. Within a half-hour of training, newborns who had initially turned in response to the tone an average of 25 percent of the time now turned 75 percent of the time. Perhaps even more striking, when a different tone was introduced and the newborns were not reinforced for turning in response to the second tone but were still reinforced for the first tone, they continued to respond to the second tone only 25 percent of the time. Thus, newborns can not only be conditioned, but they can also discriminate between different sounds.

Cognition and Language Development

Discriminating the sounds of a language is essential for one of the most formidable and important of all cognitive tasks: learning to communicate with language. And, as we saw in Chapter 2, language is basic to thinking, to creating and participating in cultures, and to communicating.

The *prespeech* stage of language learning spans most of the first year. It entails learning to take turns, to use gestures, to discriminate among different sounds, to produce sounds, and eventually to produce words. A good set of wireless headphones with cleverly designed lessons might also help.

But communication and language are not quite synonymous. A dog that walks to its empty dish, looks its master in the eye, and begins to growl is communicating but is not using language. Language is the use of arbitrary sounds or symbols in a purposeful way to convey meaning; communication is simply the transmission of a message.

The infant's first communication system is not language but a complex system of sounds and gestures. To master this communication system, the infant needs to learn five things: turn taking, the use of gestures, sound discrimination, sound production, and words. All of these are basic to adult conversation. These accomplishments are part of the *prespeech* stage of language learning.

At around age 1, though sometimes much earlier or later, the first word appears. In all cultures, the first words tend to be nouns—simple names for common, everyday objects (Salerni, Assanelli, D'Odorico, & Rossi, 2007). Often, the earliest consistent sound made by an infant is not a recognizable word but has a clear meaning. Elizabeth, at a startlingly young age, repeatedly said "buh"—an expression that her parents eventually realized meant "light" or "turn the light on and off and on and off and on and off . . ." These sorts of consistent sounds are labeled **protowords**.

Holophrases are similar to protowords except that they are real words rather than just sounds. Holophrases are words or expressions that are sentencelike in that they contain a variety of sometimes complex meanings. Holophrases usually appear by the age of 12 months. They often express meanings that an adult could not easily communicate in less than an entire sentence. For example, the holophrase "up," uttered in an unmistakably imperious tone by 1-year-old Nathan, means "Pick me up right now and sing me a song or else I may do something really annoying."

By the age of 18 months, most infants have begun to join modifiers to nouns and pronouns to make two-word sentences. At this stage, speech is still highly telegraphic; complex meanings are squeezed into simple, and sometimes grammatically incorrect, two-word utterances. For example, the sentence "Mummy gone" may mean something as complex as "my dear mother is currently on a business trip in Chicago."

During this stage, there is ordinarily a tremendous spurt in vocabulary, common to all cultures. Whereas learning the first 100 or so words can take several months, the next hundred might be learned in just a few weeks (Yu, 2008). This type of learning is called **fast mapping**.

Note that in all early stages of language learning, children's **passive vocabulary** is much larger than their **active vocabulary**. That is, they understand far more words than they actually use in their speech.

Multiple-word sentences typically appear by the age of 2 to 2½. Although early preschool speech is still often telegraphic, it includes complex grammatical variations to express different meanings. By the late preschool years, it has become adultlike.

Although average ages are assigned to each of these developments, they are simply approximations. Here, as in all areas of human development, it is normal for some to display a behavior earlier or later. An average is not an expression of normality; it is simply a point around which observations are distributed. (See Table 6.2 for a summary of early language development.)

Table 6.2 Sequence of Infant Language Development

Developmental Stage	Main Accomplishments	Sample Utterances
Prespeech (before age 1)	Turn taking Using gestures such as pointing Discriminating and producing sounds	"Waaaaaa . . ." "Gooogoooogoooogaaahgaah"
First words (around age 1)	Protowords (nonwords with consistent meaning) Holophrases (single words with sentence-like meanings)	"Bulla," meaning all umbrella-like things, including rhubarb leaves "Mama," meaning "Would you please come here mother and bring the milk with you . . ."
Two-word sentences (around age 18 months)	Vocabulary spurt Fast mapping (one-exposure learning)	"More milk" "Pretty horsie"
Multiple-word sentences (by age 2 to 2½)	Longer sentences; more grammatical variation; increasingly correct use of word classes	"Read again book" "I no can play" "I runned fast"

Social-Emotional Development in Infancy

Average vocabulary size at different ages is relatively easily calculated; uncovering average social and emotional characteristics is more challenging.

Erikson's Stages

Erik Erikson (1963; 1968) describes eight major stages in human development over the lifespan. Each of these stages is identified by a basic conflict brought about by the need to adapt to the social environment—hence it is a theory of **psychosocial development**. And at each level, new competencies are required of the individual. The first two of these stages span infancy (all eight stages are summarized in Figure 6.8).

Trust Versus Mistrust   The first task for the infant, Erikson explains, is learning to trust this bewildering and often frightening world—in the face of a strong tendency not to trust because everything is so strange and unfamiliar. The most important person in the infant's life at this stage is the principal caregiver. If that person is warm and loving, the infant soon learns that the world is a safe, warm, and predictable place. But if the caregiver is cold and rejecting, the child may grow up to be wary and anxious.

Autonomy Versus Shame and Doubt   At first, infants cannot intend to carry out an action and then do so. They have to learn to coordinate and control activities according to intentions. As they begin to realize that they can *intend* and *accomplish* things, they develop a growing sense of autonomy. But always, there is the tendency to go back to a safer period, back to the comfort and security that marked the end of the previous period. Successful resolution of this conflict depends largely on caregivers giving the child opportunities to explore and to be autonomous.

Infant States

Clearly, however, not all infants develop in the same way and at the same pace. Even very early in life, we are sometimes very different from one another in our typical behaviors and reactions. These early differences might foreshadow differences among adults.

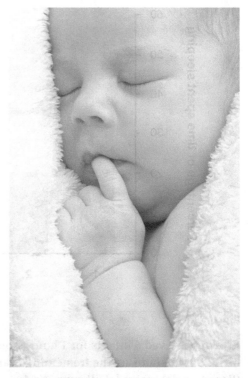

Sleep is the most common newborn state, occupying about two thirds of the day. Happily, crying is the least common state.

The most common *infant states* are described as regular sleep, disturbed sleep, drowsiness, alert activity (alert and actively responding to stimuli), alert inactivity (alert, examining environment, but inactive), and crying (Wolff, 1966).

Infants vary tremendously in the amount of time they spend in each state. For example, in a study of six infants, Brown (1964) found that although the babies spent approximately one third of their time sleeping, one infant slept 56 percent of the time, and another 22 percent of the time. One infant cried 35 percent of the time; another, 17 percent of the time. One was alert 40 percent of the time; another, 10 percent of the time (Figure 6.3).

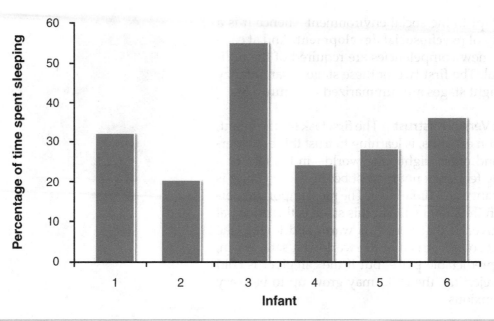

Figure 6.3

Brown observed 6 infants for 1 hour about an hour after feeding, during the first week after birth. Shown here are the tremendous variations in the amount of time each spent sleeping. (Based on data from J. L. Brown, 1964.)

Infant-Caregiver Interaction

To understand what it is like to be a child, it is essential to know which child, when, and where. We have to be aware of children's contexts and of how these contexts have changed and continue to change. We also need to know something of the ethnic, cultural, social, and political realities in the child's life. Perhaps most important, to understand the lives of infants, we need to ask about interactions in the family, because the family usually defines the most important aspects of the child's physical and social context.

Traditionally, the emphasis has been on **dyadic interactions** (interactions involving two individuals)—especially the mother-infant dyad. Father-infant and infant-sibling interactions also need to be taken into account. More complex interactions are concerned with how infants affect parents and change the family, and how these changes in turn affect the infant. The contexts in which the family functions—social, political, economic, religious, and philosophical—are all important influences in shaping the child.

Infant Temperament

Parental characteristics, such as patience or irritability, influence how parents interact with their children; so, too, do infant characteristics.

The infant's characteristic ways of behaving define **temperament**, a term that is somewhat different from *personality*. *Personality* indicates a degree of learning and experience that infants have not yet had; it is used to describe identifying traits of older children and adults. *Temperament*, on the other hand, implies an inherited predisposition to act and be a certain way. For example, some infants are habitually active, others quieter; some readily approach strangers, others hide behind their mothers; some are generally happy, others less so.

After looking at the typical behaviors of a large group of infants, Thomas and Chess (1977) found that certain infants seem to have remarkably similar patterns of characteristics. One group, the **difficult infants**, is characterized by irregularity in such things as eating, sleeping, and toilet functions; withdrawal from unfamiliar situations; slow adaptation to change; and intense and often negative moods.

In contrast, **easy infants** are characterized by regularity in eating, sleeping, and toileting; high approach tendencies in novel situations; high adaptability to change; and a preponderance of positive moods as well as low or moderate intensity of reaction.

Slow-to-warm-up infants are characterized by a low activity level, high initial withdrawal from the unfamiliar, slow adaptation to change, greater negativity in mood, and a moderate or low intensity of reaction.

Of the 141 children in Thomas and Chess's study, 65 percent could be classified as belonging to one of these three temperament types (40 percent easy; 15 percent difficult; 10 percent slow to warm up); the remaining 35 percent displayed varying mixtures of temperament (Figure 6.4).

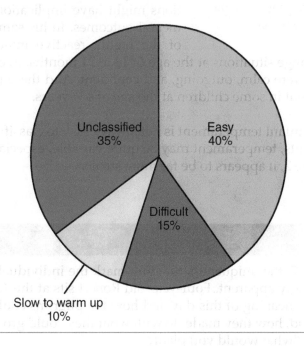

Figure 6.4

Infant temperaments. Approximate percentage of children with each temperament. Based on data reported in Thomas, A., & Chess, S. (1977). *Temperament and development.* New York: Brunner/Mazel.

The majority of children are classified as "easy" or of mixed temperaments. About 10 percent are "slow to warm up." Some take comfort behind a parent's leg; others rely on the bear.

Note that these temperaments don't exhaust all possibilities. Nor do all "easy" or "difficult" children always react predictably in a given situation. Even easy infants sometimes cry and fuss; and the most difficult of little urchins might occasionally laugh and seem approachable and adaptable.

The long-term implications of infant temperament are intriguing. For one thing, following a study of some 7,695 families, Jokela (2010) reports that the probability of parents having a second child is significantly affected by the temperament of the first. Parents whose first child adapts easily to novelty and is alert, intelligent, and sociable are more likely to have a second child than are parents of more difficult children.

Several longitudinal studies also indicate that infants rated as *difficult* are at somewhat higher risk of displaying psychiatric symptoms in adolescence (Kapornai et al., 2007). And Kagan's (1997) research with infants classified as highly *reactive* (fearful of the unfamiliar; easily distressed) or *nonreactive* (relaxed in the face of the unfamiliar; not easily frightened) shows that these classifications might have implications for later developmental outcomes. In his sample, about one third of the highly reactive infants continued to be highly fearful in strange situations at the age of 14 to 21 months. In contrast, the majority of the nonreactives were calm, outgoing, and confident. And these patterns, though less clear, were still evident in some children at the age of 4 ½ years.

Note, however, that infant temperament is not always easy to classify accurately. Furthermore, for many infants, temperament may be quite variable, especially during the first 2 years of life; after age 2, it appears to be far more stable.

6.3 Children

By the age of 6 or 7, the uniqueness that will mark the individual throughout life has become increasingly apparent. Four-year-old Robert sits at the Thanksgiving table as his dad explains the meaning of this day and how the pilgrims could not just run to the store to buy their food, how they made do with what they could grow. "If you were a pilgrim," says his dad, "what would you plant?"

"Corn," his older brother says. "And peas, and potatoes, and turnips."

"And what would you plant, Robert?"

Robert glances cleverly at his plate. "I'd plant turkeys," he answers.

That's the way Robert is: clever and entertaining. He has a wonderfully inventive mind, seldom limited by the rules that constrain our thoughts. His thinking is, as Pearce (1977) puts it, **magical thinking**; it does not always need to be checked against reality. In these early years, thinking is wishful and fantastic. It somehow assumes that reality can be changed by a thought. Thus it is that a magic spell can produce a witch or a princess, a silver thread or a pot of gold; a dream can be real, and perhaps reality too can be a dream; and a wish can make a race car of a stone, a cave of a small corner, a giant sailing ship of a discarded matchbox.

Cognitive Development in Childhood: Piaget's Theory

But, Pearce tells us, we do not gladly accept—perhaps we don't even understand—the magical child. Our approach to children and our scientific research ask instead: "How can the child be made to attend to reality?" or "How can we make the child abandon magical thinking?" (p. xv). The Swiss psychologist, Jean Piaget, provides some fascinating insights that have become a lasting part of the child development puzzle.

Mechanisms of Adaptation

Piaget was first trained as a biologist, and he brings a biologist's perspective to the questions of development. Development, he explains, is a process of adaptation. Children are not born knowing how to cope with external reality; they're born with a handful of reflexes that are crucial for biological survival (sucking, sneezing, and swallowing, for example). These ready-made responses allow the child to *assimilate* important aspects of the environment. Piaget defines **assimilation** as the use of previously acquired or innate activities without having to modify these activities.

But from the very beginning, the infant's reflexes are not always suited to the demands of the environment. For example, differently placed and shaped nipples require changes in the infant's behaviors. These changes define **accommodation**. Accommodation implies changes in the child's thought and behavior in response to environmental demands.

Throughout life, assimilation and accommodation are the two ways we have of interacting with the environment. We make use of aspects of our environment for certain activities that we already know (assimilation); and we modify our activities to be able to make use of certain aspects of the environment (accommodation).

Schemas

Children are born with a limited repertoire of unlearned abilities (sucking, for example). Mental representations of these abilities are labeled **schemas** (also called *schemata* or *schemes*). As a result of interacting with the environment through assimilation and accommodation, schemas (mental representations) change. In other words, mental growth takes place through assimilation and accommodation.

The Stage Theory

As children develop, their primitive schemas give way to more advanced representations of the world and to new ways of dealing with the world on a mental level. Piaget describes the progression of cognitive development in terms of four major stages and various substages (Table 6.3).

Table 6.3 Piaget's Stages of Cognitive Development		
Stage	**Approximate Age**	**Some Major Characteristics**
Sensorimotor	0–2 years	Motoric intelligence World of the here and now No language, no thought in early stages No notion of objective reality

Preoperational
    Preconceptual
    Intuitive
	2–7 years
	2–4 years
	4–7 years
		Egocentric thought
		Reason dominated by perception
		Intuitive rather than logical solutions
		Inability to conserve

Concrete Operations	7–11 or 12 years	Ability to conserve Logic of classes and relations Understanding of number Thinking bound to concrete
Formal Operations	11 or 12–14 or 15 years	Complete generality of thought Ability to deal with the hypothetical Development of strong idealism

Sensorimotor Thought   During much of the first 2 years of life, says Piaget, infants understand the world mainly in terms of the activities they perform and the sensations that result; hence the label **sensorimotor**. It is a world of sensation and movement, a world that is not represented in imagination and that therefore ceases to exist when it is not being perceived. If an attractive object is shown to a very young infant and then hidden, the child will not even look for it: The object does not seem to exist when it cannot be seen or touched.

One of the important cognitive achievements of this period is the realization that objects are permanent and independent. This realization, the **object concept**, is possible only when the infant can *symbolize*—that is, can represent internally. Internal representation makes it possible for the child to imagine, to begin to think, to imitate objects and people who are not immediately present, and eventually to develop language.

Preoperational Thought   Piaget labels the years from 2 to about 7 *preoperational* because children don't develop the ability to deal with **operations** (logical thought processes) until around 7. Before then, thinking is full of contradictions and errors. As an example, Piaget describes his young son's reaction to a snail they see while out walking one morning. When they later see another snail, the boy exclaims, "Here it is again, the snail," absolutely convinced that this is the same snail. He does not yet understand that similar objects can belong to the same class but not be identical. Billy, who sees four different

Santa Clauses in four places on the same day, still knows there is only one Santa Claus. He is a preconceptual thinker.

Preconceptual thinkers also tend to be **animistic thinkers**. "Does the sun move?" Piaget (1960) asks a young child (p. 215). "Yes," the child answers, going on to explain how the sun, like the moon, moves when he walks, stops when he stops, turns when he turns, that it must surely be alive. But even among preschoolers, animism has its limits. If the sun and the moon are alive because they move, Bullock (1985) suggests to a 4-year-old, then surely a car, which also moves, must also be alive. No, the child is not so easily fooled. How can this thing of metal and plastic and rubber possibly be alive?

At around age 4, the child's reasoning becomes somewhat more logical, although it is still heavily influenced by appearances rather than by logic. It is not so much logical as **intuitive thinking**.

Intuitive thought, explains Piaget, is often marked by the type of **egocentrism** evident in this simple problem: An experimenter holds one end of a string in each hand so that a male and female doll, side by side on the string, are hidden behind a screen.

This 4-year-old's logic is intuitive, egocentric, and perception dominated. He is easily fooled by appearances. There are still many head-scratching puzzles out there.

He asks the child which doll will come out first if the string is moved toward the right. Whether the child is correct or not, the boy doll is moved out and hidden again. The procedure is repeated a number of times without variation so that the boy doll always comes out first. Eventually the child will predict that the other doll will come out. Why? "Because it's her turn. It isn't fair." The child interprets the problem only from a personal point of view, from an egocentric view.

Egocentricism is also evident in many preschool verbal exchanges:

Bill: I got a red one.

Sarah: My cat is sick.

Bill: Go. Go. RRRRRR.

Sarah: We don't have a dog.

A conversation? Not really, says Piaget: More a *collective monologue*. A real conversation requires the nonegocentric ability to adopt another's point of view.

Concrete Operations   That perception tends to dominate the preoperational child's thinking is evident in this Piagetian demonstration: Michael, a 4-year-old, is asked to take a bead and place it in one of two containers. As he does so, a researcher places a bead in another container. They keep doing this until one of the containers is about half full. To confuse Michael, the researcher has put her beads in a shallow, flat dish whereas Michael's container is tall and narrow. The researcher now asks, "Who has more beads? Or do we both have the same number?" "I have more," says Michael, "because they're higher." Or he might just as easily have said, "You have more 'cause they're bigger around." In either case, his answers reflect his reliance on the appearance of the containers. This reliance on perception, even when it conflicts with logic, is one of the major differences between child and adult thought.

With the advent of *concrete operations*, children no longer make this mistake. They now rely on rules of logic rather than on intuition and perception. They know that quantity does not change unless something is added or taken away. In Piaget's terms, they have achieved **conservation**.

There are as many types of conservation as there are quantifiable characteristics of objects: There is conservation of number, length, distance, area, volume, liquids, solids, and so on. None of these is acquired before the stage of concrete operations, and even then some (volume, for example) will not be acquired until late in that period. Experimental procedures and approximate ages for different conservations are shown in Figure 6.5.

Strikingly, when faced with conservation problems, preoperational children can contradict themselves repeatedly without ever changing their minds. After the bead demonstration, for example, the experimenter can pour the beads back into their original containers and repeat the question. Michael now agrees the containers have the same number of beads; but as soon as the beads are again distributed into the tall and shallow containers, he changes his mind.

During the concrete operations period, children also develop new abilities relating to classification, seriation, and numbers. The seriation problem shown in Figure 6.6 would present insurmountable problems for a 3-year-old but would be ridiculously simple for an 8-year-old. Given the ability to classify and to seriate, understanding numbers becomes relatively simple.

By the end of the period of concrete operations, the child has acquired the ability to deal with a wide range of problems systematically and logically and is very much at home in the world of symbols. But there remain a number of limitations to thought during this period, the most obvious of which is the child's continued inability to deal with the hypothetical; hence the label *concrete*. The logic of concrete operations is tied to real things. Children don't yet have the freedom made possible by the more advanced logic of formal operations.

Formal Operations   According to Piaget, the single most important achievement of formal operations is the transition to a more advanced logic that deals with hypothetical states and events. Piaget illustrates this with the following problem: Edith is fairer than Susan; Edith is darker than Lilly. Who is the darkest of the three?

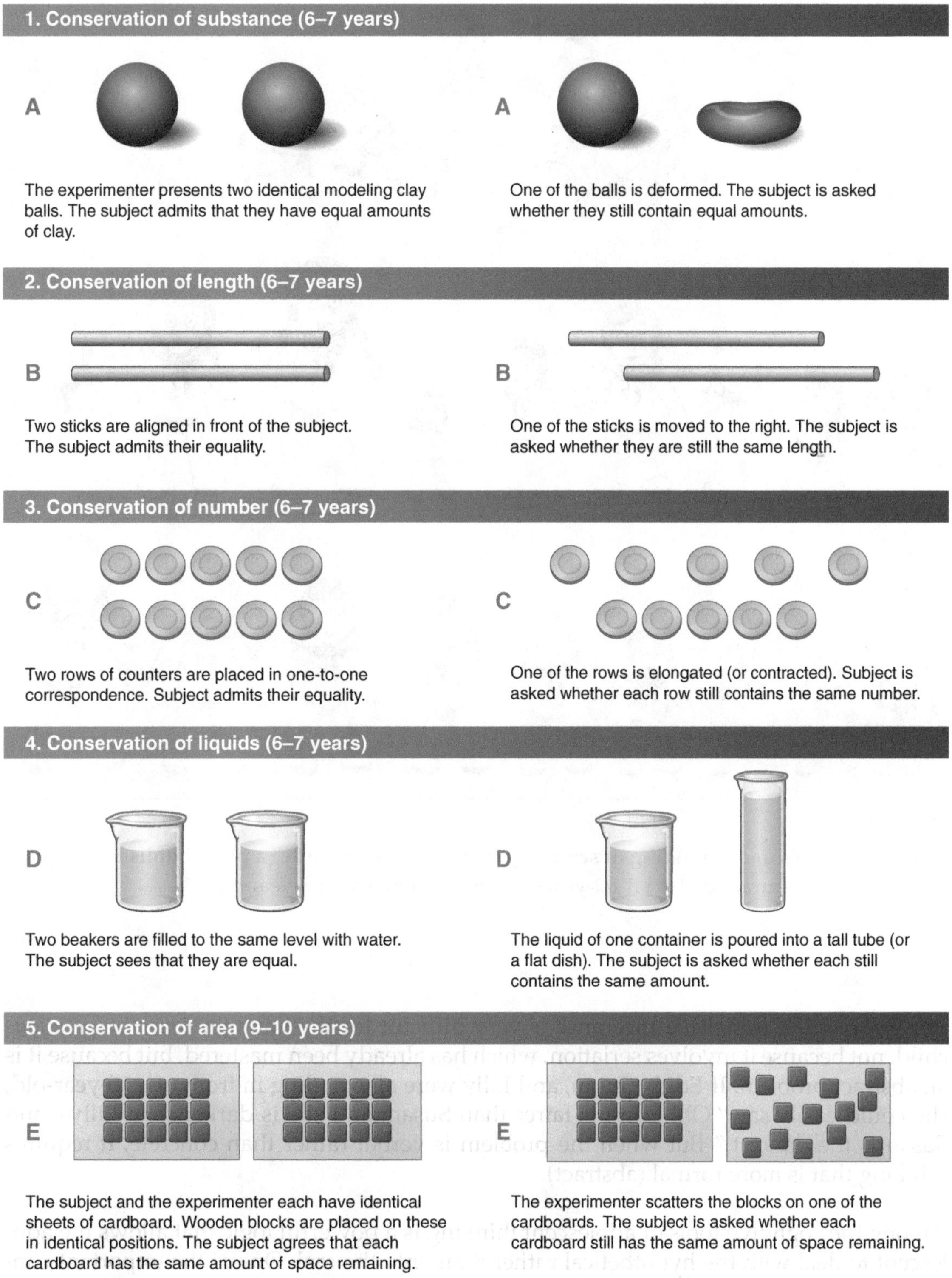

1. Conservation of substance (6–7 years)

A

A

The experimenter presents two identical modeling clay balls. The subject admits that they have equal amounts of clay.

One of the balls is deformed. The subject is asked whether they still contain equal amounts.

2. Conservation of length (6–7 years)

B

B

Two sticks are aligned in front of the subject. The subject admits their equality.

One of the sticks is moved to the right. The subject is asked whether they are still the same length.

3. Conservation of number (6–7 years)

C

C

Two rows of counters are placed in one-to-one correspondence. Subject admits their equality.

One of the rows is elongated (or contracted). Subject is asked whether each row still contains the same number.

4. Conservation of liquids (6–7 years)

D

D

Two beakers are filled to the same level with water. The subject sees that they are equal.

The liquid of one container is poured into a tall tube (or a flat dish). The subject is asked whether each still contains the same amount.

5. Conservation of area (9–10 years)

E

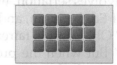 

E

The subject and the experimenter each have identical sheets of cardboard. Wooden blocks are placed on these in identical positions. The subject agrees that each cardboard has the same amount of space remaining.

The experimenter scatters the blocks on one of the cardboards. The subject is asked whether each cardboard still has the same amount of space remaining.

Figure 6.5

Some tests for conservation with approximate ages of attainment.

Figure 6.6

To test children's understanding of seriation, they are asked to order a pile of dolls by height. The top row was arranged by a 3 1/2-year-old; the bottom, by an 8-year-old.

This problem of **transitive inference** is very difficult for the younger *concrete operations* child, not because it involves seriation, which has already been mastered, but because it is an abstract problem. If Edith, Susan, and Lilly were all standing in front of a 10-year-old, she could easily say, "Oh! Edith is fairer than Susan, and she is darker than Lilly—and Susan is the darkest." But when the problem is verbal rather than concrete, it requires thinking that is more formal (abstract).

Among the cognitive tools of adolescent thinking is a powerful logic that allows the adolescent to deal with the hypothetical rather than only the real. One of the important consequences of this newfound ability is an increasing concern with the ideal. Once children are able to reason from the hypothetical to the real or from the actual to the hypothetical, they can conceive of worlds and societies that, hypothetically, have no ills.

It should be noted, however, that the ability to deal logically with the hypothetical is not a characteristic that governs all adolescent and adult thinking. Rather, it is a form of thinking that is now *possible*, whereas it had previously been beyond the child's abilities. Although formal thought may be clearly evident in individual instances, it is by no means evident in all cases.

Evaluation of Piaget's Theory

Piaget's critics typically agree on a number of standard complaints. One is that he used very few subjects in his research, which is true but not especially important unless studies with larger groups contradict his findings. In fact, as Fuson (2009) notes, of the thousands of studies that have followed Piaget's research, the majority support his description of the general sequence of intellectual development.

However, most critics also agree that Piaget underestimated the abilities of young children. That might be because Piaget's investigations, even with very young children, were largely verbal. When tasks are made simpler, children sometimes respond quite differently. For example, Charles and Rivera (2009) found that 5- and 6-month-old infants will often actively *look* for an object before they can actually reach for it. Looking for an object is a strong sign of some understanding of object permanence. Similarly, Aubrey (1993) points out that pre-schoolers have a far more advanced understanding of number than Piaget thought.

Critics also agree that whereas Piaget underestimated what younger children can do, he overestimated the capabilities of children at the stage of formal thinking. More recent studies often fail to find much evidence of formal operations thinking among adults, let alone adolescents (for example, Modgil & Modgil, 1982).

A final caution is in order: The stage aspect of theories such as Piaget's gives the impression that one day a child of a certain age is at stage X; the next day, the child wakes up at stage Y. But that, of course, is not really the case. The boundaries between stages are never entirely clear, and transitions are seldom entirely abrupt and irreversible.

Children's Social-Emotional Development

As we saw earlier, Erik Erikson describes eight stages of *psychosocial* development. The theory explains how, in the very beginning, parents are all-important. Not only are they essential for the baby's comfort and survival, but they provide for all of the newborn's psychological needs. They are the infant's source of love, and that is not a small four-letter word.

As children grow older, peers become progressively more important. But that does not mean that parents immediately become less important. Even in adolescence, peers and others outside the family don't ordinarily completely replace parents either as a source of love or as a source of profound influence on interests, values, and decisions. Two of Erikson's stages span childhood (see Figure 6.8).

Initiative Versus Guilt

By the age of 4 or 5, Erikson explains, children have become relatively autonomous. They have discovered that they are capable and independent. Now they will spend the rest of their childhood trying to discover exactly who they are. In early childhood, they do this by trying to be like their parents—that is, by *identifying* with them. At the same time, their world expands beyond the family, and as they explore this wider environment, they're called upon to exercise initiative and to overcome the sense of inferiority that threatens.

Industry Versus Inferiority

From about ages 6 to 11, children interact extensively with peers. It now becomes increasingly important that they be accepted as worthwhile. They need to discover that they are competent, that they can do things—in short, that they are *industrious*. During this stage, children are anxious to learn what their culture offers them and requires of them. Failing to do so can result in a lasting sense of inferiority.

Play

The **socialization** of the child begins in the family and continues with peers, schools, and other social institutions. Through these, children become aware of the many implicit and explicit rules that govern behavior in their culture. Much of the child's early socialization occurs through play.

And what is **play**? Sadly, many of us have forgotten. We abandon ourselves reluctantly and guardedly to the joys of madness and the ecstasies of whimsy. We know too carefully what reality is, and we fear too passionately the possibility of confusing the imaginary with the real.

There is no such fear in the hearts of children. The games they play, unlike the games we play, are played solely for their enjoyment. They are designed neither to impress nor to deceive; neither to persuade nor to annoy.

Children's games may be classified into three broad categories: sensorimotor play, imaginative play, and social play. Many games obviously share characteristics of all three.

Sensorimotor Play   *Sensorimotor play* is mainly physical activity such as skipping, hopping, jumping, running, and the countless solitary games of young children. It is the only type of play of which young infants are capable.

Imaginative Play   *Imaginative* (or *pretend*) play begins very early, continues throughout life, and takes a variety of forms. Most obvious are the host of make-believe games and activities prevalent in the preschool years. Even infants as young as 1 can pretend, often by simulating common activities like pretending to eat or pretending to sleep. And by age 2, a wide range of make-believe games becomes possible as children learn to transform objects, people, and activities into whatever they wish. Many of these pretend games are suggested by the immediate environment, notes Jaffke (1996). Thus, a picture, a crooked stick, a broken teacup, a squished worm—each can inspire a new game.

Another type of imaginative play becomes increasingly common in the later preschool years and continues well into adulthood, although we spend little time talking about it.

Daydreaming is a normal and healthy form of play. Evidence suggests that daydreaming may be very important in the resolution of fears, anxieties, and a wealth of related problems (Barber, Bagsby, & Munz, 2010). It very likely contributes significantly to creative output (Singer, 2009) and probably is also centrally involved in the development of interpersonal skills, providing as it does an opportunity for the imaginary exercising of these skills.

There is, too, the **imaginary playmate** with whom as many as one third of all preschool children play constantly (Singer, 2009). These imaginary friends are loved, spoken to, taken on trips, dressed, and played with. Psychology has not yet interviewed any of them in depth. Most of them go away in the earlier school years and never come back.

Social Play   *Social play* is any type of play that involves interaction among two or more children. Thus, both practice and pretend play are social when they involve more than one child. Skipping rope alone in the darkness of one's basement is a solitary sensorimotor activity; skipping rope out on the playground with others turning the rope and chanting "salt, mustard, vinegar, pepper . . ." is a cooperative or social activity. Similarly, creating daydreams in the solitude of one's bedroom is private imaginative play, but playing "let's pretend—you be the veterinaman [sic] and I'll be the dog" is social imaginative play.

Note, too, that children play solitary games before they engage in more social games, and that even when two children are playing side by side, they are often playing independently. Piaget (1951) drew attention to this progression in children's games, pointing out that, prior to truly *social play*, there is *parallel*

Three categories of children's play: (a) imaginative, (b) social, and (c) sensorimotor. Note that these forms of play are not mutually exclusive. A rope-tug competition can be every bit as sensorimotor as social. And playing cowboy roles may be highly social as well as imaginative.

play where children play together (in the sense of being in physical proximity) but neither share the activities employed in the game nor follow mutually accepted rules.

True social play requires interaction between two or more children, the use of rules, and cooperation. It is hardly surprising that it is considered one of the most important means of fostering language growth as well as cognitive, social, and emotional development in children.

Earlier research had suggested that as children begin to play more socially, they engage in less solitary play. Solitary play among older children has sometimes been seen as evidence of social immaturity. Xu's (2010) research suggests that this is really not the case. She explains that cultural changes have resulted in an increasing amount of solitary play among today's children. These changes include smaller families, frequent social isolation in larger urban centers, the mushrooming availability of games designed for solitary play on computers and hand-held devices, and the enormous amount of time children spend watching television.

6.4 Adolescents

Social play continues through the transition from childhood to adolescence and beyond.

Physical and Sexual Changes

It is not always an easy transition, complicated as it is by the gap that often exists between newly achieved biological maturity and social maturity. Although biological maturation readies the adolescent for adult roles of mating and procreation, social constraints often delay the adoption of these roles.

Biologically, adolescence is the period from the onset of **puberty** (sexual maturity) to adulthood. Puberty is defined as the capacity to ejaculate semen for boys and the first menstrual period (**menarche**) for girls. The changes that result in sexual maturity define **pubescence**. These changes are initiated by a dramatic increase in hormones produced by the **gonads** (*testes* in boys and *ovaries* in females), culminating in the ability to produce mature ova and sperm. Other signs of pubescence include the appearance of pigmented pubic hair, breast enlargement in the girl, the growth of armpit and facial hair, and a lowering of the voice. There is also a dramatic increase in height and weight just before adolescence (the *growth spurt*). Puberty (sexual maturity) typically immediately follows the growth spurt.

Because of wide individual variations in the ages at which these changes occur (typically much earlier for girls than for boys), the beginning and end of adolescence are not easily defined. Age 12 is often used as an approximation for the beginning of adolescence and age 20 for the beginning of adulthood—although the "legal" age of adulthood varies widely in different jurisdictions.

Early and Late Maturation

In North America, sexual maturity (puberty) is reached at around age 12.8 for girls and 14 for boys. However, some girls may reach sexual maturity as young as 9; others, not until age 16; some boys, as young as 11 or 12; others, not until age 18. Evidence suggests that sexual maturity has been occurring earlier across the United States, especially for girls. Herman-Giddens et al. (1997) looked at the age of menarche among more than 17,000 girls in the United States. They found that average age of sexual maturation has dropped from around 17 in the middle of the 19th century to just below 13 at present.

Research indicates that early maturation is sometimes an advantage for boys. Early-maturing boys are often better adjusted, more popular, more confident, more assertive, and more successful in heterosexual relationships. They are also likely to begin dating earlier and to have first sexual intercourse earlier (Kim & Smith, 1999). However, they are also more likely to use illegal drugs and to smoke cigarettes (Engels, 2009; Jaszyna-Gasior et al., 2009).

Early-maturing girls, too, are more likely to engage in behaviors of which parents don't approve, including an increased likelihood of drug use (Arim & Shapka, 2008). However, there

The most important changes of adolescence are those that lead to sexual maturity. These changes occur very early for some and much later for others. Early maturation is sometimes associated with a higher likelihood of engaging in behaviors—and displaying hairstyles—of which parents don't approve.

is good evidence that most of the negative effects of early maturation disappear by young adulthood (Copeland et al., 2010).

Adolescent Egocentrism

And much of the adolescent's egocentrism will also have disappeared by then—with exceptions.

In Piagetian theory, egocentrism is not a derogatory term; it refers less to a selfishness than to a cognitive and emotional *self-centeredness*. Egocentrism is apparent in children's inability to be completely objective in their understanding of the world. For young infants, objects exist only when they are being looked at, tasted, felt, or smelled. And in the preschool period there is evidence of egocentrism when children focus on the perceptual features of objects and respond incorrectly to conservation problems. The egocentrism of the adolescent is of a different nature.

The Imaginary Audience and the Personal Fable

When 15-year-old Rosa was getting ready to go to a concert, she agonized over her hair. It seemed that her mop had gone wild overnight, so now she was desperately trying to find some way of making it look decent enough that she would not be an absolute dork.

"Nobody'll notice, you look fine," said her mother.

"Everybody'll see," she retorted.

Her **imaginary audience** that night would consist of 30,000 people. *Everybody* would be watching; everybody would care. And Rosa is not exceptionally egocentric.

The adolescent's imaginary audience is an imagined collection of all who might be concerned with the adolescent's self and behavior. It is the "they" in all those expressions "they think . . ." "they say . . ." The imaginary audience is an expression of adolescents' belief that they are the center of attention.

In some ways, argue Bell and Bromnick (2003), the adolescent's imaginary audience is not entirely *imaginary*. In fact, there are important social and personal consequences attached to what people think of the adolescent's dress and behavior. And there may be negative consequences attached to ignoring the audience.

The adolescent's *personal fable* includes feelings of being special and powerful and invulnerable and, as this lad proves, capable of awesome bicycle feats. Not surprisingly, high-risk behaviors—and accidents—are more common in this age group.

The imaginary audience, says Elkind (1967), is not a highly critical, but an admiring audience. It makes sense that adolescents' **personal fables** would include a supportive audience. Personal fables are fantasies adolescents invent in which, not surprisingly, they are the heroes. They're stories characterized by a feeling of being special and unique, as well as by a sense of power and invulnerability. Unfortunately, this feeling of invulnerability is often sadly inappropriate, as is evident in the fact that adolescents aged 16 to 19 are four times more likely to have vehicle accidents than older drivers (Insurance Institute for Highway Safety, 2009).

Identity Formation

A higher probability of accidents is just one of the risks of adolescence; there are others. As G. S. Hall claimed many decades ago, adolescence can be a time of storm and stress. And when there are storms in adolescence, they sometimes have to do with the problem of developing an **identity**, a sense of wholeness and purpose.

In Erik Erikson's theory of *psychosocial* development, the conflict that labels the stage descriptive of adolescence is *identity versus identity diffusion* (see Figure 6.8). During this stage, the adolescent is faced with the daunting task of developing an *identity*. This involves decisions and choices not so much about who one is but rather about who one can be among all potential selves. The source of conflict lies in the various possibilities open to adolescents.

While in the transition between childhood and adulthood, the adolescent's *identity status* typically changes as crises come and go and as the adolescent explores various options. Building on Erikson's work, Marcia (1966, 1980) identifies four distinct types of identity status on the basis of whether the adolescent has undergone or is currently undergoing a crisis and on whether a commitment has been made to a specific identity.

Identity Diffusion

Adolescents in the state of *identity diffusion* have made no commitment and experienced no identity crisis. These are adolescents whose political, social, and religious beliefs are ambiguous or nonexistent and who have no vocational aspirations. It is a state that's very common in early adolescence.

Foreclosure

Some adolescents, by virtue of religious, political, or vocational commitments, achieve a strong sense of identity without experiencing a crisis. This is often the case, for example, in close-knit religious communities where roles and beliefs are predetermined. It may also be the case when adolescents simply allow parents or others to make important identity-related decisions for them. The most striking characteristic of these adolescents, says Marcia (1980), is high adherence to authoritarian values (obedience and respect of authority).

Moratorium

Erikson believed that one of the functions of adolescence was to serve as a *moratorium*—a period during which adolescents could experiment with various identities without having to make a commitment. Moratorium adolescents have vague, changing commitments; in this sense, they are in crisis. But it is a useful crisis because without it, there is a danger of premature commitment (as in the case of foreclosure) or of continuing lack of commitment (as in identity diffusion).

Identity Achieved

Those who have gone through the moratorium and made a commitment are described as *identity achieved*. Marcia (1980) reports that identity achieved adolescents are more independent, respond better to stress, have more realistic goals, and have higher self-esteem than adolescents in any of the other three categories. However, he also emphasizes that identities are never static and absolutely permanent. Even when the adolescent appears

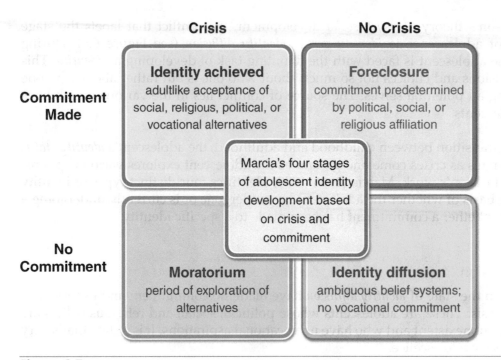

Figure 6.7

Marcia's four states of identity development.

to have achieved an identity, further changes often occur. For example, some college students move in and out of identity crises before finally achieving a permanent commitment (Figure 6.7).

6.5 Adults

And even when they are adults, some never achieve any lasting commitment, never develop a strong sense of identity. They're recognizable later in life as the full-time "fun seekers," says Marcia (1980), or as disturbed, highly anxious individuals with low self-esteem and low confidence.

Erikson's Stages of Adulthood

As we saw, Erikson describes human development in terms of progression through a series of adaptations that the culture requires. At every developmental stage, growth and development require new competencies. And always, there are opposing tendencies. Thus, the infant must develop trust in a world that is initially strange and sometimes terrifying. If the opposing tendency, fear and mistrust, is not overcome, it is difficult for the toddler to go out into the world, to explore and learn and develop. And the main task of adolescence is to overcome the crisis that comes with conflicting choices and the need to make a commitment.

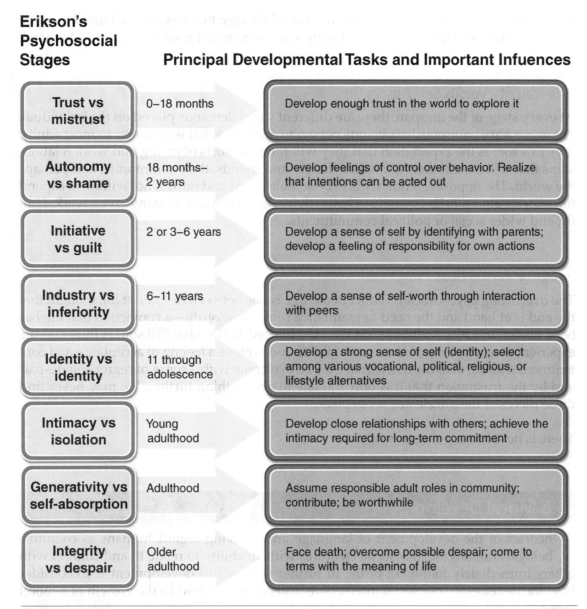

Figure 6.8

Erikson's developmental tasks. Based on Erik H. Erikson (1959).

Adulthood brings with it a whole new set of challenges, each with powerful conflicting tendencies. Three of Erikson's eight stages of the human lifespan cover adulthood (Figure 6.8).

Intimacy Versus Isolation

One of the commitments that many adolescents and young adults are called upon to make requires forming intimate relationships, often, though not always, with someone of the opposite sex. But here, as in all stages of the lifespan, there is a conflict between the need to make a commitment and an unwillingness to do so. Often, says Erikson, there is a reluctance to give up or compromise the hard-won sense of identity that has been achieved. And, of course, in many cases, the search for identity and commitment goes on well into adulthood.

Generativity Versus Self-Absorption

At every stage of the lifespan, there are different social demands placed on the individual. These can vary enormously from one person to another. What is common to most adults, says Erikson, is the expectation that they will form the sorts of caring and work relationships that will benefit their immediate family and friends, their community, and perhaps the world. The opposing tendency is to be self-absorbed and selfish, not willing to expend the effort required to be *generative*. Generativity can be evident in many areas: work, family, and wider social or political commitments.

Integrity Versus Despair

The overriding psychosocial conflict in old age is one between despair at the thought that the end is at hand and the need to maintain a sense of *integrity*—a conviction that life has been useful and worthwhile. What the elderly need to do, says Erikson, is integrate the experiences of a lifetime, make sense of them, and achieve a feeling of acceptance and contentment. Failing that, the individual may be overcome with a sense of regret and despair and by the frustration that it is now too late to do anything further. We may never find those pieces of the puzzle not yet in place.

There is not always going to be a tomorrow.

6.6 Moral Development

Theories of the development of language and thinking regard humans as cognitive beings. Humans are also social creatures with an ability to relate to and connect with others immediately following birth. To further understand development is to consider how the development of social interactions and cognitions lead to the growth of a moral sense.

Moral development is the process by which children acquire a perception of which behaviors and attitudes are right and which are wrong. While different schools of thought conceptualize moral development differently, the behaviorists claiming it involves a reinforced system of moral and/or immoral behaviors and a cognitive theorist espousing the importance of thinking and comprehension of increasingly complex concepts, all seem to agree that morality grows and develops parallel to thinking and language.

Specifically, Piaget thought that his theory of cognitive development could be used to understand our moral development as well postulating that there are age-based consistencies in moral judgments. Piaget's contemporary, Lawrence Kohlberg (1981), suggested a model explaining humans' development as moral beings, capable of understanding the dimensions of right and wrong. Kohlberg suggested that all humans progress through a sequence of moral stages that are linked not only to stages of cognitive development but also to social experiences and interactions with other people. In his research into the realm of moral development, Kohlberg asked many people across most age groups (children, adolescents, and adults) to think through different moral dilemmas and decide if the actions posed in the dilemma were right or wrong. What he found led him to conclude that humans develop through three levels of moral reasoning. Kohlberg's stages of moral development are shown in Table 6.4.

Table 6.4 Kohlberg's Stages of Moral Development

Stage	Age	Process
Preconventional Morality	By age 9	Focus is on self-interest and avoidance of punishment.
Conventional Morality	By adolescence	Caring for others emerges. Law and rules are upheld for their own sake.
Postconventional Morality	Adulthood	Universal, human ethics and rights are recognized.

TRY IT AT HOME – Kohlberg posed different moral dilemmas to many different groups of people across many different age groups. Although he was fascinated with children's responses to different problems involving ideas of right and wrong, it was children's rationale for their decisions that led Kohlberg to believe that morality is a developed concept, like thinking.

Pose a problem similar to Kohlberg's dilemmas to a child under the age of 9 and ask her if the character's actions were right or wrong.

Mr. Brown has three children, and they are all hungry because they have not eaten in many days. While there is a baker down the street with plenty of bread for all the children to eat and not be hungry, Mr. Brown does not have enough money to pay for the bread. Late at night, when the baker's shop is closed, Mr. Brown breaks in and steals enough bread for his family to eat for a week. Was it right for Mr. Brown to steal the bread? Explain.

What sort of answers do you get from younger children? What sort of answers would you expect from older children or from adolescents? From adults? What do you notice about their reasoning for their answers? Is there an answer to this dilemma that is *more* right than the other? Why?

6.7 Parenting Styles

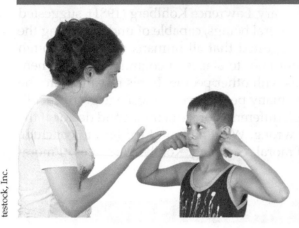

© artproem, 2011. Used under license of Shutterstock, Inc.

Raising psychologically healthy children can be a difficult endeavor offering no guarantees or instructions. However, psychological research does shed some light on what it means to be a psychologically healthy human and what sorts of parents raised such an individual. Some guidelines have emerged over the years and primarily discuss basic *parenting styles* and their effects on children. Psychologist Diana Baumrind (1971) outlined three parenting styles as a result of her many years of observing of parents: *authoritarian, authoritative,* and *permissive.* The main variables at play in each are the control and responsiveness of each parent to their child's wishes. Let's break these down.

© Monkey Business Images, 2011. Used under license of Shutterstock, Inc.

© Elena Kouptsova-Vasic, 2011. Used under license of Shutterstock, Inc.

- **Authoritarian parenting:** These parents are demanding of their children, often outlining very strict expectations and consequences for not performing. In addition to their demanding style, these parents are also unresponsive to their children's needs or desires. They believe that they need to control the child's behavior so that it adheres to a set of predetermined standards. They expect their children to obey the rules without question and are mostly closed to any input from them.
- **Authoritative parenting:** These parents are warm, nurturing, and involved with their children's experiences. Like authoritarian parents, they are demanding of their children; however, they feel a need to consider their children's point of view and wishes. There is more of a democratic process in this style of parenting and, although the demands are high and rules are clear, they are discussed with the children, and the children know they are safe and that they have a voice in the family.

- **Permissive indulgent parenting:** These parents, like authoritative parents, are warm and nurturing; however, they lack rules, structure, or clear expectations of their children's behavior. They are not unresponsive to their children's basic needs; however, they are lacking in responsiveness to their behavior and lack consistency in their reinforcements and punishments.

© Cheryl Casey, 2011. Used under license of Shutterstock, Inc.

- **Permissive neglectful parenting:** These parents, like permissive indifferent parents, lack clear rules and structure, but in addition, they lack warmth and nurturance. Children who grow up with parents like this are often left to their own devices with regard to navigating the world around them.

THINK ABOUT IT – How do you think these parenting styles affect young children?

There is a slew of research on this topic. What does this literature suggest about children with parents of different parenting styles?

Imagine you are hired by a psychologist to write a book on how to be the best parent possible. What would your chapters be titled? What would your advice be? What cautions would you give?

What type of parent are you *or* what type of parent do you hope to be?

6.8 Death and Dying

© Viktor Gladkov, 2011. Used under license of Shutterstock, Inc.

When we started this chapter, we discussed the whole person, which is the individual as made up of many different "parts" with varying traits distinguishing them from others with their own individual sets of traits. When you discussed how people are all different, you likely alluded to differences in personality, varying degrees of temperament, and diversity of people's behavior. We discussed the development of language, thinking, and of morals. In this final section, we will discuss the end of these traits in the death of the individual but also, and perhaps more importantly, the changing and diminishment of these traits.

Although it is nice to think of only the elderly dying and while it is obviously the case that all people die, there is also a large level of protection from the harsher elements of death built into our society. It is also nice to think that older adults are prepared for their demise and that they are at peace. What appears to be more the case is that all humans of all ages die, that they all have some anxiety, whether significant or miniscule, about the prospect of dying and that not everyone, whether elderly or youthful, has a peaceful, wisdom-filled exit.

Elisabeth Kübler-Ross (1969) is the most widely recognized person associated with the psychological study of grief, death, and dying. Her research with hundreds of terminally ill patients led her to her stage theory of death. In short, she believed that people come to terms with their own death the same way that they come to terms with the death of others. She outlined five stages of dying: *denial* ("It's not true"), anger ("Why me?!"), *bargaining* ("I'll do anything to reverse this"), *depression* ("I've lost everything"), and *acceptance* ("I accept my time is near"). While her theory is continually criticized in many social and academic circles, it survives as a template for human movement within the knowledge of death.

THINK ABOUT IT – There are many protective factors against death. Each culture seems to have its own stories of life and death, the process of dying, and all have ceremonies or ritualized behaviors that honor, celebrate and even keep at bay the dead.

What is your cultural experience with death? What times in your life have you come into contact with a person who has beliefs about life and death that are completely different than your own? What were your reactions?

Finally, religion seems to be a common cultural component that weighs in on the ideas of life and death perhaps more than any other subject. What are different ideas that different religions offer about death? Despite their differences, do they have anything in common?

© Ashley Whitworth, 2011. Used under license of Shutterstock, Inc.

What are your thoughts? Beliefs?

Main Points

1. **The Beginning: Prenatal Development:** The beginning involves sperm and ovum forming a zygote containing 23 pairs of chromosomes, 1 pair of which determines biological sex. Chromosomes contain the tens of thousands of genes that give each of us our unique genetic code.

2. **Infants:** There is an enormous amount of motor and cognitive learning during the first 2 years of life, including locomotion and language. This learning is made possible by relatively well-developed perceptual systems coupled with an impressive brain. Infants vary in the amount of time they spend sleeping, crying, being alert, and being active. They also vary in terms of their predominant temperaments (easy, difficult, slow to warm up).

3. **Children:** A sort of *magical* thinking characterizes childhood. But as children adapt by assimilating (using previously learned responses) and accommodating (modifying responses), they become more closely attuned to reality and less given to magic. In Piaget's description, the *here-and-now* world of the infant gives way to the egocentric, perception-dominated, intuitive world of the preschooler, then to the reality-based, concrete-operations world of the young child, and finally to the more logical and idealistic world of the adolescent. Play has a fundamental role in the socialization of the child.

4. **Adolescents:** The transition from childhood to adulthood is defined by sex-related changes (pubescence) leading to sexual maturity (puberty). The adolescent's egocentrism is evident in the imaginary audience and the personal fable (which brings with it a sometimes dangerous sense of invulnerability). The principal task of adolescence is to arrive at a commitment (a decision regarding who one can and should be) and to overcome related crises.
5. **Adults:** Adulthood brings new challenges having to do with establishing intimate relationships, making worthwhile contributions (being generative in various spheres), and, in the end, reconciling one's life and developing a notion that it has been worthwhile.

Thoughts and Suggestions

1. In order to grow, one must change. If we don't change, we don't grow. We become stuck or fixated if you will. We are actually to go from glory to glory. Looking back on your past stages of development, can you think of at least one developmental change that you are aware of and is important to you?
2. When considering Erikson's stages of development, which stage issue (i.e., trust vs. mistrust or identity vs. role confusion) which of the traits do you think you are strongest in. What trait, if any, do you think is a personal weakness, or area that needs development?
3. Where would you place yourself according to Kohlberg's stages of moral development?

Suggested readings from Hock, R. R. (1999). *Forty studies that changed psychology* (3rd ed.). Upper Saddle River, NJ: Prentice Hall. (ISBN #: 0-13-922725-3):

*   Reading 17: Discovering Love
*   Reading 18: Out of Sight, But Not Out of Mind
*   Reading 19: How Moral Are You?

Study Terms

accommodation	egocentrism
animistic thinkers	embryo
assimilation	identity
conception	imaginary audience
conservation	imaginary playmate
daydreaming	infancy
deoxyribonucleic acid (DNA)	intuitive thinking
difficult infants	magical thinking
dizygotic	menarche
easy infants	monozygotic

nature-nurture controversy

object concept

operations

personal fables

placenta

play

psychosocial development

puberty

schemas

sensorimotor

slow-to-warm-up infants

socialization

temperament

zygote

Personality

Focus Questions

*By the end of the chapter, you should be able
to answer the following questions:*

- How is personality defined?
- What are trait-type approaches to personality?
- What are the *Big Five*?
- What are the main beliefs of biological approaches to personality like Sheldon's
  and Eysenck's?
- How does Freud describe normal and abnormal personality development?
- What is *self-actualization*?
- What are some common examples of *projective* personality measures?
- What are the uses of some common *nonprojective* personality tests?

Part of me suspects that I'm a loser, and the other part of me thinks I'm God Almighty.

—John Lennon,
The Beatles Anthology

Inspirational Words

For God hath not given us the spirit of fear; but of power, and of love, and of a sound mind. 2 Timothy 1:7

And beside this, giving all diligence, add to your faith virtue; and to virtue knowledge; And to knowledge temperance; and to temperance patience; and to patience godliness; And to godliness brotherly kindness; and to brotherly kindness charity. For if these things be in you, and abound, they make you that ye shall neither be barren nor unfruitful in the knowledge of our Lord Jesus Christ. 2 Peter 1: 5–8

But the fruit of the Spirit is love, joy, peace, longsuffering, gentleness, goodness, faith. Meekness, temperance: against such there is no law. And they that are Christ's have crucified the flesh with the affections and lusts. If we live in the Spirit, let us also walk in the Spirit. Let us not be desirous of vain glory, provoking one another, envying one another. Galatians 5: 22–26.

7.1 Personality

The fact is, we are all different (although we are not all geniuses): We all have a **personality**—a collection of characteristics that defines our person. In a general sense, personality can be defined as stable characteristics, including abilities, talents, habits, preferences, weaknesses, moral attributes, and predominant moods, that vary from one person to another.

The word *personality* comes from the Latin word *persona*, which referred to the masks worn by Roman actors. Using these masks, an actor could play many different roles in a single play. A persona was, in a very literal sense, a way of changing one's personality, a way of becoming somebody else.

In one sense we all make use of *personae* (masks or roles): We appear to be different people in different situations. The type of behavior expected of us in formal situations is often quite different from that which we display in less formal circumstances. There is a type of self-revelation made possible in intimate circumstances that is impossible for most people when interacting with strangers. In public, our masks are more impenetrable.

But we do not have an unlimited choice of masks. Our roles are limited by our abilities, our inclinations, and our talents. We cannot just decide that we will be unselfish and all wear unselfish personae. For some, tendencies toward jealousy and greed make it impossible to be unselfish at all times. Their prevailing personality is simply incompatible with that persona. So too with each of us: There are some "selves" that you and I will never be, much as we might like. And there are many selves we sometimes see in others that we would never select for ourselves.

Personality and Self

Note that the terms *self* and *personality* are very closely related. The self is essentially the person viewed from inside. My self is me as I see myself. Personality is the self, too, but from a different view; it is the self as viewed from the outside. In other words, it includes those aspects of my *self* that I present to the world. The correspondence between the two may be very high (as in an "open" person) or quite low. Presumably, the more closely our personae resemble our true selves, the more similar will be our *selves* and our personalities.

We all make use of masks, personality theorists tell us: We're different in different situations. And though our masks might not be as obvious as this guy's, they are often no easier to see behind.

Although the behavior of those we know well is sometimes unexpected, it doesn't often violate our expectations. Generally, those who are friendly and outgoing, as is this woman, greet us warmly. Unless we've done them wrong.

The Real Person

When someone does some horrendous thing to a cat or a car, neighbors are often shocked: "I would never have guessed in a million years. I can't believe that's the *real* him." But, *at least in one sense*, it *is* the real him, because we cannot easily separate people from their actions.

Striking as one person's violation of his neighbors' expectations might be, we should not overlook the other 40 people on his block whose behavior surprises no one. The woman who is known to be friendly and outgoing can always be counted on to organize block parties; the man who is conscientious continues to be thoughtful and well organized; and it is expected that the person who is somewhat neurotic will sometimes be moody and anxious. All these people exhibit behaviors consistent with what psychologists would identify as their dominant personality characteristics.

Understanding how to identify and measure the factors that determine consistency in behavior is the piece that personality theorists have struggled to contribute to the human puzzle.

7.2 The Common-Sense Approach

Being effective in a social environment requires a basic understanding of others—of their likely and unlikely behaviors, their probable actions and reactions. Those unlucky individuals who are less skilled at understanding others often seem inept and tactless and maybe a little socially unintelligent.

But even those who pride themselves on their "social intelligence" tend to operate with highly global notions of what other people are like and of what they are like themselves. Stagner (1958) provides a striking demonstration of this fact. An unethical salesman (experimenter) approaches a number of personnel managers with a new personality test. The test is absolutely worthless, but managers are told that it is an excellent personality test. They are invited to take it themselves and to buy it only if they are impressed with reports of their own personalities. After taking the test, each of 68 personnel managers is presented with statements such as these:

> *You prefer a certain amount of change and variety and become dissatisfied when hemmed in by restrictions and limitations.*

While you have some personality weaknesses, you are generally able to compensate for them.

You have a tendency to be critical of yourself. (Stagner, 1958, p. 348)

In this study, 91 percent of the managers thought the first statement was "rather good" or "amazingly accurate"; 89 and 92 percent thought the same thing of the second and third statements, respectively. This phenomenon is labeled the **Barnum effect** (after the founder of the famous circus, who claimed he had something for everyone). A large number of studies have since reported corroborating findings (for example, Claridge, Clark, Powney, & Hassan, 2008; Wyman & Vyse, 2008). Rogers and Soule (2009) also found the Barnum effect among both Western and Chinese participants who were asked to rate the accuracy of astrological predictions. But they also found that those who were better educated or who had some background in psychology were less likely to fall victims to the Barnum effect.

The Barnum effect describes our tendency to believe vague but plausible generalities such as might be offered by a fortune-teller or a palm reader. "We've got something for everybody; come into the big tent!!"

It is little wonder that graphologists (handwriting analysts), phrenologists (those who interpret personality on the basis of head contours), astrologers (those who look to the alignment of stars, planets, and moons), and palmists (palm readers) have sometimes not required a great deal of training in their respective endeavors.

The point of the Barnum effect research is that there are certain things that most people believe about themselves. A common-sense approach to personality might accept these beliefs as descriptive of all people. In fact, however, the vague and general statements typically used in this research are not very revealing at all. They say nothing about what makes people different from one another, or even very much about how people might be alike.

Psychology, for its part, offers a variety of approaches and theories, none of which is exclusively correct or categorically wrong. They simply represent different orientations and different emphases. They may also focus on things the other abuse leave out, or under emphasize, in another theorists opinion.

Since personality is a function of many different forces, it is not surprising that different theories often concentrate on different things. Much of what you are is a function of your genetic composition; biological factors are therefore important in determining manifested personality. Similarly, private experience, social situations, cognitive factors, and psychodynamic forces may all be involved in personality. This suggests at least six approaches to personality theory: common-sense, trait-type, biological, psychodynamic, learning-based, and humanistic (Table 7.1).

Table 7.1 Approaches to Understanding Personality

Approach	Major Concerns	Representative Theorists
Common-Sense	Why did she do that? Does he like me? What is she really like?	You
Trait-Type	Discovering and verifying the existence of related clusters of traits that compose personality types	The Greeks Jung Costa and McCrae
Biological	Looking at genes (genomics) and at brain structures and functions (neuropsychology) to identify processes and structures underlying personality	Eysenck Sheldon Researchers in *genomics* and *neuropsychology*
Psychodynamic	Clarifying the interplay of unconscious forces; understanding the conflict between basic inclinations and social/environmental constraints	Freud Jung
Learning-Based	Personality as learned habits, predispositions, attitudes; also look at rational contributions to behavior and emotions, decision making, attributions	Watson Pavlov Skinner Bandura Rotter
Humanistic	The self; worth, dignity, individuality	Maslow Rogers

Note that some of the theories and principles discussed in relation to each of these approaches include aspects of other approaches. The decision that one position is a trait-type approach rather than social, or biological rather than psychodynamic, is based on the main characteristics of the position, but not on all its characteristics; some approaches represent more than one orientation.

7.3 The Trait-Type Approach

The thousands of adjectives, nouns, and phrases that can be used to describe people are all examples of **trait** names. A trait is any distinct, consistent quality in which one person can be different from another. There are physical traits (blond, big, buxom), behavioral traits (quick, quiet, quarrelsome), moral traits (bad, base, benign)—more than 17,000 possible traits (Allport & Odbert, 1936).

One approach to personality has been to attempt to reduce the total number of possible traits to a few highly representative adjectives. The most useful would be those most often displayed in human behavior, most variable from one person to another, and most distinct. Typically, all synonyms or near-synonyms are excluded from such lists, and an effort is made to pair the words as opposites. Thus, a person can be emotional or stable, humble or assertive, outgoing or withdrawn.

Figure 7.1

Some of Cattell's 16 personality traits, based on popular adjectives that can be used to describe people in meaningful ways. The traits are arranged in pairs of opposites.

Another way of looking at a trait is to say that it implies a prediction about behavior. To say that an individual is bold is to predict that that person is more likely to act boldly than are other people in similar circumstances. That, however, is some distance from saying that a bold individual will always act boldly. Knowledge of predominant personality traits simply allows predictions that are more probable than those based solely on intuition.

Among the best known of the trait approaches is that proposed by Cattell (1946), who reduced Allport and Odbert's list of more than 17,000 adjectives by eliminating all synonyms, obscure and infrequent words, and apparently irrelevant terms. After extensive analysis of individuals who had been rated by close friends using Cattell's adjectives, he further reduced the list to 16 traits by combining separate but closely related traits using a process called **factor analysis**. This is a statistical procedure that analyzes correlations among variables and combines those that are closely related. It is commonly used to reduce large numbers of related variables—such as traits—to a smaller number of meaningful categories. Some of the 16 personality traits that resulted from Cattell's work are shown in Figure 7.1.

Cattell is now widely recognized as the founder of current personality and trait measurement (Denis, 2009). His approach to identifying and measuring personality traits continues to be widely used.

Type is a more inclusive term than *trait*. Whereas a trait is inferred from a tendency to behave in a given way in certain situations, a type is a grouping of related traits. For example, *Type A* personality is defined as individuals who are characterized by *traits* such as aggressiveness, competitiveness, high need for achievement, and perhaps other traits such as low frustration tolerance, impatience, and rudeness.

It is important to note that traits and types are not the causes of behavior, but indicate, instead, certain identifiable consistencies in behavior. Thus, people do not fight because they are hostile; but because they fight, we describe them as hostile. If causes can be identified, they may be as much in the situation as in the person.

Early Trait-Type Approaches

An ancient approach to personality types was suggested by Greek philosophers, who described four distinct types of individuals: the *sanguine* (optimistic and happy); the *melancholic* (unhappy, depressed); the *choleric* (of violent temper); and the *phlegmatic* (apathetic, not easily moved to excesses of emotion). They thought that each of these personality types depended on fluids in the body—then called "humors." The sanguine individual had a preponderance of blood; the melancholic, of black bile; the choleric, of ordinary bile; and the phlegmatic, of phlegm. Unfortunately, science has revealed us not to be so simple; that piece of the puzzle is now only of historical interest (Figure 7.2).

A widely accepted typology was originated by Carl Jung (1923), whose theory, like that of Sigmund Freud, was a **psychodynamic theory**. Psychodynamic theories are based on the belief that behavior is motivated by unconscious forces. These theories emphasize the interplay between unconscious and conscious motives. Freud, as we see shortly, believed that

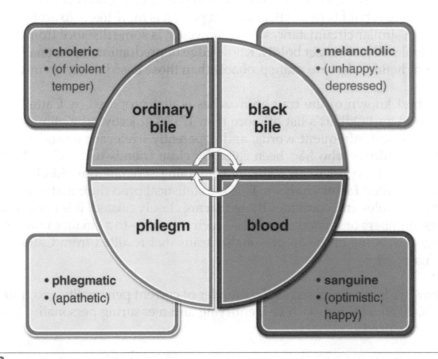

Figure 7.2

The ancient Greek classification of personality types and their biological bases. Unfortunately, we are not quite so simple.

the most important of these unconscious motives were sexual; Jung didn't agree. He, unlike Freud, believed that many of our unconscious motives stem from **archetypes**. Archetypes are a sort of unconscious shared historical memory—part of what he labeled the *collective unconscious*.

Among the most common archetypes, explains Jung, are the man/woman dichotomy (his labels are *anima/animus*). In a sense, these archetypes serve as motives that impel us to accept masculine and feminine characteristics. Similarly, there is an archetype relating to God, and this, he suggests, accounts for the existence of religions.

In his personality theory, Jung proposed two main *types* that include great clusters of traits: **extraversion** (also spelled *extroversion*) and **introversion**. These represent the two possible attitudes with which all people approach life, Jung explained. On the one hand, there are extroverts—those who run toward life, adventurous, bold, eager to live

Jung's typology describes *introverts*, who are more timid and quieter, and *extroverts*, who, like this young girl, are bold, adventurous, outgoing, and not averse to being the center of attention.

and to experience, concerned with others, with sports, with all the external world. *Extroverts* are fun-loving, outgoing, friendly, and active.

Introverts, on the other hand, are those who turn inward and away from the world (*intro* meaning inward). They are concerned more with subjective than objective reality. Introverts are described as timid and quiet. They avoid social interaction and dislike adventure and physical risk.

The Big Five

Jung's ancient typology is a puzzle piece that has withstood the test of time: Today's personality theorists agree overwhelmingly that extraversion and introversion represent a consistent and important dimension of human personality. But they also agree that these two labels represent only one of five personality types—commonly labeled the **Big Five factors** (or the *Five Factor Model*).

The five factors were discovered independently by different researchers and have been extensively investigated over the years (Digman, 1990). Much of this research uses factor analysis to look at how different traits tend to co-occur. This has allowed personality theorists to reduce a very large number of traits to five *big* factors, each of which is one extreme of a pair of opposite types. Thus, *extraversion* is one of the five factors, but *introversion* is not: It is simply the opposite of extraversion.

The Big Five factors, which are thought to include most of the traits that describe personality, are **c**onscientiousness, **a**greeableness, **n**euroticism, **o**penness, and **e**xtraversion. As a memory aid, note that the first five letters spell the acronyms CANOE or OCEAN.

Extraversion

Those who are extraverted tend to be outgoing, to seek stimulation, to want to be in the company of others. They are engaged in the world, highly sociable and lively. At the other extreme are the introverts—those who shy away from social interaction. Whereas extraverts tend to be gregarious, assertive, and bold, introverts tend to be solitary, withdrawn, and more timid. This does not mean that introverts are necessarily shy and have no friends. But research indicates they are likely to have fewer friends, that they are more socially reserved (Selfhout et al., 2010).

Openness

Openness is characterized by a high degree of inventiveness, adventurousness, and curiosity. Those who are highly open seek out new experiences; they want to know, to discover, to find out things. Openness implies an appreciation for things that are different and unusual, for art and imagination. The opposite dimension is characterized by a more rigid, conventional, traditional approach to life. Those who are *closed* rather than open prefer that things be straightforward and obvious rather than complex and ambiguous. Highly creative individuals tend to score high on the openness factor (Sung & Choi, 2009).

Neuroticism

Neuroticism is marked by fluctuating emotions, high anxiety, and a tendency toward negative moods such as anger and depression. Those who score high on this factor are sometimes described as *emotionally unstable*. They tend to be more vulnerable to the effects of stress and are more often in a bad mood. In contrast, those who score low on the neuroticism scale tend to be emotionally stable and calm when faced with stressful events. They are generally characterized by positive rather than negative moods.

Conscientiousness

Those who are careful and highly responsible score high on the **conscientiousness** scale. They are marked by a high degree of organization, self-discipline, thoroughness, and a need to achieve. Such individuals are often described as perfectionists or workaholics. They tend to be highly diligent, well-prepared workers (Woodman, Zourbanos, Hardy, Beattie, & McQuillan, 2010). In contrast, those who score low on conscientiousness display a lower need for achievement. They are more laid back, less disciplined, less compulsive.

Agreeableness

Agreeable people are those who are friendly and easygoing. They strive to be pleasant and cooperative. They are polite and compassionate, they value friendships, and they tend to have an optimistic view of people. In contrast, those low on the **agreeableness** factor are more suspicious of people, have a lower opinion of human nature, and are less likely to try to be accommodating and friendly. Research suggests that anger and hostility may be associated with low agreeableness scores (Sanz, Garcia-Vera, & Magan, 2010). (See Figure 7.3 for a summary of the Big Five approach to personality types.)

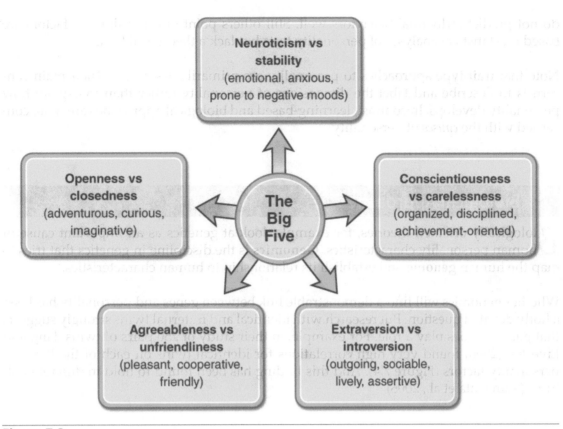

Figure 7.3

The Big Five factor model. A typology of human personality.

Stability of Personality

Some theorists believe that personality changes dramatically depending on the situation. For example, Mischel (2004) showed that scores on personality tests are not very useful in predicting a given individual's behavior in any specific situation. Behavior often seems to depend on the specific situation, taking into account the person's immediate emotions and goals.

On the other hand, there is strong evidence that personality traits are relatively stable over much of the lifespan (Bolkan, Meierdiercks, & Hooker, 2009). And there is considerable evidence that measures of the Big Five factors are highly useful in predicting typical patterns of behavior (McCrae & Costa, 1997). Although such measures do not lead to highly reliable predictions of what Sam will do tonight, they allow us to make very useful *general* predictions about how Sam is likely to behave in a wide variety of situations over a long period of time.

Although the Big Five factors are widely researched and widely accepted in personality theory, the approach has its critics. Some suggest that there are other important factors not included in the model—factors such as honesty, sense of humor, masculinity-femininity, and conservativeness (Block, 1995). Others, such as Mischel (2004), argue that the factors do not predict individual behaviors well. Still others point out that the five factors are based on statistical analyses of personality tests but lack a theoretical basis.

Note that trait-type approaches to personality are primarily *descriptive*: Their main concern is to describe and label the dimensions of personality rather than to explain how personality develops. In contrast, learning-based and biological approaches are more concerned with the *causes* of personality.

7.4 Biological Approaches

Biologically oriented theories, for example, look at genetics as an important cause of human personality characteristics. **Genomics** is the discipline in genetics that tries to map the human **genome** and establish its relationship to human characteristics.

Whether genomics will find a demonstrable link between genes and personality has been a hotly debated question. But research with identical and fraternal twins strongly suggests that genetics does play a role. For example, in their study of 250 pairs of twins, Jang and Livesley (2006) found very high correlations for identical twins on each of the Big Five personality factors (Figure 7.4). And this finding has been found to hold in different cultures (Yamagata et al., 2006).

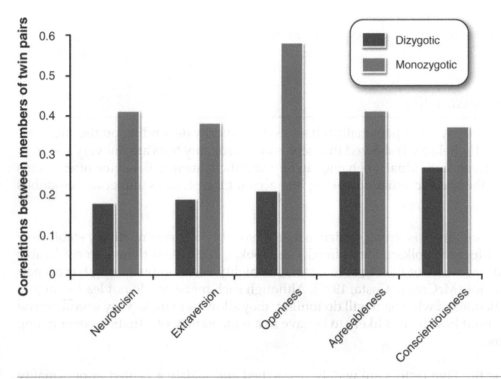

Figure 7.4

Correlations between 123 identical and 127 fraternal twin pairs for the Big Five personality factors—strong evidence of a genetic contribution to personality. (Based on Jang and Livesley, 2006.)

Research in neuropsychology also looks for the biological bases of personality characteristics and disorders. For example, some research indicates that high impulsivity may be linked with deficits in frontal and temporal lobe functioning—deficits that might be due to injury, disease, or genetics (Seres, Unoka, Bodi, Aspan, & Keri, 2009). In its extreme forms, impulsivity is a trait that may be characteristic of *borderline personality disorder* (discussed in Chapter 8).

Although the links between genes, neurological functioning, and personality are still not very clear, the area is an exciting and promising field of current research. There, neuropsychology and genomics may well uncover some key corner pieces of the human puzzle.

Sheldon's Body Types

Among the first well-known systematic investigations of the relationship between biologically determined characteristics and personality traits was Sheldon's (1954) monumental study of body type. He began by looking at some of the common stereotypes people have about physical appearance and personality. Is the fat person really happy and outgoing? Is the well-built person athletic and adventurous? Is the frail person intellectual and artistic?

Sheldon approached this problem by sorting 2,000 photographs of people into three categories based on general body types: *endomorph, mesomorph,* and *ectomorph.* **Endomorphs** are the larger individuals. **Mesomorphs** are muscular and strong and of medium weight. **Ectomorphs** are frail and slender.

After classifying body types into categories, Sheldon and his coworkers interviewed large groups of individuals to determine the relationship between body type and personality. They report an extremely high correspondence between the two, with the principal characteristics of each being as shown in Figure 7.5. Thus, Sheldon apparently confirmed that endomorphs are complacent, tolerant, concerned with eating, and highly sociable; that ectomorphs are withdrawn, secretive, and concerned with intellectual matters; and that mesomorphs are adventurous, bold, and loud.

Sheldon cautioned, however, that very few individuals fall solely into one category. Although many people tend to be more one type than another, most are actually a combination of all three body types. Thus, it is possible to identify the predominant temperament of an individual by analyzing body type, but personality characteristics pertaining to other body types may also be present.

Research on Somatotypes

Many investigations of the relationship between body type and personality have found very low relationships between the two (for example, Hood, 1963). Still, there are a handful of studies that report findings very similar to some of Sheldon's.

Why should body build be related to personality characteristics? Sheldon's argument was that temperament is constitutional (hereditary) in the same way as is body build, and

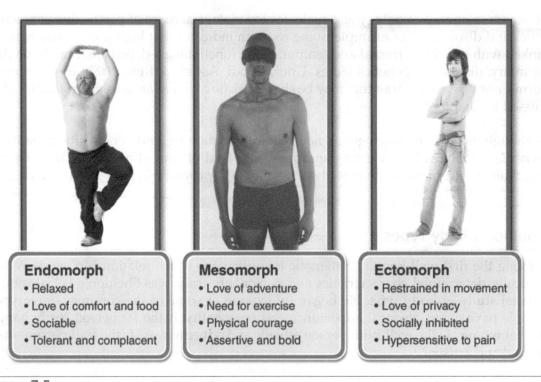

Endomorph
- Relaxed
- Love of comfort and food
- Sociable
- Tolerant and complacent

Mesomorph
- Love of adventure
- Need for exercise
- Physical courage
- Assertive and bold

Ectomorph
- Restrained in movement
- Love of privacy
- Socially inhibited
- Hypersensitive to pain

Figure 7.5

Sheldon's classification of body types and corresponding personality traits; an interesting but controversial approach to personality that has received both support and criticism.

that environmental influences are of minimal importance. It may be, as some genomics research with animals suggests, that personality characteristics are, at least to some extent, determined by genetics (for example, van Oers & Mueller, 2010).

Other explanations suggest that it is the types of activities and interactions facilitated by body build that may be most responsible for any relationship that might be found between personality and physical characteristics. The mesomorph, whose body is better suited to robust physical activity, is more likely to be athletic. Not surprisingly, research provides corroboration: Athletes in many sports are more likely to be mesomorphs (Galaviz & de Leon Fierro, 2007). Similarly, a mesomorphic build may lead more easily to violence and aggression—as Sheldon had predicted. A study by Maddan, Walker, and Miller (2008) provided some evidence for this prediction by comparing body type to the kinds of crimes a sample of prisoners had committed. And that mesomorphic builds are more attractive to the opposite sex than either ectomorphic or endomorphic builds has been confirmed in various studies (for example, Dixson, Dixson, Bishop, & Parish, 2010). This, too, may explain some of the mesomorph's personality traits.

The frail ectomorph, by contrast, may experience more difficulty with physical activity. One of the consequences of this trait may be subsequent difficulty with social interaction, since much of the early learning that is important for effective socialization occurs in the physical activities of childhood. Consequently, the ectomorph turns inward, becomes withdrawn, and is more likely to develop solitary interests such as those exemplified by the arts. And the endomorph may be seen as compensating for a tendency toward obesity by becoming gregarious and outgoing, by adopting a loving, good-willed, hedonistic approach to life.

There is another possible explanation based on the effects of social expectations. This argument maintains that the frail person is expected to be interested in intellectual matters; the person who looks like an athlete is expected to be aggressive and active; and the larger person is expected to be friendly and relaxed. According to this explanation, the pressures of social expectations influence personality development.

Eysenck's Biological Theory

But social expectations, explains Hans Eysenck (1947, 1967), are not as important as biology. One of Eysenck's basic premises is that we are born with tendencies to behave in certain ways. He initially thought that only two dimensions (types) were needed to describe human personality: extraversion and neuroticism (as opposed to introversion and emotional stability). Later, in collaboration with his wife, he added a third dimension: psychoticism (as opposed to self-control) (Eysenck & Eysenck, 1976).

Eysenck uses the terms *extraversion* and *introversion* in much the same way as they are used in the Five Factor model. *Neuroticism* refers to a personality dimension ranging from emotional instability to stability. And *psychoticism* denotes high aggression, antisocial tendencies, and high egocentrism—contrasted with high self-control and respect for authority, rules, and laws.

Analysis of numerous personality tests led Eysenck to the conclusion that these dimensions of personality are essentially independent. An individual can be high on one without being high on the other, or can be high or low on all three. And although the tendency to be neurotic or extroverted (or their opposites) is largely genetically based, Eysenck does not rule out the influence of the environment. What he says, essentially, is that individuals who score high on the neurotic factor have less stable (more labile) types of nervous systems and are more likely to acquire conditioned anxieties. This is principally because they react too strongly to situations that would evoke less intense emotional responses from individuals lower on a neuroticism scale (Figure 7.6).

Research Evidence

Much of Eysenck's experimental work has been directed toward establishing the validity of these personality dimensions and their biological bases. A basic assumption underlying the theory is that the nervous systems of extroverts and introverts differ, as do those of neurotics or psychotics and normal people. Accordingly, he predicted that extroverts should have lower levels of cortical excitation (low arousal levels) than introverts. Pavlov had already demonstrated that conditioning is closely related to level of cortical activity, with animals whose brains were most active conditioning more rapidly than others whose brains were typically at lower levels of arousal. If extroverts have more inhibited cortexes (lower arousal levels at resting states), they should condition more slowly than introverts. This prediction is supported by research (Eysenck, 1967).

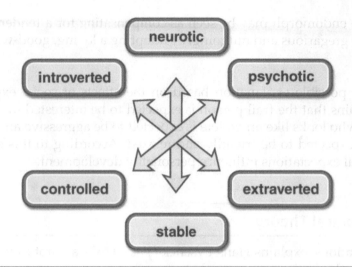

Figure 7.6

Eysenck's three dimensions of personality. Each dimension is independent of the others, so that one individual might be high on two different factors and low on the third; another might be high on one and low on the other two.

Other indirect tests of Eysenck's theorizing come from studies of personality disorders and in countless practical applications of the personality test he developed (Revised Eysenck Personality Questionnaire). Using this test, researchers have found strong relationships between high introversion and suicide attempts (Li & Lei, 2010). Others have reported a relationship between happiness and low neuroticism (Robbins, Francis, & Edwards, 2010). The test has been found to be generally useful for identifying individuals at risk of mental disorders in a wide variety of different settings and cultures (Kokkinos, Panayiotou, Charalambous, Antoniadou, & Davazoglou, 2010).

Eysenck's Organization of Personality

Eysenck's view of the structure of personality may be summarized as follows: Our nervous systems differ in important ways from those of people who have fundamentally different personality characteristics. Basically, we inherit greater or lesser tendencies toward introversion-extroversion, neuroticism-stability, or psychoticism-self-control. These tendencies are evident in the functioning of our nervous systems. In turn, the tendencies give rise to behavioral predispositions, labeled traits. The traits themselves are translated into patterns of responding that we label habits. Specific habits manifest themselves in our actual responses. Thus, personality is hierarchically structured.

As an example of the hierarchical nature of personality, consider Ebenezer Goring, who finds himself telling jokes to a group of strangers on a commuter train out of New York. There is a high probability that he would score near the top on an extroversion scale; hence his type is *high extrovert-low introvert*; the trait he is manifesting might be labeled *sociability*; the relevant habit is entertaining strangers; and the specific behavior is telling this story at this time, in this situation.

Had we known beforehand the extent of Ebenezer's extroversion, we might have predicted a behavior not unlike that observed. Theorists who have been more concerned with the identification and measurement of specific traits, however, would point out that, had we been aware of the extent of his trait of sociability, the same prediction could have been made. And if we had known of his habit of telling jokes to strangers, our prediction would have been even more accurate. Consider, however, how much simpler and more economical it is to be able to classify traits or types than to classify habits. In addition, habits change; traits and types are more enduring.

7.5 A Psychodynamic Approach: Freud

And even more enduring than traits and types, claimed Freud, are deep-seated psychological forces, sometimes instinctive, often unconscious, that interact with the environment to produce personality and guide behavior. Like Jung's, his is a *psychodynamic* approach to personality—so called because it emphasizes the interaction of unconscious emotional and mental processes and their influence on personality and behavior.

Freud's Basic Ideas

Among the most basic of Freudian notions is the belief that powerful instinctual tendencies account for human behavior and development (Freud, 2003; Lear, 2005; Roazen, 1975). Most important among these are the urge to survive and to procreate (labeled **eros** after the Greek word for love). Because survival is not ordinarily threatened by reality, it is of secondary importance. Far more important in Freud's theory is the urge to procreate, which meets with considerable social resistance. Sexual urges are so important in this theory that they warrant a separate label: **libido**.

A second important instinctual urge in Freud's system is the death wish (labeled **thanatos** after the Greek word for death). Freud thought that this instinct is sometimes manifested in high-risk behaviors (such as car-racing, skydiving, and related sports) and, more importantly, in aggressive behaviors. As a result, he gives sexuality and aggression a central position in his theory. These two forces are the main motivators of our behaviors, Freud explained, but their influence is largely unconscious: We are not ordinarily aware that many of our behaviors have sexual or aggressive significance.

Three Components of Personality

There are three broad, sequential stages of personality development, says Freud. These are manifested in the development of id, ego, and superego.

Id   The Freudian infant is all primitive instincts, a bundle of unbridled psychic energy seeking almost desperately to satisfy urges that are based on the drive to survive and to procreate. These urges, labeled **id**, are a lifetime source of energy; they are the basic, underlying motive for all we do.

The Freudian infant is all *id*, says Freud—desperate to satisfying immediate urges, with no notion of what is possible or realistic. Feed me now!! Or, of course, I'll cry.

Unlike older children and adults, the infant has no idea of what is possible or impossible, no sense of reality, no sense of right and wrong, no internal moral rules that govern conduct. As a result, says Freud, the infant is driven by an almost overwhelming urge to obtain immediate satisfaction of impulses. An infant who is hungry does not wait; right now is the time for the nipple and the sucking!

Ego But life is harsh, and almost from birth, there is an abrupt clash between these powerful libidinal urges and reality. Even hunger, the most powerful of the survival-linked drives, cannot always be satisfied immediately. The reality is that the infant's satisfaction has to be delayed or denied. Even defecation cannot always occur at will; mother says "no!" This constant conflict between id impulses and reality results in the development of the second aspect of personality, the **ego**.

This rational component of human personality grows out of a realization of what is possible and what is not. It develops as a result of a child's experiences that lead to the realization that delaying gratification is often a desirable thing, that long-term goals sometimes require the denial of short-term goals. Although the id wants immediate gratification, the ego channels these desires in the most profitable direction.

Superego The id and the ego work together. Both have the same goals: satisfying the needs and urges of the individual. But the third component of personality—the **superego**—has a different agenda.

The superego (or conscience) begins to develop in early childhood, says Freud, and results mainly from the child's identifying with parents. **Identification** involves attempting to become like others—adopting their values and beliefs as well as their behaviors. By identifying with their parents, children learn the religious and cultural rules that govern their parents' behaviors; these rules become part of the superego. Because many religious, social, and cultural rules oppose the urges of the id, the superego and the id are often in conflict. Freud believed that this conflict underlies many mental disorders and accounts for much deviant behavior (Figure 7.7).

Psychosexual Stages

Parallel to the development of the three aspects of personality is the child's progression through what Freud labels the *psychosexual* stages. A psychosexual stage is a developmental

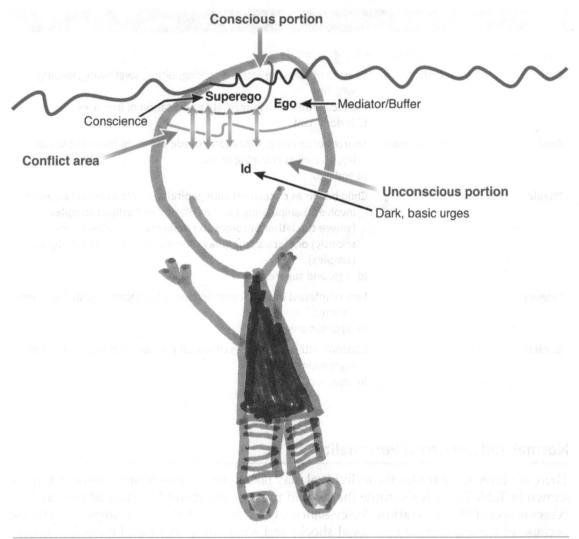

Figure 7.7

Freud's three components of personality. The part of which we are conscious is like the tip of an iceberg; most is unconscious. Instinctive urges (the id) are present from the beginning. The ego develops as the individual becomes aware of what is possible and what is not. The super-ego builds as a result of contact with social reality, and it is typically in conflict with the id.

stage characterized by identifiable sources of sexual gratification and by behaviors related to these sources of gratification. Through the course of development, these sources of gratification change; with each major change, a new developmental phase appears.

To make matters simple, the stages are labeled according to the area or activity that provides the greatest source of sexual gratification. In chronological order, they are oral, anal, phallic, latency, and genital. The ages corresponding to each of these stages and their major characteristics are summarized in Table 7.2.

Table 7.2 Freud's Stages of Psychosexual Development

Stage	Approximate Age	Characteristics
Oral	0–18 months	Sources of pleasure include sucking, biting, swallowing, playing with lips. Preoccupation with immediate gratification of impulses. Id is dominant.
Anal	18 months–3 years	Sources of sexual gratification include expelling feces and urinating, as well as retaining feces. Id and ego.
Phallic	3–6 years	Child becomes concerned with genitals. Source of sexual pleasure involves manipulating genitals. Period of **Oedipus complex** (where the father becomes the male child's rival—unconsciously) or **Electra complex** (a female version of the Oedipus complex). Id, ego, and superego.
Latency	6–11 years	Loss of interest in sexual gratification. Identification with like-sexed parent. Id, ego, superego.
Genital	11–	Concern with adult modes of sexual pleasure, barring fixations or regressions. Id, ego, superego.

Normal and Abnormal Personality

There are three main routes the individual may take in the course of development. One is shown in Table 7.2. It is the route that would presumably result in a normal personality. A second possibility is **fixation**, the cessation of development at a given stage, sometimes because of trauma (severe emotional shock) and sometimes because of excessive sexual gratification at that stage. The third possibility is **regression**, which involves reverting to a previous development stage, again sometimes because of trauma, or perhaps because of insufficient sexual gratification at a later stage.

The behavior of adults who are fixated at a certain stage, or who have regressed to that stage, is related to the forms of sexual gratification characteristic of the stage. Thus *oral characters* (fixated or regressed at the oral stage) are those who chew their nails, bite their lips, smoke, chew gum, and otherwise exercise their mouths. *Anal characters* are compulsive, orderly, stingy, and perhaps aggressive—these characteristics presumably being related to the pleasure (sexual gratification) associated with the retention and expulsion of feces during the anal stage. *Phallic characters* are concerned with the immediate satisfaction of their sexual urges without regard for the object of their satisfaction: they are sadists and rapists (according to Freudian theory).

Defense Mechanisms

In both normal and abnormal development, explains Freud, the id constantly strives for gratification. Meanwhile, the superego battles against the id, raising moral and cultural objections to unbridled gratification. And through all this, the ego struggles to find some way of finding the gratification that the id craves, but within the constraints imposed by the superego.

Anal characters, says Freud, are compulsive, orderly, and, like this man, stingy. Unfortunately, our personalities have proven more difficult to classify than Freud's typology would imply.

In trying to compensate for not being able to satisfy all of the id's urges, the ego often resorts to **defense mechanisms**. Basically, defense mechanisms are ways of channeling urges and of reinterpreting (and often distorting) reality. The ego is successful, explains Freud, when it eliminates or reduces the anxiety that accompanies the continual struggle between the id and the superego. In a sense, these mechanisms are the ego's attempt to establish peace between the id and the superego so that the personality can continue to operate in an apparently healthy manner. Thus, at one level, defense mechanisms are normal, healthy reactions to the world. What sometimes happens, however, is that the individual comes to rely on them too much. The result may be a dramatically distorted view of self, of others, and of reality, and may be evident in various personality disturbances.

Several dozen distinct defense mechanisms have been described by Freud and his followers. The most common of these are summarized and illustrated in Table 7.3.

Table 7.3 Some Freudian Defense Mechanisms

Mechanism	Example
Displacement: Undesirable emotions are directed toward a different object.	A man who is angry at his wife yells at his dog or drives his car unusually aggressively.
Reaction formation: Behavior is the opposite of the individual's actual feelings.	A woman loves an unobtainable man and behaves as though she dislikes him.
Intellectualization: Behavior motivated by anxiety-provoking emotions is stripped of its emotional meaning.	A football player who enjoys hurting opponents convinces himself he is moved by the desire to win and not by his desire to inflict pain.
Projection: Undesirable feelings or inclinations are attributed to others.	A student who is extremely jealous of another who has received a scholarship convinces himself it is the scholarship winner who is jealous of him.
Denial: Unpleasant, anxiety-provoking aspects of reality are distorted.	A heavy smoker, unable to give up the habit, concludes that there is no substantial evidence linking nicotine with human diseases.
Repression: Unpleasant experiences are buried deep in the subconscious mind and become inaccessible to waking memory.	A person who was sexually abused as a child remembers nothing of the experience.

Review of Freudian Theory

Freud's theory is one of the most comprehensive and influential of all psychological theories. It continues to have an enormous impact on psychotherapy. For example, the psychology database *PsycINFO* lists well over 1,000 articles, published in the first decade of this century, that refer to defense mechanisms. In the first 6 months of 2010, it listed more than 200 articles that relate to Freudian theory.

Freudian theory has had a tremendous influence on our attitudes toward children and child rearing. More than anyone else, Freud was responsible for making parents realize how important early experiences can be.

Freudian theory has also had an enormous impact on the development of other theories. However, many of Freud's students and followers have rejected important aspects of the theory. For many, Freud paints too dark and cynical a picture of human nature: In his view, primitive forces over which we have no control drive us relentlessly toward the satisfaction of instinctual urges and bring us into repeated conflict with reality. In addition, the theory is clearly weak from a scientific point of view, based as it is on a limited number of observations collected by a single individual (Freud himself) and not subjected to any rigorous analysis.

In spite of these criticisms, Freud's work still stands as an immensely rich basis for thinking about and understanding human personality.

7.6 Learning-Based Approaches

Biological approaches to understanding personality focus on the relationship between inherited predispositions and manifested behavior; psychodynamic approaches are concerned with interactions among competing or cooperating psychic (mental) impulses; learning-based approaches are more concerned with the role of the environment, of social interaction, and of cognitive processes. The unifying theme of learning-based approaches is that much of personality is acquired through experiences rather than genetically determined or influenced.

Behaviorism

Behaviorism provides one explanation for how personality traits might be learned. Some early behaviorists such as John Watson were absolutely convinced that the metaphor of the mind as a *blank slate* (*tabula rasa* in Latin) was correct. "Give me the child and my world to bring it up in," he wrote, "and I'll make it crawl or walk; I'll make it climb and use its hands in constructing buildings of stone or wood; I'll make it a thief, a gunman, or a dope fiend. The possibility of shaping in any direction is almost endless" (Watson, 1928, p. 35).

The clear assumption of behavioristic approaches to personality is that we are born with few genetically determined personality characteristics; what we become is a function of the experiences we have. In other words, personality characteristics are *learned*.

Skinner was another behaviorist who wholeheartedly accepted the *tabula rasa* doctrine. He believed that the consequences of our actions shape our behaviors and ultimately determine what we are most likely to do. Hence our environments and not our inherited natures shape our traits. It is the experiences we have that make us brave or fearful, outgoing or shy, altruistic or selfish.

Few personality theorists now believe that personality is entirely determined by environmental experiences. As Robins (2005) notes, about half of the variability in personality traits seems to be related to genetics. But the other half is clearly shaped by environmental influences. And especially important among these are early social experiences.

Bandura's Social Cognitive Theory

Bandura's social cognitive theory, the details of which are included in Chapters 4 and 6, is one of the best-known and most useful learning-based theories that looks at the effects of social experiences.

Observational Learning

Much of our learning results from *observational learning*, explains Bandura—that is, from observing and imitating models. Learning to drive a car, for example, is not a question of classical conditioning, of trial and error, or of reinforcement of emitted behaviors. Instead, we instruct the learner in certain fundamentals, we show her the positions and purposes of various controls, we demonstrate their operation, and we allow her to attempt the task with verbal and sometimes physical guidance. In effect, what has happened is that a number of models have been presented and imitated.

A model is not simply a person doing something that can then be imitated by a learner; it includes all the patterns for behavior that complex societies present to their members, including books, verbal directions, film and cartoon characters, and a variety of other real or symbolic objects. Their prevalence is highly evident, as is their effectiveness.

Western societies present a preponderance of achievement-oriented, assertive, outgoing models for men. Not surprisingly, many males in these societies are achievement-oriented, assertive, and outgoing. In contrast, the Zuni culture presents models of cooperation and self-effacement, and these are the primary characteristics of its members (Roscoe, 1991).

Manifested personality is highly influenced by context. We can't easily determine how naturally aggressive this soldier is by observing his behavior in war.

It seems clear that manifested personality characteristics are highly influenced by social context. This does not mean that theories based on the notion that there are inherited predispositions toward specific personality traits are incorrect. What it does indicate is that biological predispositions will not necessarily be dominant over social influences.

Reciprocal Determinism

A central belief of all learning-based approaches is that our behaviors are strongly influenced by their outcomes. But, explains Bandura, what is most important is our understanding of the relationship between our behaviors and their consequences, and our ability to anticipate consequences. And because we can anticipate consequences, we not only direct our behaviors toward the most desirable ends, but we deliberately arrange our environments to maximize positive outcomes. So, in the end, we affect the environment and it affects us in what Bandura labels *triadic reciprocal determinism.* Our actions and the environment are two aspects of the triad; our personalities (what we know and feel; our wishes and desires; our inclinations) constitute the third.

Personal Agency

Unlike Freud, who described human behavior as moved by instinctive and often unconscious forces and warring factions, Bandura insists that we are agents of our own actions. Being agents, he explains, requires intentionality (being able to do what we intend), forethought (foreseeing the consequences of our actions), and self-efficacy (having a notion of our likelihood of success).

Relevance of Bandura's Theory

The importance of Bandura's social learning theory of personality is not that it contributes to the identification of personality traits or to their measurement; nor is it particularly useful for understanding the structure of personality or the biological and dynamic forces at play. But it does facilitate an understanding of the manifestation of personality.

Most of the personality traits that have been identified are meaningful only in social interaction. Agreeableness, extroversion, sociability, dependency—these are all qualities of human interaction. They describe typical ways of relating to social realities. Furthermore, they are not characteristics that individuals manifest regardless of their immediate social context. For example, highly aggressive individuals might well display their aggressive tendencies in athletics and other physical activities where aggression is socially approved; few are likely to display aggression in a church choir or university classroom.

In summary, social approaches to personality highlight the tremendous influence of social customs, traditions, expectations, and situations on the manifestation of personality characteristics. They argue that acceptable and unacceptable social behaviors are learned.

Rotter's Cognitive Approach

In the course of learning socially acceptable behaviors, we learn what to expect when we choose this behavior rather than that one. Expectations, Julian Rotter (1982) explains, guide our behaviors.

Externality-Internality

In effect, expectations are beliefs about sources of reinforcement. Basically, claims Rotter, we can have one of two different attitudes toward our behaviors and their outcomes. We can be *externally oriented* or *internally oriented*—a notion later borrowed and elaborated by Weiner (2008) in his theory of motivation.

As we saw in Chapter 6, those who are internally oriented tend to take responsibility for the consequences of their actions. They see themselves as being in control; they attribute success or failure to internal factors (ability or effort). Those who are externally oriented believe that they have little control over what happens to them. They attribute success or failure to external factors (luck and task difficulty). Expectations of reward, and behaviors, will be affected accordingly (Figure 7.8).

Various studies have uncovered a large number of situations where expectations based on *locus of control* affect behavior. Not surprisingly, those who think they are in control of outcomes (the internally oriented) are less likely to be obese (Adolfsson, Andersson, Elofsson, Rossner, & Unden, 2005); they are more likely to participate in and profit from treatments to counter various delinquent behaviors, including alcoholism (Cavaiola & Strohmetz, 2010); they are more likely to be successful at work and integrate more readily into new social environments (Vonthron & Lagabrielle, 2002); they are less likely to behave aggressively toward an intimate partner (Gallagher & Parrott, 2010); they are less likely to have

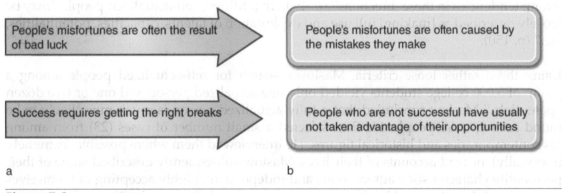

a   b

Figure 7.8

Items similar to those used by Rotter to assess a person's locus of control. An internally oriented person is more likely to select the second statement (**b**) of each pair.

eating disorders (Scoffier, Paquet, & d'Arripe-Longueville, 2010); and they tend to have generally more positive attitudes (Gianakos, 2002).

Personality theorists such as Bandura and Rotter look for regularities in individual decisions and beliefs, and they search for ways in which people can be identified on the basis of differences in their dominant modes of functioning. Their theories provide strong indications that important personality differences are evident in learned social interactions and that they reflect our expectations.

7.7 Humanistic Approaches

But surely, the humanists protest, there is more to human behavior and personality than inherited predispositions, basic instincts, warring psychic forces, and learned expectations and beliefs. We need to take into consideration what it means to be human. We need to emphasize the worth and dignity of every individual.

Abraham Maslow's Self-Actualized Person

Like most humanistically oriented psychologists, Maslow's principal concerns have been with the development of the healthy person. As we saw in Chapter 6, fundamental to his position is the notion that we are moved by a hierarchy of needs, the lowest of which relate to physiological survival and the highest to the fullest and most desirable blossoming of the person. The process of growth is one of *self-actualization—of becoming* in the most abstract sense of the term. This involves a recognition of what one is, of what one can and should be, and a striving for fulfillment.

Maslow (1970) admits that the concept of self-actualization is extremely difficult to define. It is characterized by the absence of "neurosis, psychopathic personality, psychosis, or strong tendencies in these directions" (p. 150). In addition, self-actualized people "may be loosely described as [making] full use and exploitation of talents, capacities, potentialities, etc." (p. 150).

Using these rather loose criteria, Maslow's search for self-actualized people among a group of 3,000 college students yielded only one actualized person and one or two dozen "potentials." Maslow concluded that a fully actualized person is much more likely to be found among older people. He then selected a small number of cases (23) from among his contemporaries and historical figures. He interviewed them where possible (extremely informally), or read accounts of their lives. Maslow subsequently described some of their personality characteristics: autonomous and independent; highly accepting of themselves and others; tolerant; free of inhibitions; spontaneous and able to enjoy themselves; free of guilt.

Science might shudder to consider that individuals were defined as being self-actualized by Maslow and were then interviewed by him to determine what self-actualized people were really like. The process is only slightly different from deciding that authoritarian people are psychopaths, selecting a group of psychopathic-authoritarian people, and interviewing them to determine whether authoritarian people are really psychopathic. The only surprises possible are those that might arise from errors in selection or in interviewer judgment.

Maslow's Hierarchy of Needs. Humanist scholar Abraham Maslow created a model of motivation that took into account biological, psychological, and social factors (biopsychosocial). Maslow recognized that humans have many needs to be satisfied. However, he did not believe that each of these needs was of equal importance. Thus, he created a pyramid or hierarchy of needs. The basic idea is that lower-level basic needs such as access to food and water *must* be met before a person will attempt to meet higher-level needs such as love or self-esteem.

Maslow believed that physiological needs must be met before any other needs. These are basic needs such as food and water. The second level included safety and security needs. These needs include seeking shelter, as well as a basic drive to seek pleasure and avoid pain. The third level is love and belonging, where Maslow believed people tried to form meaningful relationships with others and experience a sense of community. The fourth level is often referred to as esteem needs. Here, the person attempts to obtain competence in meaningful life activities, achieve, excel, and gain approval from others. The apex of the pyramid is self-actualization. As a humanist, Maslow believed that we were born with an innate drive to fulfill our potential. Self-actualization is a state of inner fulfillment and a realization of one's true potential.

Maslow's theory is not without its critics. One common criticism is that Maslow's ideas are only applicable to more Western cultures. Others point out examples of people who have not met lower-level needs but have still attempted to move up the hierarchy (Hanley & Abell, 2002; Neher, 1991). How does one explain how people who exist in a war zone on a day-to-day basis still form tight bonds and a sense of community? How do people who live in countries in a perpetual state of starvation still manage to form loving relationships with others?

Perhaps the most appropriate way to interpret Maslow's model in a contemporary context is to say that most often humans are driven to seek at least partial fulfillment of lower-level needs first. That doesn't mean, however, that under a certain set of circumstances that people won't attempt, and perhaps be successful at, achieving higher-level needs without first fulfilling lower-level needs.

Rogers's Phenomenology

Phenomenology is concerned with the world as it appears rather than as it actually might be. Humanistic positions are typically phenomenological in that their main concern is with the individual at the center of realities that are, in essence, self-created. The argument is that no two people see the world in exactly the same way, and that understanding people requires understanding their notions of the world.

Carl Rogers's theory of personality is well summarized by this abbreviated list of his theoretical beliefs (Rogers, 1951, Chap. 11):

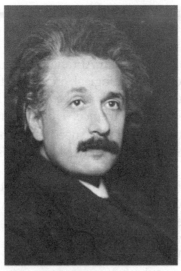
Albert Einstein

Eleanor Roosevelt

Ralph Waldo Emerson

Abraham Lincoln

Maslow defined the actualized personality as being free of defects such as neuroses and as having made full use of all capabilities and talents. He searched far and wide for examples of fully actualized individuals but found only a few, including these four. Although self-actualization may be evident among these historical giants, it's less easy to detect among plumbers and taxi drivers.

1. Every individual exists in a continually changing world of which that person alone is the center. The person's world is thus private, unknown and unknowable by anyone else. As the existential philosophers have pointed out, existence is lonely; it is necessarily always alone.
2. My perception of the world is real. So is yours. We have our separate realities. If we are to understand each other, you must try to understand my world, and I yours.

3. We have one basic tendency—*actualization*. In short, we have an inner, directing need to develop ourselves in Maslow's sense of the word.

4. The structure of self—notions of I or me—develops as a result of interaction with the environment and, particularly, interaction with others.

5. Values attached to notions of self are obtained either as a result of direct experience or indirectly. Thus, I can learn that I am good as a result of engaging in good behavior; or I can infer that I am good as a result of having people tell me I am.

6. Most of our ways of behaving are consistent with our notions of self. We tend to engage in behaviors that do not violate our internalized conceptions of what we are like—our values and ideals.

Humanistic approaches do not present theories so much as a renewed emphasis on human worth and dignity. They look more to glorify the importance of the individual, the nature of being, and the sanctity of personal experience than to analyze and dissect in the sometimes impersonal laboratories of science. Their impact on approaches to mental health and counseling has been considerable. Carl Rogers's *person-centered therapy* continues to be widely applied in therapeutic settings (Cain, 2010).

7.8 Measuring Personality Variables

Say I want to hire somebody and I want to make sure he or she is cooperative, agreeable, not highly neurotic, and not afraid of the dark (the work is carried out in an unlit basement); how can I uncover somebody's personality?

I have four choices, Funder (2007) explains: I can look at *life outcomes* (whether candidates are married, have graduated, what work they have done, whether they sleep in the dark); *self-reports* (I can ask candidates about themselves, maybe give them questionnaires, ask them if they leave their lights on at night); *observer ratings* (I can ask their friends, families, former teachers, or expert judges what they are like and whether they willingly eat in dark places); or *objective tests* (instruments designed specifically to measure personality). Objective personality tests are typically described as being *projective* or *nonprojective*.

Projective Measures

I might also find out whether my candidates are afraid of the dark by asking them to respond to ambiguous descriptions, pictures, or sounds and trying to find evidence of fear or confidence projected into their descriptions. **Projective measures** of this kind have been used extensively in personality assessment. The assumption underlying the use of projective tests is that unconscious fears, desires, and other personality traits may be projected in descriptions of stimuli apparently unrelated to the underlying personality characteristics. Since these traits are unconscious, the argument goes, they would not ordinarily be revealed in conventional measures of personality.

The Rorschach

Among the best known of the projective measures is the *Rorschach inkblot test*, so called because it presents the subject with 10 stimulus cards with printed figures that resemble elaborate inkblots (Figure 7.9). The scoring procedure is complicated, detailed, and not well validated, and interpretations of different experts vary a great deal. Furthermore, the relationships of scorer interpretations to the actual behavior of testees has been very difficult to establish, although there is evidence that it can be used to discriminate between psychotic and nonpsychotic populations (Wood et al., 2010). It continues to be one of the most widely used personality measures in clinical practice (Sendin, 2010).

The Thematic Apperception Test

Another well-known projective test is H. A. Murray's (1938, 1943) *thematic apperception test* (*TAT*). It consists of 30 black-and-white pictures showing people in various situations and asks subjects to tell a story suggested to them by the pictures. Clinicians often use the TAT as a way of gaining insight into the subject's fantasies. Although the test does not measure specific personality characteristics, it may be highly suggestive of preoccupations, fears, unconscious needs and desires, personal relationships, and related themes. It is widely used in clinical practice as well as in research (Teglasi, 2010). For example, it has been the

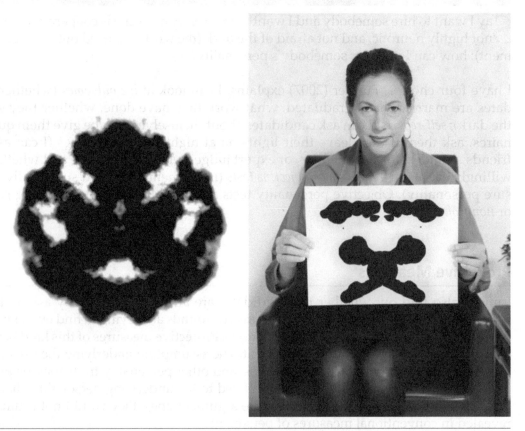

Figure 7.9

The Rorschach inkblot test. Subjects are shown 10 such stimuli and asked what the stimuli look like to them and why.

basis of many investigations of need achievement, with scorers looking for achievement-related themes in subjects' descriptions of the pictures. It has also been used to look at the concerns and interests of highly creative children (Garces-Bacsal, 2010).

Nonprojective Measures

There are hundreds of paper-and-pencil or computer-based personality tests, usually referred to as scales or *inventories*. Scales measure specific dimensions of personality (sociability, neuroticism, and so on); inventories are more inclusive. Typically, inventories consist of a number of different scales and yield a profile of personality characteristics.

The NEO-PI-R

The *Neuroticism Extraversion Openness Personality Inventory, Revised (NEO-PI-R)* (Costa & McCrae, 1992) is an inventory designed specifically to assess the Big Five personality factors (**c**onscientiousness, **a**greeableness, **n**euroticism, **o**penness, and **e**xtraversion). It is available in a longer 240-item format or in a shorter 60-item inventory. Items are presented on what is called a Likert scale—that is, on a scale where the responder selects an option ranging from *strongly disagree* to *strongly agree*.

Research indicates that this personality inventory has relatively high reliability (consistency) and validity in terms of its usefulness for predicting outcomes such as adjustment to career requirements. For example, scores on the NEO-PI-R correlate well with job success (Denis, Morin, & Guindon, 2010). It has been translated into many different languages and is reportedly useful across many cultures (Ortet et al., 2010; Plaisant, Courtois, Reveillere, Mendelsohn, & John, 2010).

The MMPI-2

One of the best-known, most rigorously developed, and most widely used personality inventories is the *Minnesota Multiphasic Personality Inventory-2 (MMPI-2)*. There are various forms of this test, which is normally computer scored. Ordinarily, it yields measures on a wide number of dimensions. Ten of the original scales are *clinical scales*. Closely related to these are newer *Restructured Clinical (RC) scales*. These clinical scales provide scores on dimensions such as depression, hypochondriasis, hysteria, paranoia, schizophrenia, and social introversion. Some scales are *validity scales*: They provide indications of the extent to which an individual's responses may be considered reliable and valid. In addition, there are various *supplementary* scales that measure things such as proneness to substance abuse and anxiety.

MMPI-2 items were first developed with groups of individuals who had been clearly diagnosed with disorders such as hypochondriasis, depression, or psychopathy. Scores obtained by these groups were then compared to scores obtained by a normal "control" group, and items were selected on the basis of how well they discriminated between groups. If, for example, hypochondriacs always responded in one way to 10 items, and controls always responded differently, these 10 items would then make up the hypochondriasis scale. It would then be possible to identify people who respond in the same way as hypochondriacs by looking at their scores on that scale.

In many ways, the MMPI-2 is a masterpiece of objective test construction. Evidence suggests that it is useful in making discriminations among groups of people and in preliminary diagnosis of abnormal behavior—which is the purpose for which it was designed. It appears to have impressive validity when used for that purpose. However, it is also often used for personnel assessment or as a screening tool with presumably normal individuals—purposes for which it has questionable validity. Indications are that it remains an extremely powerful tool for identifying emotional and mental disorders (Caldwell, 2006). Few instruments have been used more widely in psychological diagnosis, and few have stimulated more research.

Some Cautions

Although personality inventories and other assessment devices have proven useful in a number of situations, both practical and theoretical, it cannot yet be argued that any specific personality trait can be measured with unquestioned validity and reliability. Results obtained from different inventories for the same individual are sometimes different, and not all predictions made on the basis of diagnostic instruments have been entirely reliable. For these reasons, interpretation of test scores requires both restraint and wisdom. Tests such as these can be dangerous in the hands of those who are not fully aware of their weaknesses. Users must constantly bear in mind that the stability of personality characteristics is still a matter of debate. A test that reveals an individual to be tense does not establish that anxiety is a pervasive and predominant personality characteristic in that person. Personality tests measure mood, fatigue, feelings of happiness or dejection, and a variety of other affective states. And we know from our private experience that none of these is necessarily permanent.

Main Points

1. **Personality:** Personality is defined as an individual's stable characteristics, including habits, preferences, weaknesses, strengths, moral attributes, and customary ways of thinking, feeling, and behaving. The Barnum effect labels our tendency to believe vague generalities about ourselves.

2. **The Types and Traits Approach:** A personality trait is a specific quality that differentiates among different individuals (for example, good-hearted or selfish); types are clusters of related traits. The Big Five personality factors are five independent personality dimensions, each of which can range from very high to very low: conscientiousness, agreeableness, neuroticism, openness, and extraversion.

3. **Biological Approaches:** Biological approaches emphasize the genetic underpinnings of personality. Historical biological approaches include Sheldon's suggestion that body type (ecto-, endo-, and mesomorph) is strongly associated with different temperaments. Eysenck's biological approach holds that inherited differences in nervous system activity underlie the two main dimensions of personality, extraversion and introversion, as well as a third dimension, psychoticism. Recent approaches use genomics and neuropsychology to look for genetic and neurological structures and functioning underlying personality differences.

4. **A Psychodynamic Approach: Freud:** Psychodynamic approaches look at the interaction of basic inherited tendencies with physical and social reality to

explain personality. In Freud's system, sexual and survival urges (id) often drive us in directions incompatible with social reality and conscience (superego). This leads to conflict that our conception of reality (ego) mediates and tries to resolve. Objects of sexual gratification progress from oral through anal, phallic, latent, and genital as we develop. Fixation and regression are two unhealthy possibilities, as is overreliance on defense mechanisms.

5. **Learning-Based Approaches:** These approaches look at the role of the social and physical environment in determining personality. Behavioristic approaches describe how personality traits might be shaped and conditioned. Bandura's social cognitive theory describes personality development in terms of the effects of observation and the reciprocal determinism at play in person-behavior-environment interactions. It emphasizes the extent to which we are agents of our actions, anticipating and intending their outcomes, and estimating our likelihood of success in our endeavors (self-efficacy). Rotter's expectancy theory explains how locus of control (external and internal orientation) affects our personalities as reflected in our choice of behaviors.

6. **Humanistic Approaches:** Both Maslow and Rogers describe the development of human potential as the highest goal. They emphasize healthy human functioning and the uniqueness and worth of the individual.

7. **Measuring Personality Variables:** Personality variables may be evident in life outcomes and observer ratings. They can also be measured with projective tests such as the Rorschach and TAT (where the individual reveals unconscious traits in responding to ambiguous stimuli), or with nonprojective written tests like the NEO-PI-R (which measures the Big Five personality types) and the MMPI-2 (which is designed mainly to measure personality disorders).

Thoughts and Suggestions

Suggested readings from Hock, R. R. (1999). *Forty studies that changed psychology* (3rd ed.). Upper Saddle River, NJ: Prentice Hall. (ISBN #: 0-13-922725-3):

- Reading 25: Are You The Master of Your Fate?
- Reading 26: Masculine or Feminine… or Both?

Study Terms

archetypes	Electra complex
Barnum effect	endomorphs
Big Five factors	eros
conscientiousness	extraversion
defense mechanisms	factor analysis
ectomorphs	fixation
ego	genome

genomics

id

identification

introversion

libido

mesomorphs

neuroticism

Oedipus complex

openness

personality

phenomenology

projective approach

psychodynamic theory

regression

superego

thanatos

trait

type

8

Psychological Disorders, Problems, and Struggles

Focus Questions

By the end of the chapter, you should be able to answer the following questions:

- How are the terms *insanity* and *mental disorder* differentiated?
- What are the identifying characteristics of the principal models used to understand mental disorders?
- What are symptoms of the principal *anxiety disorders*?
- What are the identifying characteristics of *impulse-control disorders* in childhood?
- What are the most common mood disorders?
- How are bipolar disorder and schizophrenia different?
- What are the main sexual and gender identity disorders?
- What are the identifying characteristics of different personality disorders?

Psychology: The Human Puzzle by Guy R. LeFrancois © 2013 Bridgepoint Education. Reprinted by permission.

> *"'But I don't want to go among mad people,' Alice remarked.*
>
> *'Oh, you can't help that,' said the Cat. 'We're all mad here. I'm mad. You're mad.'*
>
> *'How do you know I'm mad?' said Alice.*
>
> *'You must be,' said the Cat, 'or you wouldn't have come here.'"*
>
> —Lewis Carroll,
> Alice's Adventures in Wonderland

. . . .

Inspirational Words

A double minded man is unstable in all his ways. James 1:8

For we know that the law is spiritual: but I am carnal, sold under sin. For that which I do I allow not: for what I would, that do I not; but what I hate, that do I. If then I do that which I would not,

I consent unto the law that it is good. Now then it is no more I that do it, but sin that dwelleth in me. For I know that in me (that is, in my flesh,) dwelleth no good thing: for to will is present with me; but how to perform that which is good I find not. For the good that I would I do not: but the evil which I would not, that I do. Now if I do that I would not, it is no more I that do it, but sin that dwelleth in me. I find then a law, that, when I would do good, evil is present with me. For I delight in the law of God after the inward man. But I see another law in my members, warring against the law of my mind, and bringing me into captivity to the law of sin which is in my members. O wretched man that I am! who shall deliver me from the body of this death? I thank God through Jesus Christ our Lord. So then with the mind I myself serve the law of God; but with the flesh the law of sin. Romans 7: 14–25

8.1 Historical and Current Views of Mental Disorders

Of special interest to students is **brain fag**, which, thankfully for North Americans, is found almost exclusively in West Africa. It is triggered by prolonged periods of intense study resulting in difficulty concentrating, insomnia, anxiety, and depression (Katona & Robertson, 2005).

Historical Views of the Causes of Mental Disorders

Not surprisingly, many ancient human cultures attributed madness to the work of gods or to possession by evil spirits. *Windigo* and *susto* are two examples. Witches were often thought to be responsible. As a result, in 1484, Pope Innocent VIII issued a papal bull (edict) exhorting all clergy to search constantly for witches. Two well-intentioned monks subsequently compiled a manual documenting the existence of witches and explaining how they might be hunted. They described the various signs that could be used to prove that a suspect was a witch. Most important among these were the red marks sometimes left by the devil's claw on the witch's skin, and the fact that witches do not sink when bound and tossed into water. In addition, this "divinely inspired" manual described the many methods of torture that might be used to convince the devil that a confession would be in order. Those found guilty of being witches were generally executed publicly. By around 1700, an estimated 40,000 to 100,000 witches had been executed in Europe and North America (Levack, 2006).

Current Definitions and Models

Insanity is a legal term, defined by law and determined by a court in consultation with mental health experts. Hence it is a legal issue that might determine whether a convicted person is *responsible* for a crime. Individuals found not guilty by reason of insanity are frequently provided with treatment rather than punishment.

The term *insanity* is seldom used in medicine and psychology, although it has been retained by the courts. The terms *abnormality, mental illness, personality disorders, psychological disorders, emotional disorders, mental disorders,* or other more specific descriptions are preferred.

How we look at and define mental disorders depends greatly on the **models** we use. In one sense, models are guides or ways of looking at things. Models tell us what to look for when we're trying to understand, explain, and define what we mean by mental disorders. Among the various models used for this purpose are the *statistical,* the *medical/biological,* the *behavioral,* the *cognitive,* and the *psychodynamic.*

The Statistical Model

One way of determining whether a behavior is abnormal is in relation to the prevalence of the behavior in the general population. According to this model, those whose behaviors or personality traits violate social norms and are therefore demonstrably different from the majority are abnormal in a statistical sense (Figure 8.1). Significant departure from normality with respect to emotional functioning, social behavior, perception, and so on may be directly related to mental health. Deviance is evident in behaviors and characteristics that have low frequency. To be afraid of red dirt is deviant because most people are not afraid of red dirt. But if you live where everybody knows red dirt is toxic, not being afraid of it might be abnormal.

The statistical model is useful in that it provides an objective method for identifying abnormal behavior. For example, **intellectual disabilities** (still often called *mental retardation*) are defined as a significant departure from average intellectual and adaptive

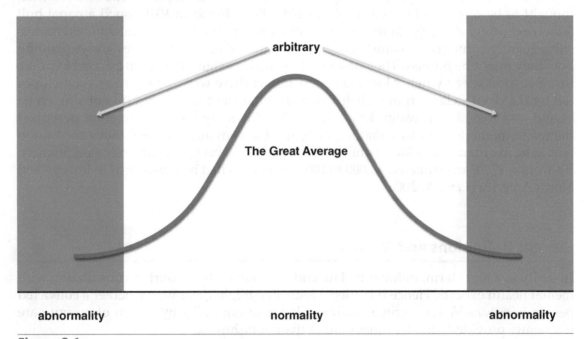

arbitrary

The Great Average

abnormality   **normality**   **abnormality**

Figure 8.1

The statistical model of abnormality. According to this model, being significantly different from other people is abnormal.

functioning. Similarly, disorders such as **autism, Asperger's syndrome**, and **specific learning disabilities** are all defined in terms of behaviors that are not age-appropriate in a statistical sense.

Medical/Biological Models

Medicine deals with physical (organic) malfunctions that are due to injury, infection, chemical imbalances, genetics, or other causes and that can often be treated surgically or chemically. The medical view of psychological malfunction is analogous. Accordingly, psychological abnormality is sometimes seen as a disease or illness caused by internal factors (infection, system malfunction, or genetic causes) and amenable to the same sorts of treatment that might be employed for organic malfunctions. The finding of high heritability of disorders such as bipolar disorder and schizophrenia suggests that, at least for these diseases, there may often be an underlying genetic cause (Walsh, McClellan, & McCarthy, 2008). For example, there is evidence that as much as one third of the risk of acquiring schizophrenia is due to identifiable genetic variations (Massachusetts General Hospital, 2009).

The most obvious advantage of the medical models is that they encourage the search for specific organic causes of various disorders and suggest means of dealing with them. They look not only at genes as a possible cause, but also at neurological functioning and especially at the role that various neurotransmitters play. The development of highly effective drug therapies for disorders such as depression is related directly to information that neuroscience provides about the role of neurotransmitters in areas of the brain involved in emotion.

Behavioral Models

The principal difference between medical models of abnormality and the behavioral models lies in their explanations of causes. Whereas medical models ascribe abnormality to internal causes such as disease, injury, or chemical imbalances, behavioral models claim simply that abnormal behavior is learned just as is any other behavior. Most behavioral models are premised on conditioning theories, or variations thereof, and concentrate principally on manifestations of abnormal behavior without paying much attention to supposed causes. Whereas medical models lead to treatments designed to eliminate the causes of malfunctioning, behavioral models concentrate instead on "unlearning" unacceptable behavior and learning (or relearning) more "normal" forms of behavior.

Cognitive Models

The cognitive interpretation of psychological disorders revolves around the notion that these disorders involve cognitive problems that are often expressed in distortions of reality (Beck, 2008). Patients view themselves as worthless, unhealthy, and unhappy, have unrealistic appraisals of their future, and react inappropriately. Distorted views of reality are, in fact, one of the principal characteristics of the more serious mental disorders.

Contemporary cognitive models also take into account the interaction of genetic and neurological events with cognitive problems. For example, neuropsychological research provides a great deal of evidence that an overactive amygdala may be associated with a higher risk of depression (Gaffrey et al., 2011). And genomics research (research on the contributions of genes) has discovered a variety of links between genome (genetic complement) and a variety of disorders, including *bipolar* disorder (for example, Choi et al., 2011).

Although the cognitive model considers these genetic and neurological causes, their emphasis is on the *cognitive* (intellectual) distortions that underlie maladaptive behavior. For example, in this view, overreaction to stress may be genetically based, but it is mediated by cognitive distortions. Accordingly, therapies are directed toward altering subjects' perceptions of the world and of themselves—in other words, toward changing cognitions.

Psychodynamic Models

The *psychodynamic* model describes how our basic libidinal urges (*id*) are continually being impeded by our immediate circumstances (*ego*) as well as by the fact that society does not permit unbridled expression of sexuality or aggression (*superego*). The result of this conflict is anxiety, which we try to reduce in various ways including through defense mechanisms.

If the anxiety is sufficiently severe, or if there is an overreliance on defense mechanisms, the result may be mental disorders of various kinds. Also, if the individual stays stuck in a developmental stage or regresses back to an earlier stage, development is said to be abnormal.

Which Model?

These various models show how complicated this part of the human puzzle is. It is not possible to say that one of the models is correct and the others not. Nor is it possible to state categorically that one is more useful than any other. Each leads to a different view of mental disorders; and each leads to different forms of intervention or treatment.

The statistical model is useful in providing a relatively objective means of identifying bizarre, unconventional behavior, although its value in increasing our understanding of abnormal behavior or our ability to deal with it is clearly limited.

Medical models are valuable in providing methods for identifying and describing malfunctions, and often in providing specific treatments for them, as is clear in the widespread use of medications that are often highly effective treatments for a variety of mental disorders.

The principal contribution of the behavioral and cognitive models has been the development of systematic learning-based therapies that have been highly effective in many situations.

Psychodynamic approaches, despite their historical influence, tend to be imprecise and speculative. The various models of mental disorders are summarized in Table 8.1.

Table 8.1 Models of Mental Disorders

Model	Abnormality	What the Therapist Looks For	Therapeutic Approach
Statistical	A rare behavior	Uncommon behavior in a statistical sense	None
Medical/Biological	System malfunction	Organic, systemic, or genetic basis	Drug therapy, surgery, electroconvulsive shock therapy
Behavioral	Learned behavior	Symptoms, not causes	Learning therapies (such as behavior modification)
Cognitive	Inappropriate cognitions (beliefs, thoughts, perceptions)	Irrational or inappropriate beliefs about self or others	Attempts to change cognitions, sometimes through learning therapies
Psychodynamic	Psychic conflicts, anxiety	History, relationships	Psychoanalysis

A Definition

Four Criterion Used to Determine What Is Abnormal Behavior or a Mental Disorder Is

1. Is the behavior considered strange or rare within the person's own culture?
2. Does the behavior cause personal distress?
3. Is the behavior maladaptive?
4. Is the person a danger to self/others?

The Most Common Disorders

A survey of mental disorders in the United States reveals that the most commonly diagnosed mental disorders are anxiety disorders, followed by impulse-control disorders, mood disorders, and substance-abuse disorders (Kessler et al., 2005; Figure 8.2). When nicotine dependence is included among substance-abuse disorders, it becomes the most frequently diagnosed disorder, at 35 percent (National Comorbidity Survey Replication (NCS-R) (2010).

Of these disorders, anxiety and impulse-control disorders appear earliest at a median age of 11; substance-use disorders, at age 20; and mood

Different models of mental disorders provide different explanations and different treatments. Most agree that mental disorders involve problems in coping with the world and, as in the case of the boy shown here, significant distress and unhappiness.

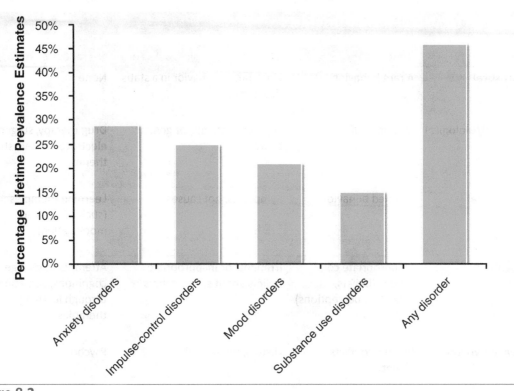

Figure 8.2

The four most commonly diagnosed mental disorders in America, based on a sample of 9,282 English-speaking participants over age 18. Based on data reported by Kessler et al., 2005.

disorders are the latest to appear, at a median age of 30 (Kessler et al., 2005; Figure 8.3). We look at these most common classes of disorders before looking at related therapies.

8.2 Anxiety Disorders

A wide variety of disorders, initially labeled **neuroses** by Freud, are characterized by anxiety. Anxiety is among the most devastating and the most baffling of human emotions. It can range from mild trepidation to acute terror and can occur in response to a wide variety of situations, or sometimes without any apparent provocation. In many cases it is both natural and normal; but sometimes it is maladaptive and irrational, and is the basis of a number of disorders.

Panic Attacks

A relatively common anxiety disorder involves recurring episodes of very intense fear and anxiety, often accompanied by physical symptoms such as shortness of breath and heart palpitations. These **panic attacks** occur for no apparent reason. Victims often feel they might be having a heart attack or that they're in danger of fainting or even dying. In some individuals, attacks occur only once or twice. Those who suffer from recurrent and persistent panic attacks are diagnosed as suffering from **panic disorder**. It is not uncommon

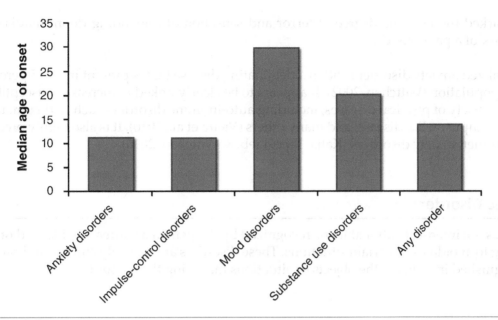

Figure 8.3

Median age of onset for the four most commonly diagnosed mental disorders in the United States. Based on Kessler et al., 2005.

for patients suffering from other mental disorders to also suffer from panic attacks (Ulas, Polat, Akdede, & Alptekin, 2010).

Panic attacks are relatively common, affecting an estimated 10 percent of the population (Panic Disorder, 2010). Among well-known people who have reportedly suffered panic attacks are Sigmund Freud, Kim Basinger, Tom Cruise, Donny Osmond, Princess Diana, Johnny Depp, and many others (*Famous People Affected by an Anxiety Disorder*, 2011).

Generalized Anxiety Disorder

Generalized anxiety disorder is marked by general rather than episodic subjective sensations of anxiety in the absence of specific situations or objects that might be associated with anxiety reactions. The hallmark of this disorder is worry. Individuals suffering from generalized anxiety, sometimes termed *free-floating anxiety*, recognize themselves as being predominantly tense, nervous, and fearful and cannot associate their anxiety with anything specific. Generalized anxiety is

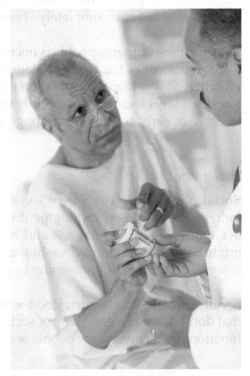

The most commonly diagnosed mental disorders are anxiety disorders. Drug therapy is currently the treatment of choice.

not marked by the same degree of terror and sensation of impending doom that is the hallmark of a panic attack.

Generalized anxiety disorder is often a debilitating disease that is present in 3 to 5 percent of the population (Wittchen, 2002). It appears to be clearly linked to increased susceptibility to a variety of physical diseases, including auto-immune disorders such as rheumatoid arthritis, lupus, celiac disease, and many others (Vieira et al., 2010). It is also highly predictive of other anxiety disorders (Katja, Pine, Lieb, & Wittchen, 2010).

Phobic Disorders

Phobias are intense, irrational fears, recognized by the person as unreasonable, and often leading to avoidance of certain situations. These disorders are typically chronic and can be distinguished in terms of the objects or situations that bring them about.

Agoraphobia

Literally, **agoraphobia** means fear of open or public places. It manifests itself as severe anxiety related to places or situations from which departure or return home may be difficult and, often, avoidance of such places. Subjects may experience anxiety at the thought of leaving home or when traveling alone, being apart from friends, or being in strange places. Agoraphobia is often associated with serious personal distress. In extreme cases, subjects may become completely "house-bound" for prolonged periods.

The prevalence of agoraphobia is uncertain, although some estimates suggest that between 3 and 5 percent of the U.S. population may have the disorder (Kessler, Ruscio, Shear, & Wittchen, 2008). Many people who experience panic attacks later develop agoraphobia. The disorder is seen more frequently in women than in men and most often begins in adolescence or early adulthood, although it may occur considerably later.

Social Phobias

Social phobia involves fear of social situations—that is, fear of situations in which the individual is exposed to judgment of others. Its most common manifestations include avoidance of social situations and of public behaviors such as speaking formally to a group. Fear of using public washrooms, eating in public, appearing at certain social gatherings, and writing or performing in public are other manifestations of social phobia.

Because social phobias often lead the individual to adopt a lifestyle and occupational role that don't demand a great deal of social contact, thus permitting adequate adjustment and functioning, relatively few people seek clinical help for this disorder.

Specific Phobias

Specific phobias include the variety of other specific fears that are not agoraphobic or social. Some of the most common phobias are listed in Figure 8.4.

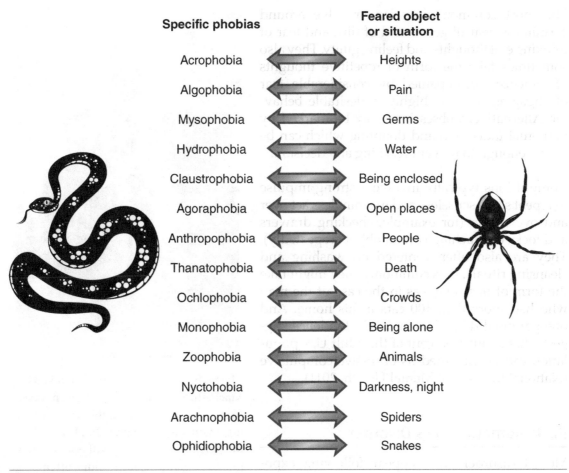

Specific phobias		Feared object or situation
Acrophobia	⟷	Heights
Algophobia	⟷	Pain
Mysophobia	⟷	Germs
Hydrophobia	⟷	Water
Claustrophobia	⟷	Being enclosed
Agoraphobia	⟷	Open places
Anthropophobia	⟷	People
Thanatophobia	⟷	Death
Ochlophobia	⟷	Crowds
Monophobia	⟷	Being alone
Zoophobia	⟷	Animals
Nyctohobia	⟷	Darkness, night
Arachnophobia	⟷	Spiders
Ophidiophobia	⟷	Snakes

Figure 8.4

Some common and uncommon specific phobias. Most phobias make some sort of evolutionary sense. Snake and spider phobias are relatively common; fear of the moon or of brussel sprouts, not so much.

The criterion for a phobia is simply that the fear be irrational, completely out of proportion to the potential danger of the feared object or situation, and not shared by a significant number of other people. It is interesting to note, however, that human phobias tend to be limited to a number of common situations, most of which imply some sort of danger. Thus, although very few people have furniture or vegetable phobias, a much larger number are afraid of open spaces, heights, closed spaces, insects, snakes, and darkness.

Obsessive-Compulsive Disorders

Obsessive-compulsive disorders are defined by the presence of recurring thoughts or impulses that appear irrational to the person having them (*obsessions*) and/or behaviors that are not perceived as the result of the individual's wishes but that give rise to intense urges to engage in them and result in anxiety when they are resisted (*compulsions*). Thus, a compulsion is a *behavior* and an obsession is a *thought*. Both obsessions and compulsions are perceived as incompatible with the individual's nature, but neither can easily be resisted.

The most common obsessions revolve around cleanliness, fear of germs and of dirt, and fear of thinking evil thoughts and feeling guilty. They also sometimes take the form of repetitive thoughts of violence, accompanied by considerable fear of engaging in some highly undesirable behavior. Alternatively, obsessions may be marked by perpetual indecision and doubting which can be severe enough to prevent reaching any decision.

Compulsions typically involve a strong impulse to repeat some senseless and meaningless act over and over again (for example, checking drawers and locks or touching certain objects repeatedly). They are also often centered on washing and cleansing rituals. Less commonly, they might take the form of hoarding—as in the case of the man who had more than 100 cats in his home. And one paranoid dog (Gerson, 2010). Evidence suggests that about 1 percent of the adult U.S. population can be classified as obsessive-compulsive (National Institute of Mental Health, 2011).

MACBETH. Act. 5. Sc. 1.

Macbeth, Act V, scene 1, in which Lady Macbeth, after murdering Duncan, says, "Yet, here's a spot." And this after imploring, "Out, damned spot! Out, I say. All the perfumes in Arabia will not sweeten this little hand." Compulsions often involve cleaning rituals. Sometimes they take the form of collecting and hoarding.

Posttraumatic Stress Disorder

Mental disorders that appear following exposure to an extremely traumatic event—such as war, rape, or a horrendous accident—sometimes take the form of **posttraumatic stress disorder (PTSD)**. Symptoms may include flashbacks or nightmares during which the individual reexperiences the event. PTSD is often marked by sleep disturbances, anger and aggression, numbing/avoidance, hypervigilance, and significant impairment in social functioning. Compared with other military personnel, alcohol-related disorders are twice as likely for veterans who meet the criteria for PTSD (Jakupcak et al., 2010).

Estimates of the prevalence of PTSD vary widely. One study that looked at the results of 19 different investigations that had attempted to determine the prevalence of PTSD among veterans returning from Iraq found estimates ranging from a low of 1.4 to an astounding 31 percent (Sundin, Fear, Iversen, Rona, & Wessely, 2010).

8.3 Impulse-Control Disorders Usually First Diagnosed in Children

Almost one in three people meet the criteria for diagnosis of an anxiety disorder at some point in their lives. Median age of onset is surprisingly young, at age 11—meaning that half of all those diagnosed with an anxiety disorder will be diagnosed *before* that age.

Impulse-control disorders, which are primarily childhood disorders, are almost as frequent as anxiety disorders—approximately one in four people. They manifest at about the same age (Figures 8.2 and 8.3). Impulse-control disorders are marked by failure to resist an impulse to engage in a behavior that is harmful either to the person or to others. They include a range of often aggressive behaviors.

Aggression-Based Impulse-Control Disorders

Intermittent explosive disorder is marked by the repeated failure to resist aggressive impulses. Children diagnosed with this disorder have typically engaged in a number of excessively violent acts against people or property, or both. As adults, they are at higher risk of aggression in their romantic relationships (Murray-Close, Ostrov, Nelson, Crick, & Coccaro, 2010).

Another aggression-based impulse-control disorder is **oppositional defiant disorder**. It is characterized by a pattern of hostile, disobedient, defiant behavior toward authority figures. The disorder is sometimes apparent in children given to violent temper tantrums and persistent negative moods. Bullying, stealing, and vandalism are other possible symptoms.

Conduct Disorder

Conduct disorder, which is often preceded by *oppositional defiant disorder*, is a disorder that begins in late childhood and often becomes more severe in adolescence. A related disorder among adults is *antisocial personality disorder*.

Conduct disorder is far more common among boys than girls, affecting between 6 and 16 percent of boys and between 2 and 9 percent of girls (Searight, Rottnek, & Abby, 2001). The disorder is marked by a persistent pattern of behaviors that violate the rights of others or that are socially inappropriate for the child's age. Children with a conduct disorder are often selfish, relate poorly with others, and typically don't display a normal sense of guilt. They are frequently the school bullies, given to threatening, fighting, abusing animals, and vandalism.

Attention Deficit Hyperactivity Disorder

The national survey summarized in Figure 8.2 includes **attention deficit hyperactivity disorder (ADHD)** as an impulse-control disorder. Some research indicates that as many as half of all children diagnosed with ADHD also meet the criteria for oppositional defiant disorder or conduct disorder (Connor, Steeber, & McBurnett, 2010). Adolescents who were diagnosed with ADHD as children are more likely to display oppositional defiant disorder as adults. They're also more likely to fail or drop out of school and to abuse drugs and alcohol (Bussing, Mason, Bell, Porter, & Garvan, 2010).

ADHD is often marked by excessive activity for the child's age, persistent inattention that is maladaptive, and high impulsivity. Not all children diagnosed with ADHD manifest all symptoms.

ADHD is the most frequently diagnosed childhood mental disorder. In fact, many think it is grossly overdiagnosed as a result of parents and teachers wanting explanations for child misbehaviors and pharmaceutical companies wanting to sell medication (Cohen, 2006). Another reason for overdiagnosis may be as simple as the fact that many young boys are still relatively immature when they start kindergarten. As a result, their behaviors are marked by higher levels of activity and lower impulse control than is characteristic of older children. Following a study of some 12,000 kindergarten children, Elder (2010) reports that the youngest children were 60 percent more likely to be diagnosed as ADHD. By his estimates, as many as 1 million children in the United States may be wrongly diagnosed.

That some of the causes of ADHD are genetic seems clear. One line of evidence is the fact that only about 10 to 20 percent of cases are female. In addition, genomic researchers have now identified genetic markers closely related to ADHD (Ribases et al., 2011).

The most common treatment for ADHD involves stimulant drugs such as dextroamphetamine (Dexedrine) and methylphenidate (Ritalin). Instead of acting as stimulants, these drugs have a **paradoxical effect** on children. That is, they appear to sedate rather than stimulate.

Other Impulse-Control Disorders

There are a number of other impulse-control disorders, most of which are relatively uncommon. They include:

- Kleptomania: an irresistible urge to steal things even when they're not needed or particularly valuable
- Pyromania: a compulsion to set fires for personal pleasure and gratification
- Pathological gambling: an overwhelming and persistent urge to gamble where gambling becomes a constant preoccupation and need that cannot easily be discontinued
- Trichotillomania: marked by the recurrent pulling out of one's hair, resulting in noticeable hair loss and considerable tension if the individual tries to resist

Impulse-control disorders include pyromania, kleptomania, trichotillomania, and, as shown here, pathological gambling.

8.4 Mood Disorders

The main feature of **mood disorders** is that they involve a significant disturbance in mood, typically expressed as depression or inappropriate euphoria (mania). Among serious mood disorders are *major depressive disorder*, *bipolar disorder*, and *dysthymic disorder*.

Major Depressive Disorder

Major depressive disorder is the most common of all mood disorders, affecting an estimated 6.7 percent of the adult U.S. population in a given year (National Institute of Mental Health, 2011). It is characterized by a conglomerate of symptoms, including apathy, listlessness, despair, loss of appetite, sleep disturbances, unwavering pessimism, and thoughts of suicide (although not all of these symptoms need be present in every case).

Criteria for major depressive disorder stipulate that there be at least one **major depressive episode**. A depressive episode is defined as a period of at least 2 weeks during which the individual suffers from a depressed mood and/or loss of interest and pleasure in normal life activities. The depressed mood typically characterizes most or all of every day.

There appears to be a clear relationship between suicide and depression. In fact, more than 90 percent of people who commit suicide suffer from depression or some other mental disorder (Suicide in the U.S., 2010).

Bipolar Disorder

Bipolar disorder, previously labeled *manic depression*, is approximately half as common as *major depressive disorder*, affecting an estimated 2.6 percent of the U.S. adult population (National Institute of Mental Health, 2011). It is marked by recurring episodes of mania or depression, although both are not always present. Occasionally the attacks are cyclical. That is, mania is followed by depression, which may then be followed by another period of mania, and so on. More frequently, subjects experience a single episode of mania and one of depression, not necessarily in that order, and may then be free of both for long periods—sometimes even decades. At other times, the condition is characterized principally by mania and is labeled bipolar disorder, Type I. Bipolar disorder Type II refers to a mood disorder where depression rather than mania dominates.

Mania contrasts sharply with periods of depression. It is characterized by periods of extreme and intense activity, irrepressible good humor, grandiose plans and involvements, and overwhelming displays of energy and joie-de-vivre.

Family and twin studies provide strong evidence of a genetic basis for bipolar disorder, where the **heritability coefficient** has been estimated at approximately 59 percent (Karege et al., 2010; Lichtenstein et al., 2009). In this context, *heritability coefficient* means the extent to which the *variability* in a characteristic is due to genetics.

Dysthymic Disorder

Whereas a major depressive episode lasts at least 2 weeks, **dysthymic disorder** (or *dysthymia*) describes a chronically depressed mood that lasts at least 2 years and that is characteristic of most days during that period. Except for its longer duration, dysthymia is marked by much the same symptoms as a major depressive episode, but of lesser severity. In effect, it is a lower-grade, chronic, long-term depression.

8.5 Substance-Related Disorders

L et's look at two kinds of **substance-related disorders**: On the one hand are the *substance use disorders*, defined in terms of the abuse or dependence on drugs such as alcohol or narcotics; on the other are *substance-induced disorders* such as might be brought about by medication.

Substance Use Disorders

Substance use disorders include substance *dependence* and substance *abuse*. Dependence is defined mainly in terms of **drug tolerance** and **withdrawal symptoms**. That is, with increasing use many drugs have diminishing effects. This, as we saw in Chapter 2, is due primarily to the fact that most abused drugs are effective precisely because they increase the release of dopamine, the neurotransmitter associated with pleasure and reinforcement, or block its reuptake. One consequence is that the brain produces *less* dopamine naturally as it becomes increasingly dependent on external sources. Hence the apparent increased tolerance and the need to use more of the drug.

Withdrawal, the physiological and psychological effects of stopping drug use, results from a sudden reduction in stimulation of those areas of the brain associated with pleasure and typ-

ically leads to feelings of **dysphoria**—the opposite of *euphoria*. Withdrawal symptoms vary depending on the drug, its manner of ingestion, and the individual. Withdrawal is often marked by depression and anxiety, as well as by a strong craving, this being the hallmark of addiction. Sudden and complete withdrawal from alcohol dependence can be fatal.

Substance *abuse* refers to a maladaptive, recurrent, and persistent pattern of drug use without the tolerance and withdrawal symptoms that mark drug *dependence* disorder.

Successful treatment of substance use disorders is difficult and often uncertain.

Prevalence and Types of Drug Use

As Figure 8.5 indicates, nearly half (46 percent) of all Americans aged 12 and up have tried one or more drugs, although only 8 percent describe themselves as current users (those who have used the drug in the last 30 days). Nicotine and alcohol continue to be the most widely used drugs.

Drugs are typically classified in terms of their effects rather than their composition. There are **narcotics** such as morphine and opium, addictive drugs that produce sensations of well-being; **sedatives**, such as tranquilizers and barbiturates; **stimulants**, such as the amphetamines and cocaine; and **hallucinogens**, such as LSD, ecstasy, and Rohypnol. Marijuana is also ordinarily classified as a hallucinogenic drug, although its effects are seldom as dramatic as those of LSD or mescaline (see Table 8.4).

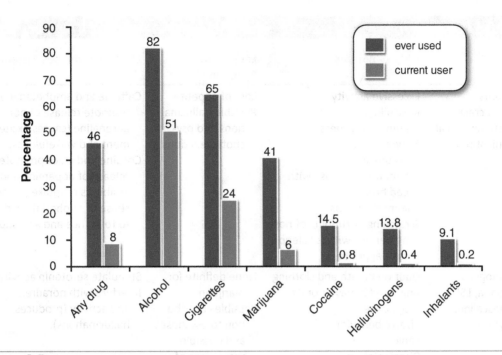

Figure 8.5

Drug use in the United States based on interviews of around 68,000 participants aged 12 or more. Current users are defined as those who used the drug at least once during the past 30 days. Based on U.S. Census Bureau (2010b). *The 2010 Statistical Abstract: The National Data Book: Table 202.* Washington, DC: U.S. Government Printing Office.

Table 8.4 Symptoms of Drug Use and Their Effects on the Nervous System

Drug	Early Symptoms	Long-Term Symptoms	Effects on Nervous System
Narcotics (opium, morphine, heroin, codeine, methadone)	Medicinal breath Traces of white powder around nostrils (heroin is sometimes inhaled) Red or raw nostrils Needle marks or scars on arms Long sleeves (or other clothing) at inappropriate times Physical evidence may include cough syrup bottles, syringes, cotton swabs, and spoon or cap for heating heroin	Loss of appetite Constipation	Bind to painkilling sites to dull sensation of pain; block reuptake of neurotransmitters such as dopamine. Mimic endorphins (cause sensations of pleasure and well-being). With chronic use, the brain may stop producing endorphins so user develops tolerance and craves more drugs to feel good.
Sedatives (barbiturates, tranquilizers, alcohol, Rohypnol, and GHB [the "date-rape" drug])	Symptoms of alcohol consumption with or without odor: Poor coordination and speech Drowsiness Loss of interest in activity	Withdrawal symptoms when discontinued Possible convulsions	Activate GABA receptors (which are inhibitory and cause drowsiness). GHB increases dopamine levels in the brain (associated with sense of well-being).

(Continued)

213

Table 8.4 (*Continued***)**

Drug	Early Symptoms	Long-Term Symptoms	Effects on Nervous System
Stimulants (cocaine, crack, amphetamines, caffeine, nicotine)	Excessive activity Irascibility Argumentativeness Nervousness Pupil dilation Dry mouth and nose with bad breath Chapped, dry lips Scratching or rubbing of nose Long periods without sleep Loss of appetite	Loss of appetite Possible hallucinations and psychotic reactions	Caffeine and amphetamines promote release of noradrenaline (causes excitement and wakefulness). Cocaine and crack promote release of dopamine and inhibit its reuptake (causes sense of euphoria); leads to tolerance and addiction.
Hallucinogens (marijuana, LSD, PCP, mescaline, psilocybin)	Odor on breath and clothing Animated behavior or its opposite Bizarre behavior Panic Disorientation	None definite for marijuana Possible contribution to psychoses and possible recurrence of experiences later	Stimulate serotonin activity. Interfere with noradrenaline activity (produces hallucinations).
Inhalants (glue, paint thinner, aerosol sprays, solvents, other combustibles)	Odor of glue, solvent, or related substance Redness and watering of eyes Appearance of alcoholic intoxication Physical evidence of plastic bags, rags, aerosol glue or solvent containers	Disorientation Brain damage	Long-term use can break down myelin, leading to muscle spasms, tremors, and other physical problems.

8.6 Psychotic-Sexual-Gender and Somatoform Disorders

The four groupings of mental disorders we've considered so far—anxiety, impulse-control, mood, and substance-related disorders—are the four most commonly diagnosed in the United States. But let's look at just a few more.

Psychotic Disorders

This grouping includes a variety of disorders characterized by *psychotic* symptoms such as **hallucinations** (perceptions of experiences without corresponding external stimuli together with a compelling feeling that these are real) and **delusions** (false beliefs or opinions). These disorders are severe, debilitating conditions.

Schizophrenia

Among the most severe and the most common of the psychotic disorders, **schizophrenia** is characterized by emotional, cognitive, and perceptual confusion and a consequent breakdown of effective contact with others and with reality. Schizophrenia includes a number of distinct disorders, each distinguishable by its specific symptoms.

Catatonic type schizophrenia is so named because of the rigid, immobile (*catatonic*) postures frequently adopted by patients, sometimes for hours. Typically, immobility is absolute during a catatonic stupor. Patients sometimes have no bowel or bladder control and have to be fed intravenously. The rigidity may be so complete that saliva runs unchecked down their chins because patients don't even swallow.

Catatonic patients often alternate between periods of immobility and periods of intense physical activity accompanied by a great deal of excitement. Changes from one to the other are sometimes violent and dramatic. Periods of intense activity may be accompanied by overtly aggressive and dangerous behavior. If precautions are not taken, catatonic patients sometimes hurt themselves as a result of prolonged immobilization and hampered blood circulation as well as muscular strain, or as a result of doing themselves violence and injury while in a frenzy of catatonic excitement.

Paranoid type schizophrenia is probably the most common of the schizophrenias. Its symptoms are not always as obvious as those of catatonia and may remain undetected for a time. Chief among these are delusions of grandeur and feelings of persecution, which go hand in hand. Paranoid type schizophrenics typically suffer from delusions that they are someone of extreme importance, believing, for example, that they are some historical figure such as Napoleon or Jesus Christ. At the same time, they are overwhelmed by the conviction that someone or something is after them—that they are being persecuted because they are important, because they know something that someone else wants, or simply because the historical figure they know themselves to be was persecuted. Such individuals may spend a lifetime running from these imaginary persecutors, gathering evidence that they are being persecuted, sometimes hearing voices belonging to their enemies and hallucinating their presence. In severe cases, subjects may seek retaliation or defense and can become extremely dangerous. Sirhan B. Sirhan, assassin of Robert F. Kennedy, was diagnosed by defense experts as a paranoid schizophrenic who believed himself to be the savior of his people.

This classification of schizophrenias is not nearly so clear in practice as it might appear in theory. Numerous apparently schizophrenic patients cannot easily be classified within a single division, since symptoms often overlap or change over time.

Causes

Various psychotic disorders appear to be related to malfunctions in the metabolic processes involved in the essential transformations that occur among synaptic neurotransmitters such as dopamine, serotonin, and epinephrine (Chapter 2). The effectiveness of many psychotherapeutic drugs appears to result from their effects on neurotransmitters, providing added evidence that these are implicated in some mental disorders. In addition, research with animals has shown that stressful environmental events may adversely affect essential metabolic processes in the brain.

Genomic research provides very strong evidence that schizophrenia in particular has a genetic component. Lichtenstein et al. (2009) summarized a large number of studies that looked at incidence of schizophrenia among twins, full and half siblings, and parents and estimated that the contribution of genetics to the disorder was approximately 64 percent. This finding is consistent with the belief that neurotransmitters are implicated in these mental disorders (Gray, Dean, Kronsbein, Robinson, & Scarr, 2010).

Sexual and Gender Identity Disorders

DSM-IV-TR recognizes three major subgroups of sexual disorders: those having to do with gender identity problems; those relating to unusual objects of sexual gratification and unusual modes of sexual expression (the paraphilias); and those relating to sexual dysfunction (psychosexual dysfunctions).

Gender Identity Disorders

These disorders are defined in terms of a conflict between anatomical sex (male or female, genetically) and gender identity. *Gender identity* refers to the subjective feelings individuals have concerning their sexuality. In the absence of gender identity problems, anatomical males and females feel that they are male or female. A **gender identity disorder** would be evident in a strong feeling of discomfort with one's anatomical sex and persistent feelings that one is or should be the other sex.

Gender identity disorders are sometimes confused with *transvestism*, which is a different disorder. Transvestism refers to the act of *cross-dressing* (dressing in clothing that is culturally recognized as appropriate for the other sex) for sexual gratification.

Gender identity disorders sometimes lead individuals to undergo sex-change procedures, which typically include both surgery and hormone treatment—as did Chastity Bono, daughter (now son, Chaz) of Sonny Bono and Cher (Chaz Bono Granted Name, Gender Change, 2010).

Paraphilias

Paraphilias are a variety of sexual deviations (*para*: deviation; *philia*: attraction or love). Among these are the fetishes, involving sexual attraction to nonliving objects such as women's undergarments, shoes, hats, and walnuts. Fetishism occurs primarily in males. Paraphilias eventually replace the person's desire for intimacy with another person.

Zoophilia denotes sexual attraction to animals and the exclusive or preferred use of animals for sexual arousal or release. It is apparently not as rare as once thought (Earls & Lalumiere, 2009).

Pedophilia describes a condition in which prepubertal children are employed as sexual partners or objects. Pedophilia is predominantly heterosexual rather than homosexual. It is the most commonly seen paraphilia in clinical practice (Fedoroff & Marshall, 2010). In particular, the use of children in pornographic books, films, and websites has increased dramatically.

Among the paraphilias are a number of other behaviors undertaken for sexual gratification. These include *exhibitionism* (flashing of private parts); *fetishism* (sexual arousal related to a physical object or situation); *frotteurism* (rubbing against a nonconsenting person); *masochism* and *sadism* (giving or receiving pain, respectively); *transvestic fetishism* (cross-dressing); and *voyeurism* (spying on people engaged in intimate behaviors).

There are no reliable statistics available on the prevalence of paraphilias, but they occur much more frequently in men than in women. One study found that 13.4 percent of adult male *psychiatric* inpatients admitted having one or more paraphilias—most commonly voyeurism and exhibitionism (Marsh et al., 2010).

Sexual Dysfunctions

The sexual dysfunctions include impediments to the enjoyment of normal sexual activity. Their principal psychological consequence is one of distress that may vary in severity depending on the individual concerned. Among sexual dysfunctions are inhibited sexual desire, inhibited sexual excitement (frigidity or impotence), inhibited female orgasm, inhibited male orgasm, premature ejaculation, dyspareunio (pain during coitus), and vaginismus (spasms of the vagina making coitus painful).

Somatoform Disorders

Somatoform disorders include a variety of conditions in which the patient has symptoms suggestive of some medical problem but no such problem can be found. People with somatoform disorder are often very anxious about their health. But the condition is not a result of consciously fabricating or exaggerating symptoms (called *malingering*) or what are called *factitious disorders* (where the patient deliberately produces or feigns symptoms). Those with somatoform disorders genuinely believe they are physically ill.

8.7 Personality Disorders

Personality disorders are evident in behaviors that are socially inappropriate, inflexible, and often antisocial. Most of these behaviors typically become apparent during childhood or adolescence and are manifested as relatively stable, although sometimes highly maladaptive, personality characteristics.

Unlike those with more serious mental disorders, persons suffering from personality disorders usually continue to function in society. Often, too, they experience little anxiety over their behaviors since they are ordinarily unaware of their maladaptive nature. Most are unlikely to seek help on their own. Many individuals diagnosed with other forms of mental disorder have a long-standing history of personality disorders.

- *Paranoid personality disorder* is marked by a profound, long-term, and unjustified conviction that other people are hostile, dangerous, and out to get them. It often leads to social isolation.

- *Schizoid personality disorder* is characterized by a disinterest in social relationships and a limited range of emotional reaction. It is sometimes evident in emotional coldness and a solitary lifestyle.
- *Histrionic personality disorder*, primarily a female disorder, is evident in excessive emotionality, attention seeking, and inappropriate flirtatiousness. People with histrionic personalities typically want to be the center of attention and are often egocentric and self-indulgent.
- *Narcissistic personality disorder*, primarily a male disorder, is evident in excessive self-love. Narcissus of the Greek legend loved himself above all else. Extreme arrogance, cavalier disregard for social convention and the rights of others, supreme confidence, and selfish exploitation of others are the principal characteristics of the narcissistic personality. Not surprisingly, such individuals appear only rarely in clinics.
- *Antisocial personality disorder* displays a pattern of pervasive disregard for, and violation of, the rights of others. Common characteristics might include lack of remorse for actions that hurt others, lack of empathy, cruelty to animals, poor and abusive relationships, and frequent problems with the law.
- *Borderline personality disorder* is evident in fluctuating and unpredictable moods that are often extreme. Those with borderline personality disorder tend to alternate between idealizing and devaluing, and they often have unstable and chaotic interpersonal relationships.
- *Schizotypal personality disorder* is marked by a need for social isolation, by what are often very different convictions and beliefs, and sometimes by odd or eccentric dress and behavior. Because the disorder is very similar to some forms of schizophrenia, its inclusion as a personality disorder is controversial.
- *Avoidant personality disorder* is characterized by an extreme and pervasive pattern of *social inhibition* evident in feelings of inadequacy and avoidance of social interaction.
- *Dependent personality disorder* describes a chronic and long-term condition in which the individual manifests excessive dependence on others for physical and emotional needs.
- *Obsessive-compulsive personality disorder (OCPD)* is different from obsessive-compulsive disorder (OCD) described earlier. Whereas OCD is an *anxiety disorder* marked by recurring obsessions (thoughts that won't go away) and compulsions (behaviors that must be carried out repeatedly), OCPD is a *personality disorder*. It is marked by a chronic and persistent maladaptive pattern of interacting with other people and with the environment. Among its manifestations are excessive preoccupation with orderliness, perfectionism, and details and a need to control all aspects of the environment.

There is a danger, when reading quick descriptions of disorders, to recognize clusters of symptoms among people we know and wonder whether they might have this or that disorder. For example, we all know people who are neat and orderly; but the fact is that probably none of them would come close to satisfying the criteria for obsessive-compulsive personality disorder. Nor are all people who are shy candidates for a diagnosis of *avoidant personality disorder*. Note that for all other personality disorders, diagnosis is made only on the basis of specific combinations of *persistent*, *prolonged*, and/or chronic beliefs and behaviors.

Main Points

1. **Historical and Current Views of Mental Disorders:** Many mental disorders are highly culture specific, typically reflecting unexpected and rare behaviors in that culture. Causes may be organic/medical or learned. They are marked by persistent patterns of thought or behavior that are distressful and/or lead to significant impairment in ability to cope.

2. **Anxiety Disorders:** Disorders characterized mainly by anxiety include *panic attacks* (sudden onset of terror); *generalized anxiety disorder* (pervasive free-floating anxiety); *phobic disorders* (a range of fears, including *social phobia* and *agoraphobia* as well as fear of specific objects or situations); *obsessive-compulsive disorder* (recurring irrational thoughts and impulses); and *posttraumatic stress disorder* (resulting from a traumatic event).

3. **Impulse-Control Disorders Usually First Diagnosed in Children:** Disorders in which the individual fails to resist an impulse to act in a harmful or inappropriate way include *aggression-based impulse-control disorders* (impulses are related to aggressive and violent acts toward people or property, sometimes evident in hostile, defiant, or criminal behaviors); *conduct disorders* (persistent and often aggressive violation of other people's rights and property); *ADHD* (marked by excessive activity for the child's age, inattention, and impulsivity); and other impulse-related disorders, such as *pyromania*, *kleptomania*, and *compulsive gambling*.

4. **Mood Disorders:** These disorders of affect include *major depressive disorder* (a common and serious disorder involving despair and unwavering pessimism); *bipolar disorder* (formerly manic-depression); and *dysthymic disorder* (a longer-term but less severe depression than major depressive disorder).

5. **Substance-Related Disorders:** These include *substance use disorders* (substance *dependence*, marked by tolerance and withdrawal symptoms, and substance *abuse*, where the criteria for dependence have not been met).

6. **Other Disorders:** *Psychotic disorders* (severe, debilitating disorders, including the various forms of *schizophrenia*); *sexual and gender identity disorders* (problems associated with discomfort with one's anatomical sex; the *paraphilias,* where objects of sexual interest are bizarre and socially unacceptable; and *sexual dysfunctions* such as impotence or frigidity); and *somatoform disorders* (marked by physical complaints that cannot be explained by injury or disease).

7. **Personality Disorders:** These are evident in persistent behaviors and thoughts that are socially inappropriate and maladaptive. They include the following personality disorders: *paranoid* (view of others as hostile, dangerous); *schizoid* (disinterest in social relationships); *histrionic* (excessive emotionality); *narcissistic* (self-love); *antisocial* (violation of rights of others); *borderline* (extreme, unpredictable, fluctuating moods); *schizotypal* (social isolation and odd or eccentric behavior); *avoidant* (social inhibition); *dependent* (excessive reliance on others for all needs); and *obsessive-compulsive* (maladaptive interactions centering on order, perfectionism, and control).

Thoughts and Suggestions

1. Labeling people and classifying people into groups has consequences. Giving someone a diagnosis can be considered giving someone a label. A psychological or psychiatric diagnosis, by definition, means someone has been classified as

having a mental disorder. What do you think are some of the advantages and disadvantages of taking such an approach to people? Do you believe there are any misuse and abuses of this approach to understanding and helping people? Please share your thoughts and perspective on this matter.

2. Some today believe that the United States in particular is too quick to diagnose, give medication, and recommend therapy. Many believe that today most psychological problems are a result of lifestyle choices, and that if people would create a healthier lifestyle a vast array of psychological problems would simply go away. What would you add to this discussion from your personal perspective?

3. What could be some possible reasons for the following statistic?

"Americans use 95% of all the psych. Meds in the world.
But make up only 5% of the world's population."

What do you this personally is the primary reason for this rather impressive statistic?

Suggested readings from Hock, R. R. (1999). *Forty studies that changed psychology* (3rd ed.). Upper Saddle River, NJ: Prentice Hall. (ISBN #: 0-13-922725-3):

- Reading 29: Who's Crazy Here, Anyway?
- Reading 30: Your're Getting Defensive Again.
- Reading 31: Learning to Be Depressed.

Study Terms

agoraphobia	hallucinogens
anorexia nervosa	heritability coefficient
Asperger's syndrome	impulse-control disorders
attention deficit hyperactivity disorder (ADHD)	insanity
autism	major depressive disorders
aversive conditioning	major depressive episode
behavior modification	mental disorder
bipolar disorder	mood disorders
conduct disorder	narcotics
delusions	obsessive-compulsive disorders
drug tolerance	oppositional defiant disorder
dysthymic disorder	panic attacks
free association	panic disorder
generalized anxiety disorder	paraphilias
hallucinations	personality disorders
	phobias

posttraumatic stress disorder (PTSD)   specific phobias

rational emotive behavior therapy (REBT)   stimulants

schizophrenia   substance-related disorders

sedatives   systematic desensitization

social phobia   transference

somatoform disorders   withdrawal symptoms

9

Therapy

Focus Questions

By the end of the chapter, you should be able to answer the following questions:

- What are the main types of mental health providers?
- What distinguishes them from one another?
- What are the main schools of thought in psychology?
- What are the treatments associated with each school of thought?
- Who are the primary founders of each perspective?
- What schools of thought work best for certain conditions.
- When is the use of medication considered to be the primary treatment?
- When is the use of medication considered supplemental or contra indicated?
- What are some of the key Biblical spiritual concepts or directions essential for mental health?
- How does the Bible address each of the concerns of the schools of thought?
- What role does spirituality and spiritual development play in mental health and growth?

Chapter Outline

. . . .

Inspirational Words

Heaviness in the heart of man maketh it stoop: but a good word maketh it glad. Proverbs 12:25.

To the chief Musician, A Psalm of David. *O LORD, thou hast searched me, and known me. Thou knowest my downsitting and mine uprising, thou understandest my thought afar off. Psalm 139:1,2*

Rejoice in the Lord alway: and again I say, Rejoice. Let your moderation be known unto all men. The Lord is at hand. Be careful for nothing; but in everything by prayer and supplication with thanksgiving let your requests be made known unto God. And the peace of God, which passeth all understanding, shall keep your hearts and minds through Christ Jesus. Finally, brethren, whatsoever things are true, whatsoever things are honest, whatsoever things are just, whatsoever things are pure, whatsoever things are lovely, whatsoever things are of good report; if there be any virtue, and if there be any praise, think on these things. Those things, which ye have both learned, and received, and heard, and seen in me, do: and the God of peace shall be with you. Philippians 4:4–9

Blessed be *God, even the Father of our Lord Jesus Christ, the Father of mercies, and the God of all comfort; Who comforteth us in all our tribulation, that we may be able to comfort them which are in any trouble, by the comfort wherewith we ourselves are comforted of God. 2 Corinthians 1:3,4*

Hear counsel, and receive instruction, that thou mayest be wise in thy latter end. There are many devices in a man's heart; nevertheless the counsel of the LORD, that shall stand. Proverbs 19:20,21

*A Psalm **of David**. Judge me, O LORD; for I have walked in mine integrity: I have trusted also in the LORD; therefore I shall not slide. Examine me, O LORD, and prove me; try my reins and my heart. Psalm 26:1,2*

Now we exhort you, brethren, warn them that are unruly, comfort the feebleminded, support the weak, be patient toward all men. *See that none render evil for evil unto any* man; *but ever follow that which is good, both among yourselves, and to all* men. *Rejoice evermore. Pray without ceasing. In everything give thanks: for this is the will of God in Christ Jesus concerning you. Quench not the Spirit. 1 Thessalonians 5:14–19*

Preview

This chapter covers five modalities or types of psychotherapy commonly used to treat or manage psychological disorders. We begin with a brief overview and discussion of a few types of mental health professionals: clinical psychologists, psychiatrists, and psychoanalysts. Following the description of the psychotherapy professionals is an overview of the historical paradigms used to explain and treat psychological disorders. Next, we discuss the psychoanalytic, behavioral, cognitive, humanistic, and medical approaches for treating psychological disorders. We end by broadly reviewing the effectiveness of psychotherapy based on research studies. By the end of the chapter you will have a better understanding of methods mental health professionals use to treat the psychological disorders that you learned about in Chapter 8, and that you understand the benefits of psychotherapy.

9.1 Therapy

People go to psychotherapy for a variety of reasons. Psychotherapy is intended to be a safe place where individuals work through a variety of issues such as family problems, relationship problems, loss of a loved one, problems with a co-worker, or the treatment of a psychological disorder such as major depressive disorder or schizophrenia, to name a few. The therapeutic experience can vary significantly from client to client and from therapist to therapist. The variability can be attributed to a number of factors such as personality differences between the client and the therapist, race differences, gender differences, educational differences, age differences, the client's reason for seeking treatment, the therapist's professional degree, which dictates the way that the therapist approaches the client's concern, or the therapist's theoretical framework. In addition, given the diversity present in our society, it is imperative that therapists be culturally competent, which means that they understand the culture of persons different from themselves and have a genuine respect and appreciation for the diversity that their clients represent. Let's examine a few different types of therapists.

Clinical psychologists hold a PhD (doctor of philosophy) or PsyD (doctor of psychology). The term clinical psychologist is being broadly applied to psychologists who integrate theory, science, and practice to address psychological dysfunction and distress among individuals (Helms & Rogers, 2015). Clinical psychologists largely consist of people with doctoral degrees in either clinical psychology or counseling psychology. Clinical and counseling psychologists make up nearly half of all doctoral degrees awarded in psychology (National Science Foundation, 2013). In addition to learning how to diagnose and treat psychological disorders, clinical psychologists are trained to conduct research as well. That is, they have to do some original research on a topic in psychology and publish their results in a doctoral dissertation. For example, they might compare how effective different therapies are in the treatment of depression, or how accurately a psychological test distinguishes depressed clients from anxious clients. Before being able to practice psychotherapy, they complete an internship in a mental health facility, pass a national exam that tests their knowledge of practice and research issues, pass a state licensing exam, and work under the guidance of a supervisor for a number of hours. Currently, clinical psychologists do not have the legal right to prescribe drugs to their clients in most states (New Mexico and Louisiana being the exceptions), so they would use a "talk therapy" approach such as behavioral, cognitive, humanistic, or psychoanalytic therapy with their clients (American Psychological Association, 2016).

Psychiatrists first receive a medical degree (MD) and then specialize in psychiatry. After receiving their MD, they complete a multi-year residency in a psychiatric facility such as a clinic or hospital. Other psychiatrists train them in the diagnosis of psychological disorders and the use of drug therapy to treat these disorders. Although they may use group and individual therapies similar to those of a clinical psychologist, the principal form of treatment by psychiatrists is the prescription of drugs. Psychiatrists treat the full range of psychological disorders from the mildest to the most severe, but because drug therapy is such an integral part of the treatment for severe disorders like schizophrenia and bi polar disorder, they tend to treat a disproportionate share of clients with more severe problems.

Psychoanalysts receive special training in Freudian analytic techniques, such as the interpretation of dreams and the analysis of free associations. Psychoanalysts focus largely on the role of unconscious drives and their impact on thoughts, feelings, and behaviors. As such, the focus of their treatment is on resolving unconscious conflict (Whitbourne & Halgin, 2014).

Other mental health professionals include psychiatric nurses and psychiatric social workers who often monitor patient adherence to a therapeutic regimen on an outpatient basis. Counselor concentrations include pastoral counselors, drug and alcohol counselors, or

People see a therapist for many different reasons.

mental health counselors, who work in a variety of settings such as private practices, hospitals, prisons, and college counseling centers. Licensed clinical social workers also provide therapy in a variety of settings. Marriage and family therapists provide therapy, but focus on working with couples and groups. Becoming a mental health professional requires at least a master's degree, the completion of licensing exams, and supervision by a licensed mental health professional for a specified amount of time.

9.2 Paradigms of Psychological Disorders and Their Treatments

The general approach people use to explain and understand something, whether it is the cause of mental illness or the creation of the world, is called their paradigm choice. A number of paradigms have been applied to the explanation of psychological disorders (Box 9.1). The importance of choosing a paradigm when explaining psychological disorders is that the choice implies a method of treatment. Here we look at some of the paradigms utilized throughout history.

BOX 9.1   Paradigms and Associated Models for Treating Psychological Problems

Paradigm	Model	Treatments
Somatogenic	Medicine	Drugs, surgery, ECT
Psychogenic	Psychology	Psychoanalysis
Psychogenic	Psychology	Behavioral therapy
Psychogenic	Psychology	Cognitive therapy
Psychogenic	Psychology	Humanistic therapy

Somatogenesis

Another early belief that is still quite prevalent today is the belief that mental illness has a physical basis. The idea that something is wrong with the body and that the body needs to be treated to cure the psyche is called **somatogenesis** or the **somatogenic view**. Hippocrates (460–377 BC) is often credited as one of the originators of somatogenesis. He rejected the idea that mental illness was due to demonic possession or a curse or spell from the gods. Instead, he believed that there were physical causes for mental disorders. Hippocrates classified mental disorders into three basic diagnostic categories: mania, melancholia, and phrenitis (or brain fever). He also had a theory about the causes of the disorders based on the relative amount of the body fluids: blood (red), black bile, yellow bile, and phlegm. Specifically, he believed that too much black bile was associated with depression and moodiness, whereas too much yellow bile was indicative of mania (see Figure 9.1). He treated the physical symptoms rather than the psychological conditions. For example, depression or melancholia (as it was referred to then) was to be treated with quiet, restful relaxation, the avoidance of sex and alcohol, and the careful selection of food and drink.

Factors contributing to the development of the somatogenic point of view are as follows:

1. During the Middle Ages, autopsy examination of the body was not permitted (Davison & Neale, 1998). After autopsy examination was allowed, this led to an increase in knowledge about brain structure and function. By the 1800s an understanding of changes in the brain was associated with senile and presenile dementia (Davison & Neale, 1998).

2. Emil Kraeplin published a book in 1883 on the classification of mental disorders based on the idea that each disorder had a specific group of symptoms that distinguished it from other disorders. The symptoms of each disorder appeared together frequently enough to suggest to him a common physical origin. A group of symptoms that appear together and follow a similar course is called a syndrome.

3. A physical cause for general paresis was discovered. People suffering from general paresis often show symptoms of paranoia and delusions of grandeur. Around 1900 the cause of syphilis was found to be a spiral-shaped bacteria, called a spirochete, that destroyed certain areas of the brain. This was clear evidence that psychological symptoms could be tied to the destruction of brain tissue.

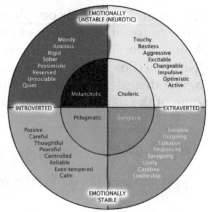

Figure 9.1

Hippocrates' bodily fluids. Eysenck, H.J and Eysenck, M.W. Personality and Individual Differences. Plenum Publishing, 1958.

Psychogenic Perspective

Although it had been known that events like disappointment, extreme fear, or a love gone wrong could induce psychological disturbances, the modern psychological approach for finding the cause and cure of psychological problems traces its roots back to hypnotism. An ailment known as **hysteria** in the 1800s, now referred to as conversion disorder, is characterized by the loss of some body function. Many different body parts can be involved; for instance, a person might display paralysis in a limb (like an arm or leg), lose sensitivity to touch on a body part, or have a deficit in his or her ability to hear or see.

When Franz Anton Mesmer (1734–1815) treated this disorder, hysteria was thought to have a physical basis. Mesmer was having some success treating the symptoms of hysteria by "mesmerizing" his patients, a process later called hypnotism. He believed his treatment had physical rather than psychological effects on the patients.

Jean Charcot (1825–1893), a leading neurologist of his time, became convinced that hysteria was a psychological condition, not a physical one. He found that he could not distinguish people who had been given a hypnotic suggestion to display symptoms of hysteria from real patients who actually suffered from the disorder.

Box 9.2   Basic Assumptions of Psychogenic Models

Model	Assumptions
Psychoanalytic	Psychological problems stem from unconscious conflicts lingering from childhood.
Cognitive	Psychological problems stem from distortions in thinking and perceptions that are self-defeating.
Behavioral	Psychological problems are learned responses. Learning desired behavior eliminates the problem.
Humanistic	Psychological problems occur when people either fail to make or avoid making choices that would be self-actualizing.

Josef Breuer (1842–1925) developed a **cathartic treatment** for hysteria, in which he would get a hypnotized patient to talk about upsetting events associated with the symptoms. He believed that when patients relived an emotional event under hypnosis they would experience a catharsis, a release of emotion that would relieve their symptoms upon awakening.

Freud worked with Breuer and adapted his method to provide more long-lasting relief of symptoms by having patients talk about their lives in a nonhypnotized state (that is, normal consciousness). This is called **free association**. Eventually, with the help of the psychoanalyst's interpretation, the free-association process would help the patient gain insight into the cause of his or her symptoms, freeing up his or her psychic energy to be used in more productive ways rather than maintaining the paralysis.

From these early beginnings the psychogenic approach, in all its many forms (behavioral, cognitive, humanistic, and psychoanalytic), along with the somatic or medical approaches, have become the predominant methods for treating psychological problems (Box 9.2).

In the late 1700s and early 1800s, asylums in the United States began to be built for the purpose of confining the mentally disturbed. Philippe Pinel in Europe and Dorothea Dix in America are recognized for their crusade for the humane treatment of people confined in mental asylums.

Today we largely ascribe to the psychogenic perspective and tend to treat psychological disorders with psychotherapy, medication, and/or physical treatments (in limited cases). We next explore several different modalities of psychotherapy.

9.3 Psychoanalytic Therapy

Psychoanalytic therapists focus on helping clients gain insight into unconscious conflict, which they consider the source of psychological problems. A client may come to a psychoanalyst complaining of low self-esteem or with problems keeping a job, but to a psychoanalyst, these are symptoms of an unconscious problem operating beneath the client's awareness (Consoli, Beutler, & Bongar, 2017). The therapist's job is to help the client gain insight into the unconscious problem—the real problem. Once the client can identify and understand his or her hidden fears, motivations, or conflicts, the energy that was tied up in repressing the problem is freed to be used more constructively in fixing the problem. This helps the person operate at a higher level of development or maturity, and thus the presenting problem (low self-esteem or keeping a job) tends to diminish. To help the client discover hidden (unconscious) fears, motives, and conflicts, psychoanalytic therapists use two basic avenues to the unconscious: free association and dream analysis.

Free Association

In **free association** the client lies on a couch, and the therapist sits behind the client to prevent any distraction. The client is instructed to talk about whatever comes to mind, without censoring anything, no matter how unimportant or shameful it might seem. In this relaxed, free-flowing atmosphere, unconscious material has a greater chance of surfacing.

The psychoanalyst is particularly interested in areas where the client shows resistance. **Resistance** is an attempt by a client not to talk about something that is threatening or upsetting and buried deep in the unconscious. Resistance, however, is usually not deliberate; the client does not even realize he or she is doing it. Changing the subject, experiencing memory lapses, dismissing something as unimportant, or simply not talking are all ways of unconsciously avoiding a particular

subject. These areas of resistance are important to the therapist because eventually the psychoanalyst may use them to identify the unconscious conflicts that the client is guarding.

Transference is different from resistance. It is also quite common and can be very useful in uncovering repressed unconscious material. **Transference** occurs when a client starts behaving as if the therapist represents an important emotional figure in the client's life. For example, a client might say to the therapist, "You know, Doctor, I wish you would have been my father; you really listen to me and think about what I have to say, not like my old man. He never took anything I had to say seriously, and when he did, he would just dismiss it with a comment like 'that's stupid.' No wonder I'm so screwed up." Freud interpreted these reactions as unconscious childhood feelings that were being transferred onto the therapist. The client's emotional reaction toward the therapist can be either positive or negative. Freud believed he was symbolically representing someone very important in the childhood of the client, like a parent or other relative, and the way the client reacted toward Freud was indicative of the emotions associated with that person in the client's childhood. Freud believed that many of the problems experienced by adults stemmed from their childhood and provided an important means of gaining insight into the origin of a person's problems.

Dream Analysis

In psychoanalytic therapy, clients are encouraged to describe their dreams to the therapist. Freud believed that during sleep, our ego defenses are weaker and unconscious material is more likely to leak into the content of the dream. The unconscious content is not laid bare for all to see—our ego defenses are still strong enough to try to mask the unconscious material so that it is not completely exposed. Freud called the description of the dream (that is, the part we remember) the **manifest content** of the dream. It is only a superficial cover-up of the real content of the dream. The unconscious message of the dream is still there, just in a disguised or symbolic form. Freud called this the **latent content** of the dream. He believed a trained psychoanalyst could see through the manifest content to the latent content and thereby uncover the true hidden meaning in the dream.

For example, a client comes to a psychoanalyst and complains that he is having problems keeping a job. He states that this is because his supervisors mistreat him. After listening to the client complain about so many different supervisors in so many different ways, the therapist may form the belief that the client has not resolved the Oedipal competition he felt toward his father as a child. His bosses symbolize the father he is still competing with. The client doesn't want to blame himself for his problems, so he projects the antagonism onto the bosses and away from himself. This brief description could be the psychoanalyst's interpretation of the client's problem and provides a context in which to interpret the following dream: This client reported a dream where he was walking a big dog that required considerable strength to rein in and control. The psychoanalyst might interpret the big dog as in reality the client's father and suggest that the dream illustrates the client's wish to control his father just as he felt controlled as a child. He now wishes to turn the tables on the father and be in the superior position. At the same time, however, the client does not want to lose the love and protection he gets from the father, and that's why he is holding on so tightly to the dog. The struggle the client experiences with the dog is symbolic of the client's own childhood struggle of wanting to be free of the father's control and yet be loved at the same time. This interpretation is the latent content of the dream and is consistent with the psychoanalyst's conceptualization of the client's problem, but there could be other interpretations. Can you think of any?

Think of a recent dream that you had. What would Freud say is the manifest and latent meaning?

Psychoanalytic Interpretation

The analyst's interpretation of the client's free associations and dreams is ultimately what allows the client to gain insight into his or her unconscious problems. This insight presumably frees the client's psychic energy so that it can be used to further the client's growth and development.

Getting the client to adopt the analyst's interpretation is not something to be rushed. Psychoanalytic therapy can take months, even years, and isn't always covered by insurance. To convince the client, the analyst needs to point out similarities in the client's behavior across a variety of situations in which the client originally failed to recognize the similarities. For example, the therapist might point out that the client's love of pets, children, and subordinates stems from a need to be in control and that his or her disdain for peers or superiors comes from the threat to that control. The therapist will also point out areas of resistance displayed by the client in an attempt to get him or her to realize the discomfort these topics pose. Ultimately, it is the therapist's job to present the evidence to the client subtly enough that the client eventually has a leap of insight into his or her own unconscious processes. If the analyst simply described his or her interpretation to the client, it is likely to be defensively rejected.

9.4 Behavior Therapy

In **behavior therapy**, contrary to the psychoanalytic approach, the presenting problem or current problem is what is focused on. For example, when a client comes to a behavior therapist because she is afraid of flying and turns down promotions because of the flight requirements, the behavior therapist is going to direct his or her attention toward reducing the fear of flying. The behavior therapist doesn't assume, as the psychoanalyst does, that the fear of flying is just a symptom of an underlying problem hidden in the unconscious. Instead, the behavior therapist believes that fear of flying is the problem and that it should be addressed directly. There is no underlying cause; the person has simply learned to be afraid of flying and that is as far as it goes. The behavior therapist will attempt to teach a new response so that the person will no longer fear flying.

Psychoanalysts argue that treating the problem directly, without finding its underlying cause, will lead to **symptom substitution**. In other words, the client would simply substitute a new maladaptive behavior for the one that has been eliminated, because the underlying cause of the problem had not been addressed. For example, if a behavior therapist was able to eliminate a client's fear of flying by teaching the client to respond with relaxation rather than with anxiety, a psychoanalyst would say that a new anxiety disorder would emerge because the underlying problem has not been treated. A behavior therapist would disagree, arguing that no underlying cause exists, and when the client has learned to respond to the situation appropriately, a new symptom will not appear. Research has supported the behaviorist position; symptom elimination does not seem to be followed by symptom substitution (Kazdin, 1982).

Classical-Conditioning Therapies

Remember the case of little Albert? He came to fear a white rat after it had been paired with a loud noise several times. John B. Watson thought if fears and phobias could be induced through classical conditioning, then they could be eliminated with classical conditioning as well. For example, if stimuli like a rabbit or riding in an airplane are associated with fear, then pairing them with pleasant feelings enough times should eventually result in the elimination of fear. This is known as counterconditioning—an undesired feeling is replaced with its opposite. The idea is that fear and relaxation cannot exist simultaneously in a person; therefore, if a stimulus can be associated with relaxation rather than fear, a person will no longer exhibit a fear response in the presence of the stimulus.

Classical-Conditioning Therapies

- Systematic desensitization
- Aversion therapy

Mary Cover Jones (1924) performed one of the first demonstrations of counterconditioning. A little boy who loved candy had a phobia toward rabbits. Jones began giving the little boy candy, which he thoroughly enjoyed, in the presence of a rabbit. She gave him candy twice a day, every day for two months. Initially, the rabbit was kept far enough away not to frighten the boy. Each day, however, Jones inched the rabbit a little closer to the boy. As the days went by, the boy became less and less afraid of the rabbit, and at the end of two months, he was willing to pet and play with the

This therapist is using behavior therapy to help this woman overcome her fear of the water.

rabbit. Evidently, the pleasant feelings the boy felt when enjoying the candy became associated with the rabbit so that fear had been replaced, or counterconditioned, with relaxation.

Systematic Desensitization

Joseph Wolpe (1958) adapted the technique used by Jones to deal with more abstract fears, like that of appearing foolish or doing poorly on a test—fears that were difficult to deal with in real-life settings. Instead of feeding adults to induce pleasant feelings, Wolpe taught his clients deep-muscle relaxation. Before Wolpe, Jacobson (1929) had found that anxiety could be reduced if clients were taught progressive relaxation. To learn progressive relaxation, Wolpe had clients sit in a comfortable recliner or couch and practice successively tensing and relaxing each of the major muscle groups in the head, arms, body, and legs, until they gained the ability to completely and totally relax the entire body. Try it for a few minutes.

Learning to relax in anxiety-producing situations, like studying for an exam, is part of the process of systematic desensitization.

The next step involves having the client create an anxiety hierarchy. In this step the client imagines 10 to 20 scenes progressing in the amount of anxiety they provoke. For example, if the problem is test anxiety, the least anxiety-provoking scene might be noticing the date of the first test on the syllabus. Somewhere in the middle of the anxiety hierarchy might be the announcement by the teacher that the test is a week away. Fairly high on the hierarchy would be having the test placed in front of the client or reading the first question.

In the next step, the client combines the relaxation response with the anxiety hierarchy in the hope of eliminating the fear response. The client first achieves a state of deep relaxation, and then the therapist instructs the client to imagine the scene that produces the least amount of anxiety. If the person's state of relaxation is undiminished, he or she then goes on to the next scene, and the next, until the person becomes anxious. When the person does become anxious, he or she is told to stop imagining the scene and to focus on relaxing again. This process is repeated over and over again during the course of several days until the person no longer experiences anxiety with any of the scenes. The technique just described is known as **imaginal exposure**. Often, when imaginal exposure is used, the client is given homework assignments between sessions, which involve placing themselves in progressively more anxiety-producing real-life situations. For example, if the person fears snakes, he or she may be asked to go to the library and check out a book with lots of pictures with snakes, and then go to a zoo or pet store and view a real, live snake.

> **Systematic Desensitization**
>
> - Step One: Learning to relax the entire body
> - Step Two: Creating an anxiety hierarchy
> - Step Three: Combining relaxation response with the anxiety hierarchy

Aversion Therapy

The case of little Albert is an example of aversion therapy. You may remember that Albert initially liked and enjoyed playing with white rats, but after a rat was associated with a loud and frightening noise, Albert began to fear rats.

Aversion therapy is like desensitization, except that a negative feeling is substituted for a positive feeling. For example, if drinking or smoking evokes a pleasurable but dangerous experience, aversion therapy can be used to replace the positive feelings created by alcohol and nicotine with negative feelings.

Many people who have overindulged in alcoholic beverages to the point where they became sick and later threw up noticed that they had an aversion to the kind of liquor from which they got sick. The smell, taste, and even the sight of it could make them feel sick. These ideas have been applied in the treatment of alcoholism. The idea is to replace the positive experience associated with alcohol with a negative experience. A drug (Antabuse) is given to clients before they enter a setting made to seem like a bar in which they consume alcohol. This drug induces violent vomiting in a person shortly after consuming alcohol. These clients do develop an aversion to alcohol; Smith and Frawley (1993) found that 60% of clients remained abstinent for at least a year. Associating vomiting with alcohol has been found to be more effective than administering electric shock (Cannon, Baker, & Wehl, 1981) when treating alcoholism.

These findings support the concept of **biological preparedness**. For example, we have an inborn tendency to associate internal stomach distress with tastes, such as alcoholic beverages, rather than with external sources of pain like electric shock (see Garcia, Kimmeldorf, Hunt, & Davies, 1956).

Aversion therapy, like the use of Antabuse, is usually combined with other therapies to make them more effective. Clients can be taught alternative techniques to cope with their stress rather than by drinking.

Operant Conditioning Therapies

Therapies that rely on the consequences of behavior are based on operant conditioning. Rewards and punishments can be used to alter behavior by shaping the behavior of people toward desired activities and away from maladaptive, undesired behavior. Operant conditioning focuses on specific behaviors. The purpose is to demonstrate that a specific act is followed by a specific consequence, thus influencing the person to change her or his behavior.

Token Economies

Severely disturbed clients living in an institutional setting often come to rely on the staff to take care of their most basic needs. Bathing, grooming, eating, and maintaining the living quarters are activities that are easily transferred from the client population onto the institutional staff. This can lead to passivity on the part of clients, which isn't beneficial to the clients' psychological well-being or to the quality of the care provided by the staff.

Token economies provide a means by which to keep the client populations active and engaged in the skills needed for living. In a token economy, clients earn tokens (often poker chips) for engaging in desirable behavior (such as brushing their teeth, eating with knives and forks, attending group therapy). Tokens are like money and can be exchanged for desirable commodities and activities (such as off-campus outings, TV/computer privileges, or sweets). Token economies have proved to be successful in developing adaptive behavior not only in psychiatric hospitals but also in grade school classes, homes for juvenile delinquents, and other settings (Kazdin, 1982).

Token economies generally rely on the use of rewards to increase the frequency of desired behaviors. There are occasions, however, in which punishment is used to stop and prevent self-injurious acts. For example, some children may bang their heads against the wall, bite, or hit themselves. Often such children are suffering from a disorder called autism. Besides self-destructive

This man is in a timeout. He has been removed from a setting in which he can obtain positive reinforcers for undesirable behavior.

behavior, children with autism often display language difficulty and social withdrawal. A therapist may apply electric shock to stop the self-injurious behavior (after a rationale for using the shock has been accepted and the parents have given their approval). When the self-destructive acts have stopped, the therapist may then use positive reinforcement to promote adaptive behaviors.

Other Operant Techniques

In operant conditioning, extinction is the withdrawal of reinforcement following a behavior. When the reinforcer is no longer provided, the behavior eventually stops occurring. Timeout is an operant technique that makes use of extinction to reduce undesirable behavior. In timeout, a person is removed from a setting in which he or she can obtain positive reinforcers. Rather than just ignore undesirable behavior, in timeout the person is removed from his or her immediate setting to a dreary location where positive reinforcers (e.g., friends, games) are unavailable.

Flooding is another technique that makes use of extinction. Anxiety-provoking situations often produce avoidance. The shy person doesn't go to the party or speak up in class; the person with test anxiety may drop a class before the test. These are examples of negative reinforcement, where the avoidance is maintained (reinforced) by the reduction in anxiety when the person escapes the disturbing situation.

In flooding, the person is prevented from escaping the feared situation; thus the avoidant behavior is not reinforced. Care has to be taken to avoid having the client become overwhelmed with fear. One way to do this is through the use of **imaginal flooding**. Another way is to use **in vivo flooding**. It is the experience of confronting the situation until the anxiety response subsides that extinguishes the fear of the situation. The hard part, of course, is getting the person into the situation feared, but once in the situation, the person's anxiety eventually subsides and he or she learns there is less to fear than originally thought. When the person first imagines the feared situation his or her anxiety spikes, but escape is impossible. Because physiologically it is impossible for the person to be revved-up forever, the person eventually begins to relax or feel exhausted. It is this relaxed feeling rather than anxiety that now becomes associated with the situation.

Modeling Therapies

Therapists can reduce anxiety in clients by demonstrating or modeling the desired behaviors the client fears. Watching films of a therapist handling snakes reduced the fear level in clients with snake phobias (Bandura, Blanchard, & Ritter, 1969).

Social skills training can also be used to teach people how to handle difficult interpersonal situations, such as asking someone for a date or asking the boss for a raise. In these therapy situations the client watches the therapist act out a scene that the client fears. The client then tries to repeat the performance, and the therapist responds with a combination of praise and constructive criticism. Very specific areas may be addressed in these role-plays, such as interaction distance, amount of eye contact, the speed of the person's speech, and so forth. The client can frequently acquire entire repertoires of behavior for several social situations, which can reduce the overall level of social anxiety, eventually leading to freer, more spontaneous responding by the client. Besides being effective in the treatment of phobias, social skills training has also been very useful in helping people with schizophrenia learn how to behave more appropriately.

9.5 Cognitive Therapies

If the emphasis of behavior therapy is to change the behavior of the person, the emphasis of the cognitive therapies is to change the cognitions, that is, the thoughts and beliefs of the person. Cognitive therapies often deal with anxiety, depression, and self-esteem problems. These are problems in which people feel badly and often blame themselves for their misery. The fundamental idea of cognitive therapy is that emotions follow from thoughts; therefore, by changing the way the person thinks, you can change the way the person feels.

The cognitive therapist argues that it is not what happens to people that causes them to feel depressed or anxious—it is the interpretation, or meaning, they give to what happens to them. It is the interpretation that leads to the bad feelings. For example, the grade a person gets on a test has no inherent meaning—an "A" could stand for awful, as easily as it could stand for outstanding. An "A" or "F" has no meaning until it is given one by the person. In our daily lives, people fall in and out of love, get and lose jobs, are promoted or passed over; none of these events in and of themselves means anything until a person assigns a meaning to it. Being laid off could be an opportunity, as much as a threat. The problem arises when people assign a meaning to an event that reflects negatively on them; they can dwell on a negative interpretation until they feel hopeless or hate themselves. People can come to believe some terrible things about themselves, and more often than not, these are simple figments of their imagination. Nonetheless, beliefs, regardless of their accuracy, affect how people feel and how they conduct their lives.

There are a number of ordinary events that people interpret in harmful ways. For example, it is not unusual after a relationship breakup for one or both parties to feel they will never find anybody else and that they will always be lonely. Even psychology and medicine have contributed to the arsenal of negative things people can believe about themselves, which in the end turn out to be untrue. At one time, the concept of a schizophrenogenic mother was an accepted explanation as a cause for schizophrenia. Unfortunately, this explanation created anguish and guilt in mothers who believed they had done something terribly wrong in raising their child, and they blamed themselves for causing the schizophrenia. The schizophrenogenic mother explanation is no longer accepted, but it highlights the idea that it is not the event itself, but the interpretation of the event that determines how people feel about themselves.

Rational-Emotive Behavior Therapy (R-E-B-T)

Albert Ellis (1962) developed a therapy to change the rigid, maladaptive thinking patterns of people. Ellis's therapy is based on the A-B-C theory of emotion. In his theory:

A is the activating event.
B is the irrational belief.
C is the emotional experience.

Most people believe A causes C; (A), the bad event, led to (C), the depression. Ellis argues that (C), the depression, is preceded by some irrational belief, (B), and it is (B) that caused (C), the depression. For example, a person applies to graduate school and is turned down (A). The person doesn't become depressed, (C), unless that person believes that not getting into graduate school means he or she is a failure and is too stupid to succeed, (B). It is the irrational belief the person has about not getting into graduate school that makes the person miserable, not the rejection itself. Ellis described a number of beliefs that people carry with them, which end up making their lives miserable. Some of these beliefs are listed here:

- I should be very anxious when events are uncertain.
- Everyone must like me.
- I have to be good at everything.
- It is horrible when things don't turn out the way I want them to.
- Everyone gets what they deserve.

Ellis directly attacks these beliefs and tries to show the client how ridiculous and absurd his or her beliefs are. Ellis's manner is often confrontational and dramatic as he attempts to help clients recognize the trap they are setting for themselves. The troubling quality of these irrational beliefs is their black-and-white quality; Ellis has come to refer to this as "demandingness" (Ellis, 1991). The belief is experienced as a demand; dire and horrible consequences will follow if it is not met. Ironically, it is often impossible to achieve the demand stated in the belief. Perfection is, after all, a very rare commodity.

Aaron Beck's Cognitive Therapy

Aaron Beck (2002) also uses a cognitive approach to explain and treat depression and generalized anxiety disorder. In Beck's view, the cognitive triad combines with illogical thinking to produce automatic thoughts that overwhelm any good feeling a person has about him- or herself. The generalized attitudes of the cognitive triad lead the person (a) to think of him- or herself as inadequate, worthless, incompetent, unattractive, and so on; (b) to see the world as overwhelming and his or her experiences as continuously burdensome (that is, everything is another unpleasant task); and (c) to see the future as hopeless, with no chance of relief.

> **Cognitive Triad**
>
> The general tendency of people to see the following in negative ways:
> 1. themselves
> 2. their world
> 3. their future

Beck also believes people make a number of logical mistakes when interpreting their experiences. **Arbitrary inference** occurs when a person takes a small, meaningless incident and assumes a larger, very negative conclusion. For example, a man might conclude that the kids in the park are deliberately being loud to distract him from his reading and then conclude further that they are doing so because he is so ugly. Beck describes a number of different ways illogical thinking contributes to depression; two other examples are magnification and minimization.

In both magnification and minimization the person misinterprets the magnitude of the incident. An example of **magnification** would be a student thinking, "I missed a

5-point exercise in my psychology class; how will I ever make up the loss? Now I am doomed and will fail the course." An example of **minimization** would be a student thinking something like, "She isn't really attracted to me; she was just desperate to get a date to the prom." Another example might be a student thinking that the "A" he received in history was because the teacher was easy, not because he was smart or studied hard.

The consequence of the generally negative outlook (cognitive triad) and illogical thinking are **automatic thoughts**. Beck calls them automatic thoughts because they don't have to be related to the immediate situation. They occur spontaneously and just seem to happen. For example, the memory of an embarrassing incident might pop into a person's head, suggesting the person is stupid; a little later a thought about his or her worthlessness passes through, and a little later a belief about how every-

The client keeping a log of his or her automatic thoughts and resulting emotions is part of Phase 2 of Beck's cognitive therapy.

one hates him or her passes through, and so it goes. By the end of the day, the person is worn out having lived a thousand painful accidents, suffered the humiliation of a thousand embarrassments, and mourned a thousand mistakes (Mendels, 1970). To get out of this trap, Beck sees four phases of treatment (Comer, 2004).

Phase 1: The person's level of activity is increased in an attempt to elevate mood and confidence. A detailed hour-by-hour schedule of activities is planned by client and therapist for the upcoming week. Activities are scheduled in order to get the person up and moving, engaged in life again, with the hope that increased activity will reduce the client's negative feelings about him- or herself.

Phase 2: Automatic thoughts and the resulting emotions are identified. Beck has the client keep a log of the content of all automatic thoughts and emotional reactions. The therapist can then challenge the automatic thought. For example, a student describes a thought that popped into her head long after the incident occurred, but nonetheless it created a sense of shame and embarrassment. The thought was about a time when the teacher called on her and asked a question. She doesn't recall her answer being wrong or getting any extraordinary response from the teacher, but she nonetheless felt extremely stupid and embarrassed. Beck would challenge the reality behind these feelings and hopefully get the client to perceive them as groundless.

Phase 3: The person's logical mistakes are identified. If the person frequently makes arbitrary inferences or maximizes or uses any of the many other logical errors described by Beck, these logical errors are recorded. The faulty logic in each error is pointed out, as are the resulting negative feelings. The client and therapist come up with alternative interpretations, and then the client practices applying these alternative explanations.

Phase 4: The therapist then teaches the client to think through negative prevailing beliefs to understand how they prevent making more realistic and positive assumptions about self and his or her life and future.

9.6 Humanistic Therapy

Carl Roger's Client-Centered Therapy

Carl Rogers (1951) believed individuals have a natural, inborn tendency to become the persons they are meant to be, and will do so if conditions allow them this freedom—a concept that he referred to as self-actualization. Rogers attempted to create the conditions for the natural, healthy tendencies of people to be expressed and, in effect, improve their own psychological well-being. Thus, Rogers strictly avoided advising clients, as well as strictly avoided interpreting or analyzing clients' statements. In fact, his therapy is often referred to as nondirective. Rogers' focus was on the **phenomenology** of the client. Only by knowing what the client was thinking and feeling about an issue could the therapist and client hope to gain any understanding of the client's true nature. It is this process of self-discovery that Rogers believed facilitated the therapeutic process. He believed that when people are healthy, they make choices that are right for them, allowing them to be their authentic person. Rogers believed, more so than the psychoanalytic and behavioral orientations, that free will allows people to make choices for themselves. The problem for most of us, Rogers argued, is that we are often forced to choose between gaining the acceptance and approval of others or being ourselves. Everybody needs love and acceptance, and to gain it, people often act as others want. This causes a person to live a life that is at odds with one's true nature, and the person's self-concept becomes distorted, followed by psychological discomfort and confusion. To feel right again, the client needs to rediscover his or her natural self-worth and develop a congruence between the choices made in life and his or her feelings. The choices, which are consistent with the self, feel right and natural because they are self-actualizing; that is, they promote the growth and development of the person. Choices that are not consistent with the self leave the person anxious, doubting, and confused. In the following section we discuss the characteristics of the therapist that Rogers believed would help the client make self-actualizing choices.

Therapist Qualities: Genuineness, Unconditional Positive Regard, and Empathy

To be effective the therapist should display three fundamental characteristics:

1. **Genuineness** means the therapist behaves as who he or she is, not as Doctor or Psychotherapist "Whoever." The therapist is, in effect, modeling for the client a person who is in touch with her or his feelings and can express them honestly and openly, as well as take responsibility for her or his actions and feelings. The therapist is open and sincere with the client about him- or herself and his or her feelings. Being genuine rather than phony is perhaps the best way to convey this quality.

2. **Unconditional positive regard** refers to an unwavering respect and acceptance of the client. The therapist "prizes" the client. The therapist avoids creating conditions of worth for the client, for example, "I will accept and approve of you, if you do this, but not accept you if you do that." Presumably, it is this kind of experience that has gotten the client into therapy in the first place. The client, feeling "prized" by the therapist, becomes more comfortable with exploring the thoughts and feelings associated with decisions in his or her life, and pursuing a self-discovery.

3. **Empathy** is concerned with whether the therapist can mirror back to the client the client's thoughts and feelings accurately. The therapist attempts to restate the thoughts and feelings of the client and summarizes the dilemmas described by the client. This allows the client to examine issues outside him- or herself in a more objective fashion. In response to the therapist's summary, a client might say, "It never occurred to me, but when you said it, it seemed as if I really did feel ...," or a client might say, "No, that's not what I mean; the feeling is more like ...." As the therapist restates the client's statements, it presumably helps the client clarify how well his or her actions and feelings fit together. As the client sorts through the choices and associated feelings he or she has made throughout life, a clearer recognition is gained with regard to how satisfying the choices were or were not. Thus, the client obtains greater insight into the true nature of the self and the sort of choices that are self-actualizing.

9.7 Gestalt and Existentialism Therapy

Fritz Perls (1893–1970), the founder of **Gestalt therapy**, believed that his clients were living lives disconnected from their immediate experiences. For example, when meeting a new person, people often do not respond only to what the person says or does, but may also respond based on the image they want to create or to preconceived ideas they have of the other person. The images and roles guiding behavior often create a phony person who is acting out scenes based on unconscious conflicts from relationships they have, or have had, with other people. People will often project their fears, desires, and insecurities into an interaction. For example, someone might be preoccupied with thoughts about past unpleasant interactions with a person, which causes him or her to respond to the person's image rather than to the immediate and specific behavior of the person. The person is not reacting to the other person's current behavior, but to a past situation. It is as if the "emotional baggage" carried into the interaction keeps the person's actions out of sync with the current situation.

In Gestalt therapy, clients are chided, cajoled, and confronted to move out of the past and respond to the immediacy of the moment. Perls (1970) uses techniques that can be quite confrontational in his attempts to get the person to respond to him, and him alone, rather than play the role of, say, the "wounded" or "pathetic" client. If the client becomes angry, the therapist would say, "See, you are now caught up in the moment and are responding to me, not the image you want me to have of you." The person is responding as an integrated whole—thoughts and feelings mesh with the situation. The goal of Gestalt therapy is to increase the frequency of "caught-up-in-the-moment" experiences, as well as to get the individual to take responsibility for his or her life and happiness, rather than hiding behind excuses of a difficult childhood or poor treatment from a spouse. Perls believes people can achieve fulfilling and satisfying lives if they are not afraid to take responsibility for their own happiness and live in the here and now.

Existential therapy helps clients deal with the fundamental issues of existence. Issues about our existence haunt our lives and generate anxiety from the background of our awareness when they are not dealt with. Irvin Yalom (1980), a well-known existential therapist, lists four basic issues each person must address:

1. Our death is inevitable.
2. Each of us is responsible for our own choices.
3. Each of us is alone in the world.
4. Each of us needs to find a meaning to our lives.

The existential therapist helps clients deal with life decisions related to these issues, such as whether to stay or leave a job or a marriage. The therapist helps the client think through the choices to find the ones that ring true for the person.

9.8 The Medical Approach

The idea of treating the body to create psychological changes may go back to prehistoric times. Skulls of Stone Age people have been uncovered with holes penetrating deep enough to get to the brain. The reason why these holes were cut into a person's skull is not clear. One explanation put forth is that the holes were a physical attempt to solve a spiritual problem. It is possible that a Stone Age man who was behaving strangely may have been subjected to trephination, the name given to cutting through the skull with a sharp instrument (a trephine) to release evil spirits trapped inside him. Although the cause wasn't believed to be physical, the attempted cure was brutally physical.

Today, many view psychological problems as having a physical cause and thus attempt a physical cure. Three primary forms of treatment are used.

Drug Therapy

In the past 50 years, the treatment of psychological disorders with drugs has exploded. Initially the most dramatic effects of drugs were observed in patients suffering the most severe disorders, like schizophrenia. Since then, however, many other disorders, such as depression and manic depression, have drug therapy as the first line of treatment.

> **Primary Forms of Treatment**
>
> 1. Drug Therapy
> 2. Electroconvulsive Therapy
> 3. Psychosurgery

Antipsychotic Drugs

The inspiration for much of modern-day drug therapy came in 1952 from two French psychiatrists, John Delay and Pierre Deniker. They administered a drug called chlorpromazine (brand name Thorazine) to a patient with schizophrenia, and the patient showed tremendous improvement.

Many patients with schizophrenia had to be warehoused in psychiatric hospitals for most of their lives. Some were kept in restraints, straitjackets, or padded rooms almost all the time. Chlorpromazine changed all that. Many patients responded so well to chlorpromazine (Thorazine) that they could be released from mental hospitals and, if they continued to take their medication, could lead more normal lives. Since then, researchers have sought not only to find even more effective antipsychotic drugs but also to find drugs to treat less debilitating disorders.

Chlorpromazine was one of a group of antihistamines called **phenothiazines** originally developed to treat allergies. Now, chlorpromazine (Thorazine) is just one of many of the phenothiazines, now commonly referred to as first-generation antipsychotic medications, used to treat schizophrenia. Others include thioridazine (Mellaril), mesoridazine (Serentil), fluphenazine (Prolixin), and trifluoperazine (Stelazine).

These drugs are all **dopamine antagonists**, meaning that they affect levels of the neurotransmitter dopamine in the brain. Five different dopamine receptor sites have been identified by researchers and are labeled D1, D2, D3, D4, and D5. The phenothiazine drugs have an affinity for the D2 receptor sites and bind most frequently to it (Box 9.3).

There are problems, however, with the use of the phenothiazines. One problem is that they are more effective for the positive symptoms and less effective for the negative symptoms of schizophrenia. The phenothiazines reduce hallucinations and delusions (positive symptoms) but have little effect on negative symptoms like flat affect, poverty of speech, and loss of volition. A much more serious problem is the damage produced by these medicines. These drugs are called **neuroleptics** because they often produce symptoms similar to neurological disease. As you may recall, Parkinson's disease is a movement disorder of the nervous system (a neurological disease) caused by the lack of dopamine. The neuroleptics or phenothiazines prevent dopamine from binding to receptor sites and can have

Box 9.3   First-Generation Antipsychotic Drugs

Generic Name	Brand Name
Chlorpromazine	Thorazine
Thioridazine	Mellaril
Mesoridazine	Serentil
Fluphenazine	Prolixin
Trifluoperazine	Stelazine
Haloperidol	Haldol
Thiothixene	Navane

much the same effect as if the brain were not producing enough dopamine, thus inducing Parkinsonian-type symptoms.

Parkinsonian symptoms include tremors, muscle rigidity, shaking gait, lack of facial expression, and problems maintaining balance, to name a few. As many as 40% of patients may show these side effects (Strange, 1992). Another side effect of these drugs is **akathisia**. In akathisia, the person feels discomfort in the limbs, which makes it difficult for the person to sit still. In an effort to relieve the discomfort, the person may appear agitated because he or she moves around a lot, for example, pacing, getting in and out of a chair, and so on. Unfortunately, these side effects are often misinterpreted, and the patient is thought to need more medication rather than less. These side effects can be lessened by other drugs that have anti-Parkinsonian properties. In some cases, the antipsychotic medication may have to be stopped altogether in an effort to reduce the neurological symptoms.

When the Parkinson-like symptoms do not appear until the person has taken the phenothiazines/neuroleptics for a year or longer, the disorder is called **tardive dyskinesia**. In tardive dyskinesia, patients may exhibit a number of other symptoms as well. For example, they may have tic-like movements in the face and body, smack their lips, make chewing movements, and may rock the upper torso back and forth, and (most seriously) they develop irregular breathing. Two other drugs, neither belonging to the phenothiazines, are also used to treat schizophrenia. They are haloperidol (Haldol) and thiothixene (Navane), and they also have been implicated in the neurological disorders just described.

A current type of psychosurgery is practiced in the form of cingulotomy. Patients suffering from obsessive-compulsive disorder or severe depression, but who are unresponsive to other forms of treatment, may have a small portion of their limbic system destroyed in an attempt to seek relief.

9.9 Is Therapy Effective?

Most psychotherapists and patients assume that psychotherapy is effective. Most people took for granted that psychotherapy helped people feel better and function more effectively in the world—that is, until Hans Eysenck, a well-known British psychologist, reported in 1952 that about two-thirds of patients not receiving psychotherapy had **spontaneous remission**. A spontaneous remission rate of 66% was just a little less than that for patients who were receiving psychotherapy. This finding led to the criticism that therapy was a waste of time and money.

Such an attack on one of the basic pillars of psychology led to a considerable effort to disprove Eysenck. Many methodological flaws were found in Eysenck's research. For example, it was argued that the patients receiving and not receiving therapy differed in terms of education, socioeconomic status, and motivation to improve. Furthermore, many of the so-called untreated patients did receive some type of treatment in the form of drug therapy or informal counseling from their physicians. Nonetheless, Eysenck's bold attack has led to considerable research on the effectiveness of psychotherapy. Although Eysenck seems to have overestimated the rate of spontaneous

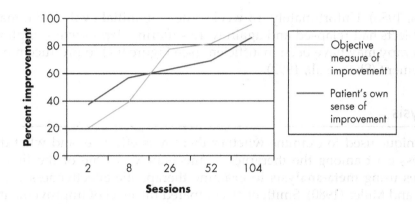

Figure 9.4

Effectiveness of therapy over sessions. (Adapted from Howard et al., 1996.)

remission—it appears to be between 30% and 40% rather than 66% (Bergin & Lambert, 1978)—much has been learned about the therapeutic process because of his criticism (Figure 9.4).

Today, decades of meta-analyses, which is a review of multiple studies, has found that in comparison to no therapy, psychotherapy is effective in reducing symptoms and distress (Wampold, 2001). We'll look at this research more in the Meta-Analysis section below.

Does the Type of Therapy Matter?

A number of studies have found that receiving therapy is more important than the specific type of therapy received. For example, a study done by Sloane, Staples, Cristol, Yorkston, and Whipple (1975) compared behavioral therapy, psychoanalytic therapy, and an untreated control group for effectiveness in reducing symptoms in clients suffering from anxiety disorders. A group of diagnosticians totally unaware of the treatment the clients had or had not received examined the clients four months after the study had begun. They found that both the behavioral and psychoanalytic groups showed statistically significant improvement over the no-treatment control group, but there was no difference in effectiveness between the behavioral and psychoanalytic therapies.

More recently, a study sponsored by the National Institute of Mental Health demonstrated similar effects of therapy for depression, but again found no difference in effectiveness among the therapies. A total of 239 depressed clients were randomly assigned to one of four conditions. In one condition, subjects received Beck's cognitive therapy; in another, subjects received a form of psychoanalytic therapy called interpersonal therapy; in still another, patients received the antidepressant Tofranil; and the last group received a placebo pill. After 16 weeks, 50 % of the subjects in the treatment conditions were depression free, but only 29% of the subjects in the placebo condition were free of symptoms. At the 16-week point, all three therapies (cognitive, interpersonal, and drug) were equally effective, although the drug therapy had brought the quickest relief (Mervis, 1986). Unfortunately, 18 weeks after the initial evaluation, many of the improved subjects had relapsed and again were suffering depressive symptoms. Three months of therapy may have been insufficient (see Figure 9.4) to produce more permanent improvement (Shea et al., 1992).

Meta-Analysis

Another technique used to examine whether therapy is effective, and what differences in effectiveness exist among the therapies, is meta-analysis. One of the first and best-known studies using **meta-analysis** to examine therapeutic effectiveness was done by Smith, Glass, and Miller (1980). Smith et al. compared the level of improvement obtained in treatment and control groups for 475 studies. These studies differed with regard to the psychological problem being treated and the way improvement was measured. However, they were all the same in that they compared a therapy versus a no-therapy condition. Smith et al. found that most of the treated individuals were better off than the people in the untreated control conditions. Furthermore, there were few, if any, differences found among the alternative forms of psychotherapy. Through a review of numerous studies, Lambert and Archer (2006) concluded that roughly 75% of people who attend therapy show some type of benefit, which is statistically better than no treatment.

Picking a Therapist

If a person feels some help would be useful in handling her or his problem or the person believes her or his current level of distress is affecting personal, family, or work life, the person may want to try therapy (Engler & Goleman, 1992). To find a therapist, a person can ask friends and family for recommendations, consult his or her insurance provider, call a community mental health center, or ask a religious leader or a physician for a referral.

A person should feel comfortable with and trust the person giving the therapy. An extremely important factor in effective therapy is the empathy communicated by the therapist. The ability to instill hope, motivate the client toward improvement, and respond empathetically varies from therapist to therapist, and it is suggested that a client shop around to find a therapist he or she is comfortable with. Even when therapists are deliberately trying to follow the same treatment regimen, and are making every effort not to deviate from it, the clients of one therapist will show more improvement than the clients of another (Norcross, 2002).

When shopping for a therapist, some general assumptions should be kept in mind. Generally, psychiatrists or medical doctors (MDs) will treat complaints with drugs, which may be helpful in the short run. However, anxiety or depressive disorders can also be treated with talking therapies or in combination with drug therapy. The skills and support obtained from the talking therapies may allow the person to stop the drug therapy sooner and provide protection from a relapse.

Clinical psychologists are more likely to focus on a person's behavior, thoughts, and feelings during therapy regardless of whether the person is treated individually or in a group (Figure 9.5). Counselors, on the other hand, may be more interested in the overall social environment of the person, that is, wanting to involve family and friends in the therapy.

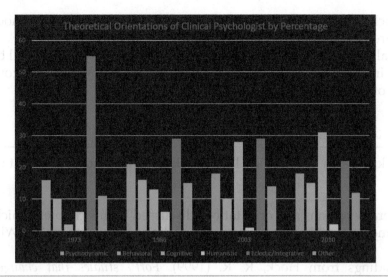

Figure 9.5

Orientation of clinical psychologists. (Adapted from Norcross and Karpiak, 2012.)

Prospective clients should inquire about a therapist's credentials. For example: What degrees does the therapist hold? Does the therapist hold a license or certification by the state to practice psychotherapy? Does the therapist specialize in the treatment of any specific disorders? Does the therapist have any specialized training in the treatment of certain kinds of problems? This last question could be particularly important for disorders like drug or alcohol abuse or sexual problems. Prospective clients may also want to ask a therapist what, if any, theoretical orientation he or she uses in therapy. It may also be useful to set specific therapeutic goals, as well as a time frame for which these goals could be achieved. This gives both the client and therapist some means of assessing the effectiveness of the therapy and whether or not changes in therapist or therapeutic strategy should be made. Finding a good therapeutic match, like any interpersonal relationship, may take some searching, but finding a good match can be one of the most important parts of a successful therapeutic outcome.

Picking a Therapist

- Get recommendations.
- Trust and feel comfortable with the therapist.
- Take into account your needs (medications, type of therapy, etc.).
- Consider the therapist's credentials.

Main Points

1. **Mental Health Providers:** There are many types of mental health providers. Psychiatrists, psychologists, licensed counselors, social workers, pastoral counselors, to name a few. Some are better qualified to treat certain conditions than others. It is important for clients and patients to understand and ask about the types of training and areas of expertise providers have in order to be wise consumers.

2. **There Are a Range of Therapies:** There are a wide range of therapeutic orientations and schools of thought in the field of psychology. From psychoanalytic to behavior therapy. There are also cognitive, humanistic, and existential therapy

approaches. It is important to know the difference between each modality as some are better suited for certain conditions and people.

3. **Medical Approach:** Depending on the condition, many people will benefit from a combination of medications and psychological treatments. This combination can be of great value for clients.

Thoughts and Suggestions

If possible, pick one area you would like to work on. That kind of therapist would you go to and why?

If all of the therapy options and orientations discussed in this chapter, which one do you believe is the most valuable, interesting, or appealing to you personally? Why?

Suggested readings from Hock, R. R. (1999). *Forty studies that changed psychology* (3rd ed.). Upper Saddle River, NJ: Prentice Hall. (ISBN #: 0-13-922725-3):

- Reading 33: Choosing Your Psychotherapist
- Reading 34: Relaxing Your Fears Away
- Reading 35: Projections of Who You Are

Study Terms

Clinical psychologists Hold a PhD or PsyD degree but typically cannot prescribe medication.

Psychiatrists Receive an MD degree, specialize in psychiatry, and can prescribe medication.

Psychoanalysts Train in Freudian analytic techniques.

Somatogenesis/somatogenic view The belief that the body needs to be treated to cure the psyche.

Syndrome A group of symptoms that appear together and follow a similar course.

General paresis Physical and mental deterioration of a person in the last stages of syphilis.

Hysteria Psychological problems characterized by the loss of some body function.

Cathartic treatment Getting a patient to talk about upsetting events associated with symptoms.

free association Talking about whatever comes to mind, without censoring anything.

Resistance An unconscious (usually) attempt not to talk about something that is threatening or upsetting.

Transference Client behaves as if the therapist represents an important emotional figure in his or her life.

Manifest content Description of a dream.

Latent content The unconscious message of a dream.

Behavior therapy Focusing on the current behavioral problem.

Symptom substitution Substituting a different maladaptive behavior for the one that has been eliminated.

Imaginal exposure Exposing the client to anxiety-provoking images through imagination.

Flooding Extinction technique that prevents the client from escaping the feared situation.

Imaginal flooding Holding the feared situation in your mind until the anxiety subsides.

In vivo flooding Exposing the client to the feared situation, often accompanied by the therapist, until the anxiety stops.

Arbitrary inference Negative conclusions based on little evidence.

Magnification Blowing out of proportion the negative consequences of an event.

Minimization Trivializing their role or a good quality about themselves when something good happens.

Automatic thoughts Self-persecuting thoughts that occur spontaneously.

Phenomenology The immediate experience of a person.

Genuineness Not pretending to be anyone other than who you are.

Unconditional positive regard An unwavering respect and acceptance of others.

Empathy The ability to identify another person's thoughts and feelings accurately.

Gestalt therapy The person is responding as an integrated whole— thoughts and feelings mesh with the situation.

Existential therapy Helps clients deal with the fundamental issues of existence.

Phenothiazines One of the first group of antipsychotics to be developed; it includes Thorazine.

Dopamine antagonists Drugs that bind in the dopamine receptor sites of a neuron's dendrite, preventing the natural effect of dopamine.

Neuroleptics Drugs that often produce symptoms similar to neurological disease.

Akathisia A drug side effect that causes the person to feel discomfort in the limbs, making it difficult for the person to sit still.

Tardive dyskinesia When the Parkinson-like symptoms do not appear until the person has been taking the drug a year or longer.

Spontaneous remission Improvement of patients without psychotherapy.

Meta-analysis Combines the results of several studies on a common measure.

10

Social Psychology

Focus Questions

*By the end of the chapter, you should be able
to answer the following questions:*

- With what is social psychology concerned?
- How are *compliance* and *conformity* different?
- How do attitudes, beliefs, opinions, and stereotypes differ?
- What are some key forces that might serve to change attitudes?
- How is aggression defined and explained?
- What are some causes and manifestations of antisocial and prosocial behavior?
- What is love?

I don't know if life is greater than death, but love was more than either.

—*Tristan's dying words,* Tristan + Isolde *(2006 movie)*

Inspirational Words

And the Lord make you to increase and abound in love one toward another, and toward all men, *even as we* do *toward you: 1 Thessalonians 3:12*

And I say unto you, Make to yourselves friends of the mammon of unrighteousness; that, when ye fail, they may receive you into everlasting habitations. He that is faithful in that which is least is faithful also in much: and he that is unjust in the least is unjust also in much. If therefore ye have not been faithful in the unrighteous mammon, who will commit to your trust the true riches? And if ye have not been faithful in that which is another man's, who shall give you that which is your own? No servant can serve two masters: for either he will hate the one, and love the other; or else he will hold to the one, and despise the other. Ye cannot serve God and mammon. Jesus in Luke 16:913

10.1 Social Psychology

What Is Social Psychology?

Social psychology is concerned with relationships among individuals or between individuals and groups. In Allport's (1968) terms, "social psychologists regard their discipline as an attempt to understand how the *thought, feeling,* and *behavior* of individuals are influenced by the *actual, imagined,* or *implied* presence of others" (p. 3). Thus, social psychology says something about why Isolde married King Mark (the powerful influence of social customs and values)—and why she later returned to Tristan (the strength of their love).

The subject matter of social psychology spans almost all facets of human behavior save those that are clearly individual and not affected by the presence of others. Most of what we learn, think, feel, and do is influenced by others. There are very few people whose lives are totally devoid of human relationships. To be completely isolated socially would require absolute geographic isolation or some form of mental disorder. Social isolation, interesting though it may be, provides no pieces of the puzzle for the social psychologist. Social psychology tries to understand the socially influenced aspects of attitudes, relationships, and behaviors.

10.2 Attitudes and Attitude Change

Understanding social influence is basic to understanding the formation and changing of attitudes, opinions, stereotypes, and prejudices.

An **attitude** is a prevailing and consistent tendency to react in a given way based on individual beliefs. Attitudes have important emotional connotations as well as behavioral and cognitive components. They may be described as positive or negative; neutral reactions don't qualify as attitudes. Attitudes have strong motivational consequences, a fact that distinguishes them from **opinions**. Although opinions are also evaluations, they don't drive people to action as do attitudes (Figure 10.1).

Stereotypes are widely held attitudes and opinions concerning identifiable groups. They usually include value-laden beliefs and are often based on emotional reaction, illogical reasoning, and faulty generalization.

Although stereotypes have often been assumed to be negative, they can also be positive. Negative stereotypes have been shown to have detrimental effects on many kinds of interactions, including, for example, between teachers and students (Marx, 2009). In the same way, positive stereotypes can have a beneficial effect on learning and performance (Kwong See & Nicoladis, 2010).

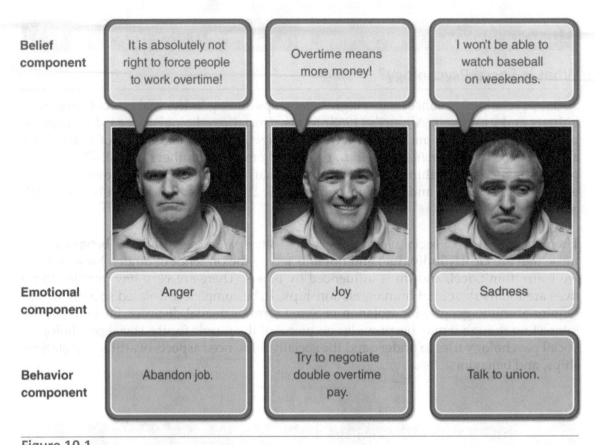

Belief component

It is absolutely not right to force people to work overtime!

Overtime means more money!

I won't be able to watch baseball on weekends.

Emotional component

Anger

Joy

Sadness

Behavior component

Abandon job.

Try to negotiate double overtime pay.

Talk to union.

Figure 10.1

The three components of attitudes, illustrating how attitudes motivate behavior.

As generalized beliefs about groups, stereotypes are virtually indispensable in daily interaction. They're like shortcuts that tell us how to react without having to wait to see how other people are going to behave. For example, we may have a stereotype that tells us that panhandlers become aggressive if we look them in the eye but throw nothing in their hats. So we don't look them in the eye, or we go ahead and toss heavy coin into their hats.

Not surprisingly, there is considerable research, much of which is summarized by Lee, Jussim, and McCauley (1995), that many stereotypes, including those applied specifically to identifiable ethnic groups, agree remarkably well with more objective evaluations. This doesn't mean that stereotypes are invariably accurate and useful; many are bigoted, inappropriate, and shockingly unjust.

Unlike stereotypes, which are widely held beliefs about groups, **prejudices** are personal rather than shared prejudgments. To be prejudiced implies having arrived at an opinion prior to obtaining relevant facts.

How attitudes, opinions, stereotypes, and prejudice are different is evident in a sample of most people's behaviors and beliefs. For example, Eddie's strong feeling that involvement in war is immoral and his attempt to persuade others they should protest illustrate an *attitude*—a personal, emotional, and clearly motivating belief. If he is convinced that military

The urge to conform is a powerful social motive. It does much to ensure that societies function smoothly. But do we all have to check our watches at the same time?

personnel are highly immoral even though he has had little exposure to them, that conviction would be a *prejudice*—a preconceived judgment. His personal belief that seatbelt legislation is unnecessary and uneconomical is an *opinion*—a personal belief not necessarily shared by others and not directed toward an identifiable group. And his assumption that Americans are sufficiently resourceful and industrious that they will easily cope with global warming and other crises illustrates a *stereotype*—a belief about a specific group that is shared by a significant number of people.

Compliance and Conformity

Attitudes are powerful motives for behavior. And although they tend to be stable and long lasting, they can change in response to various factors, including new information we acquire, social pressure, tendencies we have to obey or disobey, and the effects of persuasion. As we change our attitudes, our behavior changes as well; it can be said to *conform* or *comply* with the forces that change it. **Conformity** is defined by long-term changes in behavior where attitudes have been affected, opinions modified, or stereotypes and prejudices altered. Short-term changes in behavior that don't significantly alter any of these types of beliefs are said to lead to **compliance** rather than to conformity.

The distinction between conformity and compliance is more subtle in practice than in theory. If I hold a carrot a tantalizing distance in front of a mule, thereby inducing that clever animal to swim across a small body of water, I have simply succeeded in getting a mule to comply with my pointless wishes. Assuming that the mule still doesn't like water and doesn't develop the habit of taking off its shoes and wading for pleasure of a Sunday morning, it cannot be argued that I have developed a conforming mule simply by bullying one into complying. To become a conforming mule, the creature would have to change its attitudes toward water and deliberately wade with the other wading mules because of its attitudes rather than for a measly carrot. If you happened along and saw the mule swimming, however, you would not know whether it was complying or conforming.

To bring the illustration closer to home, you may be said to conform to social norms to the extent that you approve of them and therefore act accordingly. Complying with the same social norms might involve exactly the same behavior but would be based on motives other than your approval of the norms.

Social Pressure and Compliance

The classic studies of compliance, frequently described as studies of conformity, are those conducted by Asch (1955). In a typical experiment, "subjects" are placed in a semicircle facing an easel on which the experimenter places two large cards. One of these cards has a single vertical line on it (the standard); the other has three vertical lines of different lengths, one

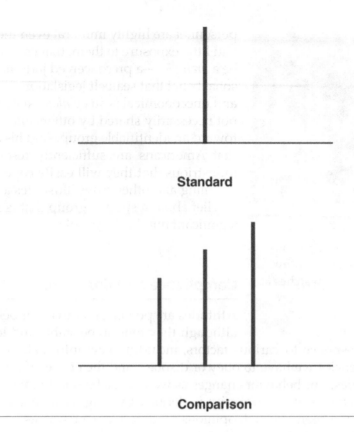

Figure 10.2

Asch (1955) used a simple visual perception test to determine the effects of social pressure. Participants, unwittingly part of a group of the experimenter's confederates, who often agreed on the wrong answer, were asked which comparison line is the same length as the standard line.

of which is clearly equal in length to the standard (Figure 10.2). In a "test of perceptual accuracy," subjects are required to determine which of the three lines is equal to the standard.

In fact, the test is not of perceptual accuracy but of social pressure and its effects on compliance. Only one of the "subjects" is actually a subject; the others are confederates. The confederates have been instructed to answer correctly for the first few trials and then to answer incorrectly but to agree on the incorrect answer. The real subject, who has no reason to suspect that the others are not also subjects, is the second last to answer.

In a series of studies carried out in three different institutions, 123 subjects answered incorrectly 36.8 percent of the time. A control group not exposed to social pressure answered correctly more than 99 percent of the time. Typically, subjects were confronted with the conflicting opinions of as many as eight confederates. However, varying the number of confederates revealed that a majority of three was equally effective in eliciting compliance with the group (Asch, 1955). This observation is strikingly similar to the ancient Chinese proverb, *three men make a tiger* (which is interpreted to mean that people will believe the most absurd things as long as enough other people seem to believe them) (Figure 10.3).

When subjects in the Asch experiment were questioned later, it turned out that they knew all along that their responses and those of the confederates were in error. But they still

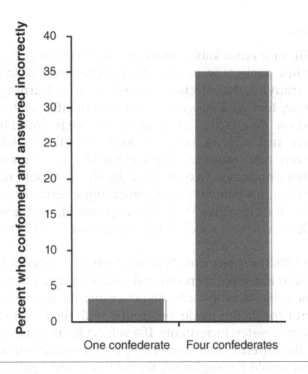

Figure 10.3

When paired with a single confederate, subjects in the Asch (1955) study were about as accurate as if they had been alone. But when paired with four, they complied with the majority more than one third of the time. Adding more confederates did not increase compliance significantly.

complied—later explaining their behavior in a variety of ways, such as by attributing it to "misjudgment" or "poor eyesight." Interestingly, however, not all were equally susceptible to the effects of group pressure. Fully one quarter of subjects continued to answer completely independently, never agreeing with the incorrect majority. In contrast, others nearly always agreed with the majority.

These experiments have often been interpreted as evidence of the gullibility of individuals and their susceptibility to group pressure. The implication is that these are undesirable qualities. In fact, however, it is precisely because we are susceptible to group pressures that complex social institutions such as governments, schools, and churches work. It is also because we are sensitive to the opinions and attitudes of others that we are able to interact effectively with them.

This should not be taken to mean that compliance and conformity are always good; it does mean, however, that they are not always bad, in the same way as stereotypes aren't always totally wrong and useless.

Obedience

Let's say your superior orders you to do something nasty like hurt some innocent person: How likely are you to rear up on you hind legs and say, "Nope, I can't do that"? Or will you just go ahead and do as you are told?

The Milgram Studies

Milgram (1963, 1965), in a remarkable series of controversial experiments, provides an answer. In these studies, subjects were duped into believing that they were confederates of an experimenter studying the effects of punishment on learning. An alleged subject (actually a confederate, termed a *stooge* in this experiment) was to be presented with a series of learning tasks while attached to electrodes so that he could be shocked whenever he made an error. The real subjects' task was to depress the switch that would deliver the shock. Subjects were first connected to the electrodes and administered a mild shock so that they would have no reason to think that the shocks would not be real. They were then seated in front of an instrument panel containing a series of switches labeled from 15 to 450 volts, in 15-volt increments. Verbal descriptions above the switches ranged from "Slight shock" to "Danger: severe shock" at 390 volts and "XXX" at 435 volts.

In the first Milgram (1963) experiment, "victims" (stooges who did not actually receive any shocks) were placed in a separate room and were instructed to make a predetermined number of errors. The subjects, who controlled the switches, were instructed to administer a shock for every error the victim made, beginning with the first switch and progressing as high as necessary, in one-step increments. If a subject hesitated or indicated any unwillingness to continue, the experimenter would employ a predetermined verbal "prod"; that prod failing, a second would be employed, then a third, and finally a fourth. In all cases, the prods were given in sequence:

> **Prod 1.** *Please continue,* **or** *please go on.*
>
> **Prod 2.** *The experiment requires that you continue.*
>
> **Prod 3.** *It is absolutely essential that you continue.*
>
> **Prod 4.** *You have no other choice. You must go on.* **(p. 374)**

Amazingly, none of the subjects categorically refused to obey from the outset. In fact, of the 40 original subjects, 26 obeyed the experimenter's instructions right to the very end ("victims" committed sufficient errors to ensure that subjects would have an opportunity to administer the most severe shock—450 volts). The remaining 14 all obeyed until at least the 300-volt level (Figure 10.4).

In related studies, Milgram (1965) looked at the effect of the distance between subject and victim using four different experimental conditions. In one, the subject could see, hear, and touch the victim, since both were in the same room. In a second, the subject could hear and see the stooge, but could not touch him. In a third condition, the subject could hear the stooge, but not see him, a curtain having been drawn between the two. In a final experimental condition, the subject could neither see nor hear the victim.

Again, subjects complied with the experimenter's requests. But now, average intensity of shocks increased in direct proportion with the distance between the subject and the victim, with the highest shocks being administered when the subject could not see or hear the victim.

One finding that is sometimes overlooked when reporting the more sensational results of the Milgram obedience studies is that most subjects, whether or not they obeyed, were disturbed by the procedure. Milgram (1963) writes:

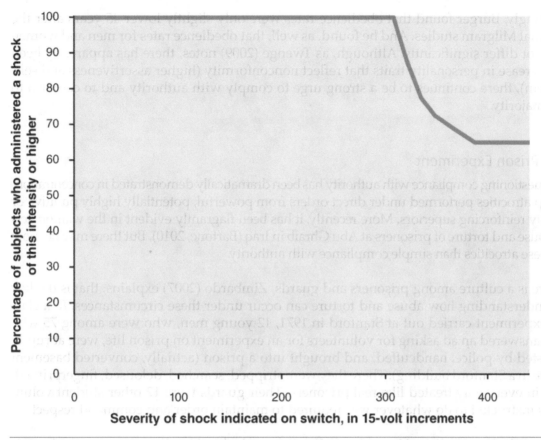

Figure 10.4

All subjects in the Milgram study "obeyed" and administered shocks beginning at 15 volts and going to at least 300 volts. The next switch was labeled "extreme intensity shock." Five of 40 subjects refused to go any further; 26 went all the way to 450 volts.

> *In a large number of cases the degree of tension reached extremes that are rarely seen in socio-psychological laboratory studies. Subjects were observed to sweat, tremble, stutter, bite their lips, groan, and dig their fingernails into their flesh. These were characteristic rather than exceptional responses to the experiment. . . . On one occasion we observed a seizure so violently convulsive that it was necessary to call a halt to the experiment. (p. 375)*

Studies such as these are disturbing for a number of reasons. They reveal aggressive aspects of humanity that many would prefer not to admit; they underline the power of authority and compliance in contrast to individual choice and freedom; and they present some serious moral issues with respect to deceiving subjects into engaging in behaviors that potentially are psychologically damaging.

Given the fact that psychological investigations now typically require approval by an ethics committee and strict adherence to ethical guidelines, the Milgram studies have not often been replicated. However, Burger (2009) did replicate these studies with one significant variation: When subjects reached the level of 150 volts (the point at which the "stooge" has been instructed to moan and protest), the experiment was discontinued.

Strikingly, Burger found that obedience rates were only slightly lower 45 years after the original Milgram studies. And he found, as well, that obedience rates for men and women did not differ significantly. Although, as Twenge (2009) notes, there has apparently been an increase in personality traits that reflect nonconformity (higher assertiveness and self-esteem), there continues to be a strong urge to comply with authority and to conform to the majority.

The Prison Experiment

Unquestioning compliance with authority has been dramatically demonstrated in concentration-camp atrocities performed under direct orders from powerful, potentially highly punitive or highly reinforcing superiors. More recently, it has been flagrantly evident in the wanton acts of abuse and torture of prisoners at Abu Ghraib in Iraq (Bartone, 2010). But there may be more to these atrocities than simple compliance with authority.

There is a culture among prisoners and guards, Zimbardo (2007) explains, that is the key to understanding how abuse and torture can occur under these circumstances. In a classic experiment carried out at Stanford in 1971, 12 young men, who were among 75 who had answered an ad asking for volunteers for an experiment on prison life, were abruptly arrested by police, handcuffed, and brought into a prison (actually, converted basement space in a Stanford building). There they were stripped, searched, deloused, fingerprinted, and in every way treated like real prisoners. Their guards were 12 other student volunteers instructed to do whatever was required to maintain order and command respect.

The results are sobering: Almost immediately, guards developed coercive, aggressive tactics, humiliating and dehumanizing prisoners. They forced them to do things like clean out toilet bowls with their bare hands, count aloud to reinforce their new numerical identities, and do protracted physical exercise as "punishment" when they made errors. The consequences were sufficiently severe that 5 of the 12 prisoners had to be "released" before the experiment ended—and this in spite of the fact that the prisoners staged a "revolt" on the second day of the experiment. The experiment was slated to run for 14 days, but it was abruptly terminated on the 6th day when one of the more than 50 outsiders who had seen the prison was shocked at what she saw and raised objections about the ethics of the experiment (Zimbardo, 2007).

The Stanford prison experiment suggests that we quickly and easily adopt roles even when they run counter to our values. And the Milgram obedience studies underscore our willingness to obey those in authority. What happened in Abu Ghraib, pictured here, may reflect both obedience and role conformity.

The effects of the Stanford prison experiment were far greater than anticipated. Both the prisoners and the guards carried their roles to an unforeseen extreme. Fully a third of the guards exhibited what Zimbardo describes as genuinely sadistic tendencies. What the study illustrates, explains Zimbardo, is the power of institutions and of institutionalized roles—dramatically illustrated once more in Abu Ghraib. In contrast, the Milgram experiments were more about the power of individual authority.

The entire Stanford prison study was photographed and filmed and is available online (Stanford Prison Experiment, 2011).

Persuasion

Social influence is a powerful and pervasive force. We know that people are influenced by norms expressed in the behaviors and attitudes of others and that they respond to authority and to the roles they're called on to play. Research and common sense also suggest that there are many subtle forms of social influence to which we are responsive. **Persuasion** is a global term for some of these influences. It refers to deliberate, usually verbal, attempts to alter beliefs or behavior. Television commercials, religious and political propaganda, newspaper and magazine advertising, and political campaigning all represent attempts at persuasion.

The most powerful forms of persuasion are those that succeed in changing attitudes rather than simply behavior. Attitudes may change as a result of events within the person, a process that is typically slow, although it may result from rational decisions and occur very rapidly. Attitudes may also change as a result of external events that are accidental rather than deliberately persuasive. Thus, an individual who is rescued from death by a member of a minority group toward which he has held highly negative attitudes may quite suddenly develop positive attitudes toward the group. Finally, attitudes may change as a result of persuasion.

Three characteristics of persuasion are important in determining its effectiveness: the nature of the message, its source, and some of the characteristics of the person being persuaded.

Importance of Message Characteristics

That the nature of the message is important is evident in the observation that it is much easier to persuade someone of something that fits in with previous beliefs or with the individual's goals and wishes. By the same token, it is difficult to change attitudes when the message runs counter to strongly entrenched prejudices and stereotypes.

Importance of Message Source

Belief in the importance of the *source* of persuasion is evident in the advertising media's use of powerful models in their attempts to persuade. Research in social psychology suggests that the belief is warranted. Persuasion that comes from a source marked by qualities such as expertise, liking, and high trust is most effective (Feng & MacGeorge, 2010). Similarly, people are more easily persuaded by opinions that are apparently shared by many, rather than by few. Horcajo, Petty, and Brinol (2010) presented subjects with strong or weak persuasive arguments, ascribing these either to a "majority" or to a "minority." Not surprisingly, whether they are strong or weak arguments, those attributed to a majority source are more persuasive than those thought to come from a minority.

Motives that might be attributed to the persuader also play an important role (Ranganath, Spellman, & Joy-Gaba, 2010). When persuaders are arguing in their own best interests,

The most powerful forms of persuasion are those that succeed in changing attitudes. That this will then result in a change in behavior is the hope of all politicians as they, like this man, try to persuade us.

the persuasion may not be nearly as effective as when the argument is opposed to the persuader's self-interest. When petroleum-linked interests suggest that no, water and air contamination are not increasing as a result of oilfield activity, you are unlikely to believe them. The same argument presented by a radical "green" group is much more convincing.

Importance of Audience Characteristics

Finally, certain characteristics of the person being persuaded, such as intelligence and independence, are also important. In one study, Cacioppo, Petty, Kao, and Rodriguez (1986) had participants read either a high-quality or a low-quality essay relating to why a university should institute comprehensive examinations. The more intelligent subjects were more convinced by the high-quality essay. In contrast, other subjects seemed less sensitive to the quality of the argument and were as easily convinced by the low-quality as by the high-quality essay.

Note that in spite of these studies, attitudes are, by definition, pervasive predispositions to respond in given ways; as such, they resist change. So, although it may be relatively simple for a skilled social psychologist to persuade individuals to vote for her, she may experience considerably more difficulty in getting them to love members of minority groups against whom they have highly negative prejudices. Persuasion is not likely to be at all effective in such endeavors, but prolonged face-to-face contact in a cooperative situation might be. Then again, it might not. When considering the power of social influence, our tendency to conform, comply, and obey, and our susceptibility to persuasion, it would be dangerous to assume that we are all highly plastic, spineless, malleable, nonopinionated, compliant, and obedient. Some are; others, not so much.

Cognitive Dissonance

Another source of attitude change, as we saw in Chapter 6, is **cognitive dissonance**. Cognitive dissonance describes a situation where there is conflict between behavior, beliefs, or attitudes. The dissonance model predicts that people will change their attitudes to conform to their behaviors when there is a conflict between the two, but only when there is insufficient justification for the behavior and when the behavior has been engaged in willingly. Thus, in dissonance experiments, subjects who are paid significant amounts for dissonant behavior, or who are forced to comply, show little attitude change later.

In studies where threats are used to force subjects to engage in dissonant behavior, cognitive dissonance theory makes an interesting prediction: Those who are exposed to the most severe threats for engaging—or not engaging—in some dissonance-inducing behavior will experience the least amount of dissonance. They would be expected to change their attitudes—and their behaviors—less than those exposed to milder threats.

To study this prediction, Wan and Chiou (2010) selected 218 college students identified as having a strong inclination toward online gaming addiction. They had these students play a new and highly engaging online game and then asked them, individually, to convince a younger adolescent that the game was not fun. They were instructed to continue until they had succeeded in convincing the "subject." In the "severe threat" manipulation, subjects were told that if they were unsuccessful in convincing the adolescent to agree with them, their parents would be informed of their addiction inclination. In the "mild threat" manipulation, subjects were told that their academic advisors would be notified if they gave up the persuasion task before completing it.

As expected, subjects in the severe threat condition were far less likely to have changed their positive attitudes toward the online game. Because of the severity of the threat, their dissonant behavior was amply justified. In contrast, those exposed to mild threats would be expected to experience more dissonance because their behavior would not be so easily justified. As predicted, they were more likely to change their attitudes.

The implication is that if you resort to severe threats to coerce someone to do or not do something, you are less likely to get them to change their attitudes and subsequent behavior than if you can bring about the same behavior with less coercion—whether it be a reward or the threat of punishment.

Attribution and Attitude Change

As we saw in Chapter 6, our **attributions** for our behaviors and feelings and for those of others (the reasons we ascribe to them) provide one explanation for attitude change in dissonance situations. In a sense, we are like naive scientists observing our own behavior, the behavior of others, and the circumstances surrounding behavior. And as we observe, we make inferences about ourselves and others, attributing causes to the behaviors we observe. In some cases our attributions are **dispositional attributions** (they involve characteristics of the actor); in others they are **situational attributions** (they involve characteristics of the situation); and perhaps in many cases we arrive at mixed attributions.

An attribution-based explanation of attitude change following dissonant behavior may be worded as follows: If I willingly do A without compulsion or reward and am then asked to express my attitudes about doing A, I will most likely attribute my behavior to the fact that I believe that doing A is right, good, and consistent with my attitudes. If, however, I am compelled to do A against my inclinations, I can attribute my behavior to causes within myself or to the situation. If the situation justifies my behavior (the reward is sufficient or the threat is compelling enough), I will likely invoke a situational attribution and I won't change my attitude. If the situation doesn't justify my behavior, I need to attribute it to a personal characteristic (a disposition). The result is that I may change my attitude toward the activity.

Overjustification

Attribution theories of attitude change in situations of forced compliance (dissonance-creating situations) maintain that when there is low justification for engaging in dissonant behavior, subjects infer that they did so because they wanted to. In contrast, when there is high justification, they attribute their behavior to external circumstances (compulsion or reward, for example).

Lepper and Greene (1975, 1978) and others have also investigated the effects of justification on *consonant* behavior. These authors have proposed an **overjustification** hypothesis which says, in effect, that large external rewards for behavior that is initially intrinsically motivated may undermine our attitudes toward the behavior. For example, if you sing songs because you like singing (intrinsic motivation: positive attitudes toward singing), and later some misguided individual promises you too high a reward for singing, you might in the end come to like singing much less.

How does this hypothesis follow from attribution theory? Bright and Penrod (2009) describe the process as follows: Given our tendency to attribute our behaviors to intrinsic or extrinsic factors, following a behavior for which external justification is very salient (a behavior that is externally *overjustified*), we are likely to attribute that behavior more to external causes than to internal causes. Having done so, we modify our attitudes (internal causes of behavior) and become less positively disposed toward the behavior.

This analysis might seem to contradict common sense. We have long assumed that people like to do things that are highly rewarded, and have perhaps naively assumed that if we increase rewards associated with a behavior, positive attitudes toward that behavior should also increase. But research on the overjustification hypothesis indicates that these beliefs are wrong at least some of the time.

10.3 Antisocial Behaviors

And how do we justify our antisocial behaviors—behaviors like aggression and violence and unbridled competitiveness and apathy in the face of human suffering? Do external rewards serve to *justify* and explain these behaviors? Or is there something in our dispositions that explains them?

Aggression and Violence

A popular stereotype of North American males is that of assertive, intrusive, domineering individuals bent on achieving their goals even at the expense of others. This view is based on the observation that **aggression**, defined as an action deliberately intended to do harm or undertaken with no consideration for the harm it might cause others, is basic to organized competitive sports such as football and hockey, is a key to success in the business and academic worlds, is one of the main themes of the entertainment media, and is characteristic of much human interaction.

Theories of Aggression

It is important to note at the outset that strong assertiveness and competitiveness are not instances of aggression when they are not intended to inflict harm on others; nor are they undesirable in all circumstances. While aggression may involve violence—actual physical

Figure 10.5

An aggression continuum. Social psychology defines aggression as actions intended to harm others or to achieve one's goals without consideration of others. Thus, in a strict sense, assertive, competitive, intrusive, domineering, and even violent behaviors (such as might be evident in sports) are not examples of aggression unless they are intended to do harm. Terrorism, a form of violence perpetrated against civilian groups, is an extreme form of aggression. Rolling pins can be too.

damage to persons or property—it might also be entirely *passive*—as when Iseult, in the opening tale of Tristan and Isolde, tells Tristan the fatal lie: The sails are black (Figure 10.5).

Frustration-Aggression   A number of beliefs have dominated social psychology's attempts to understand and explain aggression. Among them is Dollard and Miller's **frustration-aggression hypothesis**—the contention that aggression is the result of anger and the most important cause of anger is **frustration** (Dollard, Miller, Doob, Mowrer, & Sears, 1939) . To be frustrated is to be prevented from reaching a goal. The Dollard and Miller hypothesis argues that, following frustration, anger is experienced; but anger will result in aggression only if a suitable object or person releases the aggression (Figure 10.6).

This explanation of aggression has often been used to explain terrorism. The assumption is that terrorism, an extreme form of aggression, may be linked to the frustration that accompanies poverty, lack of opportunity, and repression (for example, Zinchenko, 2009). In support of the frustration-aggression hypothesis, Fischer, Greitemeyer, and Frey (2008) report that higher unemployment is associated with higher measured aggressiveness.

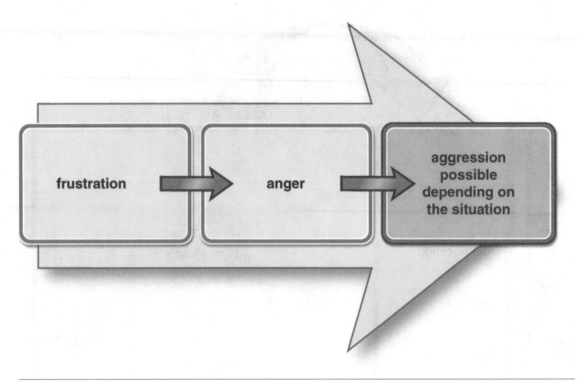

Figure 10.6

The Dollard and Miller frustration-aggression hypothesis. According to this model, frustration leads to different degrees of anger, ranging from mild irritation to blind fury. Whether it also leads to aggressive behavior depends on the situation as well as on the depth of the emotion.

Territoriality   Another explanation, attributed to **ethologists**, is based on the assumption that we are by nature aggressive. This explanation relies heavily on observations of aggression among nonhuman animals. It assumes that since aggression appears to be common among other animals, it must have a biological basis.

According to this theory, certain stimuli in the environment serve as releasers for aggression. In some cases, the stimuli are highly specific and have clear survival or reproductive significance, as when bighorn sheep fight for the right to mate. In other cases, the stimuli are less specific, as in the case of **territoriality**. For example, male chimpanzees patrol defined geographic areas, intent on aggressively repelling any encroachment by males from other communities. Those who violate their boundaries risk death (Amsler, 2010). The survival value of many aggressive behaviors in nonhuman animals and their frequent instinct like specificity (that is, the fact that aggression usually occurs only in response to specific conditions) provide strong evidence that aggression in animals is at least partly genetically based.

The situation with humans is not as clear. Although there is a possibility that we have (or had) instinctual tendencies toward aggressiveness, perhaps predicated on territoriality, learning and environment affect so much of our behavior that "instinctual" tendencies are difficult to isolate. Some argue that many wars—such as the Palestinian conflict—reflect territoriality (Fields, 2010). Others suggest that gang conflict might also be associated with territoriality (Deuchar & Holligan, 2010).

Still, the fact is that there are human societies where aggressive behavior is at an extreme minimum (the Zuni, the Hutterites, and the Amish, for example); and there are others where it is at the opposite extreme (the Ik of Uganda; the Mundugumor of New Guinea; the Yanomamo of the Amazon). Although the existence of peace-loving societies does not prove that we have no genetic tendencies toward aggression, it does indicate that environmental and social factors are important.

Social Learning   Social learning theory (see Chapter 4), a widely supported theory, argues that aggressive behavior is often learned as a result of observing aggressive models.

In a classic study that looked at the effects of aggressive models on children, Bandura, Ross, and Ross (1961) exposed 3- to 6-year-old children to one of three experimental conditions. One group saw an adult being physically and verbally aggressive with a large, inflated "Bobo" doll (punching it, striking it with a mallet, kicking it, sitting on it, while making aggressive comments like "sock him in the nose. . . ," "throw him in the air. . . ," "knock him down"). A second group watched as the experimenter totally ignored the doll. And a control group saw the Bobo doll only in the testing part of the study, during which the children were observed as they interacted with the doll or played with other toys.

The results of this study clearly illustrate the effect of aggressive models. When left alone with the doll, children exposed to the aggressive model were significantly more aggressive than children exposed to nonaggressive models. And often, their aggression was precisely imitative: If the model punched the doll, that is what they did; if the model kicked the doll instead, then that, too, is what they did. And, strikingly, those exposed to nonaggressive models engaged in far less aggressive behavior than those not exposed to any models at all (Figure 10.7).

This study provides strong support for a social learning theory of aggression. And, in fact, many predictions based on social learning theory have been supported by research. For example, we would expect that children who observe violence and aggression would themselves be more aggressive. In fact, that is often the case: Children who witness parental violence and abuse are more likely to be aggressive as adolescents (Ferguson, Miguel, & Hartley, 2009). And there is evidence, as well, that violence in children's television programs tends to increase aggression among viewers (Linder & Gentile, 2009; Strasburger, 2009).

Physiology   We know that aggression, like all emotions, also has a physiological basis. For example, it appears that aggression may be associated with hormones (injections of testosterone increase aggressiveness in monkeys); with olfaction (certain strains of mice respond aggressively to other mice who've been smeared with urine from mice that would ordinarily be aggressed upon); with brain damage or dysfunction or with stimulation of appropriate areas of the thalamus (rage can be produced in cats as a result of electrical stimulation); and with certain drugs (alcohol disinhibits aggression and is involved in a large number of violent crimes).

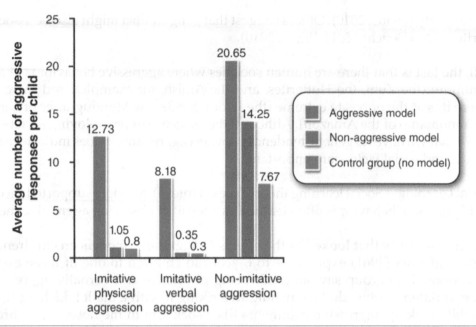

Figure 10.7

In the Bandura, Ross, and Ross (1961) study, children exposed to violent models consistently behaved more aggressively with the Bobo doll.

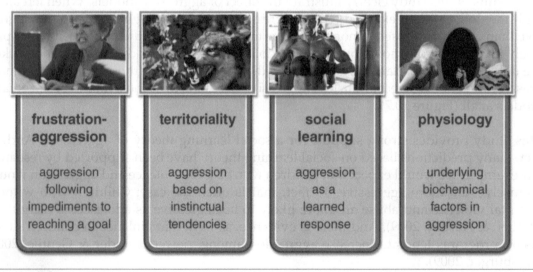

Figure 10.8

Four explanations for aggression. These aren't mutually exclusive. Aggression is often a function of several underlying factors.

Research suggests that at least five neurotransmitters and two hormones, the most important of which is testosterone, may be implicated in serious violent crimes (Beaver, 2010). But the fact that aggression has a physiological basis is not an adequate explanation for aggressive behavior because all aspects of human behavior have physiological bases. Nevertheless, knowledge of the physiological underpinnings of aggression, and of how these interact

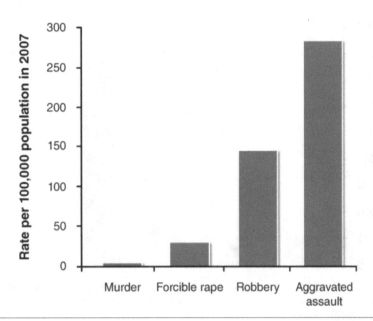

Figure 10.9

Number of violent crimes per 100,000 population in the United States in 2007. U.S. Census Bureau (2010c). *Statistical Abstract, Table 295.*

with the environment to produce aggression and violence, may prove useful in controlling extremes of violence (using psychosurgery and drugs, for example). (See Figure 10.8.)

Violence in Society

The most obvious instances of aggression in society are those involving overt acts of violence: rape, homicide, assault, and destruction of property. Interpersonal violence, which includes the first three of these, is committed primarily by males. The extent to which these acts can be attributed to frustration, deprivation, pain, or sex-related factors, and the extent to which character and personality disorders or other factors are involved, is not clear. There is little doubt, however, that each can play a significant role.

The incidence of violent crimes in Western industrialized societies appears to have declined somewhat during the last decades. Still, the incidence of violence is high, with a total of 467 violent crimes per 100,000 U.S. population in 2007 (U.S. Census Bureau, 2010c; Figure 10.9).

Violence in society is reflected not only in crime, but in international aggression as well. In the last century alone, well over half of all nations have been involved in war. Many still are. And while nations fight, so do individuals within families. Violence in the home is not always obvious. Child abuse presents one inexact index; the fact that 25 percent or more of all homicides and assaults involve members of the same family provides a second index. In fact, violence among intimate partners, surely a prime source of aggressive models for children, is alarmingly high: 260 acts of rape, robbery, assault, and homicide per 100,000 population in 2007, with almost 90 percent of these acts carried out against women (Figure 10.10). That year, 1,185 women and 346 men in the United States were killed by their

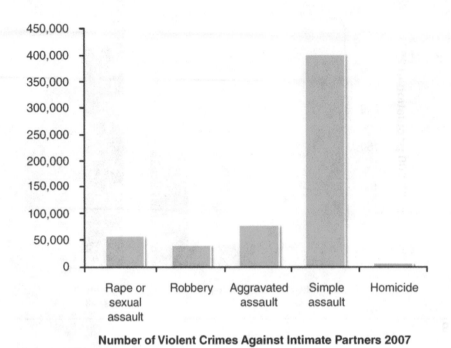

Figure 10.10

Number of violent crimes committed against intimate partners in the United States in 2007. U.S. Census Bureau (2010). *Statistical Abstract, Table 307.*

partners; over half a million women and nearly as many men were victims of reported physical assault (U.S. Census Bureau, 2010c).

Bystander Apathy

In the Monty Python movie *The Life of Brian*, Brian unintentionally inspires a group of rabid followers who think he is a messiah and who devotedly follow him around, convinced that every little thing that happens around him is a miracle. Increasingly frantic to be rid of this mob, he yells at them, "Look. You've got it all wrong. You don't need to follow me. You don't need to follow anybody! You've got to think for yourselves. You're all individuals!"

"Yes, we are all individuals!" they respond in chorus.

"You're all different," says Brian.

"Yes, we are all different!" they respond. Except for one small voice from somewhere in the crowd. "I'm not," it says.

"Shh! Shhhh! Shhh!" Brian's followers respond.

Just another movie? Or an accurate reflection of mob psychology and the effects of social pressure? How much of what we think and do is determined by the groups of which we are part?

The classic relevant case in social psychology literature is the story of Kitty Genovese, who was brutally attacked as she returned home from work at 3 o'clock one morning (Latané & Darley, 1968). What made her story remarkable was that 38 of her neighbors in Kew Gardens in New York supposedly came to their windows when she cried out in terror; none came to her assistance, even though her stalker took over half an hour to murder her, even leaving once and returning later to continue his attack. Initial reports are that no one even so much as called the police. She died.

The Bystander Effect

This episode has been widely reported and has served as the basis for the conclusion that being part of a large group witnessing an act that requires intervention often serves to inhibit helping behavior. And although this appears to be true under some circumstances, unfortunately the Kitty Genovese case has often been exaggerated. Later investigation uncovered that there were considerably fewer than 38 eyewitnesses to the murder (some only heard the attack), that Kitty Genovese had been involved in loud altercations on other occasions, and that one witness did, in fact, call the police (Manning, Levine, & Collins, 2007).

Still, there are other examples of what social psychologists call the **bystander effect**. Most of us would prefer to believe that the more people who witness an event where someone desperately needs assistance, the more likely it is that one of them will help. Sadly, it appears that we are a lot like the mob in *The Life of Brian*: In some circumstances, the more witnesses there are, the less likely it is that someone will intervene.

Latané and Darley (1970) conducted a series of experiments investigating the alleged apathy of bystanders. In one series of studies, subjects alone in a room overhear an epileptic seizure apparently suffered by another "subject" (in fact, a tape-recorded "seizure"). Experimental conditions are such that subjects either think they're the only ones listening to the person having a seizure, or they believe that there are other witnesses in different rooms. The dependent variable is whether or not the subject reports the seizure or otherwise tries to assist, and how long it takes before helping behavior occurs.

As Figure 10.11 shows, all subjects who thought they were alone with the victim responded; in contrast, when subjects thought there were four others besides the victim, only 62 percent responded.

In another experiment, subjects were left in a room supposedly to wait for an interviewer (Latané & Darley, 1968). They were asked to fill out a questionnaire while waiting. Shortly thereafter, artificial smoke was blown into the room through a wall vent, continuing in irregular gusts, eventually filling the room, irritating the eyes, and making breathing difficult. If subjects had not reported the smoke after 6 minutes, the experiment was discontinued and subjects were debriefed. In one experimental condition, subjects waited alone; in another, they waited with two other subjects; and in a third, they were paired with two experimenter's confederates who had been instructed not to react to the smoke but to continue to fill out their questionnaires.

The results of these experiments are as expected: Subjects alone reported the smoke 75 percent of the time; subjects paired with two other subjects reported it only 38 percent of

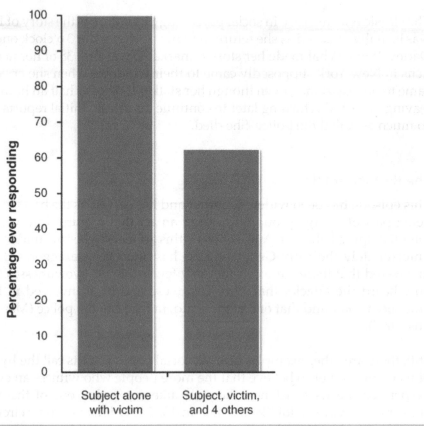

Figure 10.11

Effect of group size on the likelihood of responding in an emergency. Based on Latané & Darley (1970).

the time and took longer before doing so. Most striking, only 1 of 10 subjects paired with passive assistants reported the smoke (Figure 10.12).

An Explanation

These studies indicate that individuals who have reason to believe themselves the only witnesses and hence the only immediate sources of intervention are more likely to involve themselves, either by reporting a potentially dangerous situation or by offering direct assistance. But when there are a number of apparent witnesses, people are more reluctant to become involved. However, this doesn't necessarily mean that witnesses remain apathetic. In fact, there is considerable evidence that they do care. Subjects who did not report the "epileptic seizure" were often visibly shaken, their hands trembling, their faces pale and drawn.

A number of factors may be responsible for the greater reluctance of people to become involved when others could also be involved. They may not see themselves as the most competent; perhaps they simply assume that someone else has already intervened;

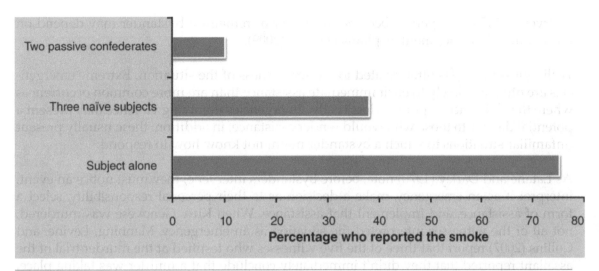

Figure 10.12

Effect of group membership in emergency situations. In the Latané and Darley (1968) study, only 1 out of 10 subjects reported the smoke when paired with two unalarmed confederates. Seventy-five percent reported it when left alone.

perhaps, too, there is a fear of making a wrong judgment and of appearing foolish.

Darley and Latané (1968) attribute the bystander effect to one of three sources (or a combination of these): a process of diffusion of responsibility, where the presence of others reduces the cost of nonintervention; a process of social influence, where the nonintervention of others leads the subject to misinterpret the seriousness of the situation; and a process of audience inhibition, where the presence of others brings about fear of making a wrong decision and acting unwisely.

How Common Is the Bystander Effect?

It is perhaps reassuring that many recent studies have not found a bystander effect, or have found a considerably less dramatic one than might have been expected. For example, McMahon and Farmer (2009) found that a majority of student athletes would be willing to intervene in a case involving sexual violence. Reluctance to do so was often related to lack of skills required to

Bystanders often ignore the plights of those who need help, especially if there are others around and if the cost of intervention is potentially high. Reassuringly, there are those, like this man, who gladly help.

intervene. Whether a person becomes a rescuer or remains a bystander may depend on level of moral development, explains DeZalia (2009).

Willingness to help is often related to the seriousness of the situation. Extreme emergencies are often less likely to elicit immediate assistance than are more common occurrences where the assistance required is less costly. Emergencies involving violence may present a potential danger to those who would render assistance; in addition, these usually present unfamiliar situations to which a bystander might not know how to respond.

As Latané and Darley (1970) note, before bystanders intervene, they must notice an event, interpret it as an emergency, make a decision as to their personal responsibility, select a form of assistance, and implement that assistance. When Kitty Genovese was murdered, not all of the witnesses interpreted the situation as an emergency. Manning, Levine, and Collins (2007) report that three of the five witnesses who testified at the murder trial of the assailant reported that they didn't immediately conclude that a murder was taking place. And none of the court witnesses actually saw the stabbing. Nor is it likely that all who saw the situation as an emergency would then decide to take personal responsibility for bringing assistance—but one actually shouted and apparently frightened the attacker away, although he returned later. Others might have thought that someone else must have called the police—and apparently someone had! In the end, the incident, shocking though it might be given our implicit beliefs in the goodness of human nature, is not entirely surprising.

Choosing a form of assistance, other than calling on someone else (the police) for assistance, also presents a real problem. The man who was killing Kitty Genovese might not have hesitated to attack anyone else who might try to come to her assistance directly.

In summary, the Kitty Genovese case presents an extreme in which the possibility of intervening and the desirability of doing so are difficult and costly. It is not surprising that the likelihood of intervention is lessened by the presence of others who might also intervene. In fact, it would be unintelligent to react without taking into account how other people are reacting. That, in a nutshell, is fundamental to understanding the nature of social influence.

10.4 Prosocial Behaviors

The influence of bystanders is not always apparent only in apathy and nonintervention: There is considerable evidence that real or imagined bystanders can have a powerful effect on prosocial behaviors like helping and giving. For example, Potter, Moynihan, Stapleton, and Banyard (2009) found that exposing students to models engaging in prosocial behavior—in this case, having to do with intervening in cases of sexual violence—increased the likelihood that the students would later try to help if they witnessed similar episodes.

Altruism

The apathy and nonintervention sometimes characteristic of situations in which a number of bystanders are involved are directly opposite to **altruistic behaviors** (self-sacrificing, helpful behaviors).

Altruism is not uncommon among animal species. When a honeybee stings an intruder, it sacrifices its life for the hive—as might, also, a bird that noisily signals an approaching hawk. While these behaviors might seem contrary to the basic biological law of *survival of the fittest*, they really aren't. That's because this law applies not to individuals but to species—or, more specifically, to the genetic material that defines a species. This form of self-sacrificing altruism among animals actually increases the likelihood of survival of the species' genetic material. The death of a single individual is a small price to pay for the survival of a swarm or a flock.

Altruism among animals has led to a *sociobiological* theory of altruism championed by Richard Dawkins (1976/2006). According to this theory, altruism is nothing more than *genetic selfishness*. Genes, Dawkins explains, can be thought of as having a selfish desire to become immortal through reproduction and survival. As a result, they push organisms toward behaviors designed to ensure the survival of the genetic material of that species—though not necessarily of the individual that carries the genes. Thus, if an altruistic act increases the probability of reproduction of genes carried by the species, the survival needs of the species have been served. So a man might take a risk in trying to save another if there is a chance that *both* will survive; but there would be no net genetic advantage to being altruistic if one or the other will surely die.

Biology clearly doesn't explain all altruism. Nor does it explain the fact that some people willingly help those in distress while others don't. In addition to this **biological altruism**, there is what is labeled **reciprocal altruism**, in which an individual behaves altruistically with the expectation that others will reciprocate. For example, a monkey will willingly pick parasites off another's back—on the surface, a selfless, altruistic act. But later, the parasite-picking monkey will turn its back and expect the other to reciprocate.

We are sometimes a little like monkeys, social psychologists inform us: We sacrifice and do good things for others in the expectation that we might one day need them to reciprocate. Some donate blood at least partly for that reason. Also, as Buchanan and Bardi (2010) show, we are sometimes altruistic because it makes us feel good—in which case, our altruism is not entirely selfless. They had participants perform altruistic acts (acts of kindness) at random over a 10-day period. Measures taken before and after this period indicated that their life-satisfaction scores had improved significantly during this period.

Studies of altruism indicate that our altruistic behavior often depends on how altruistic we think other people are (Ellers & van der Pool, 2010). We are more likely to be altruistic if we think others are, or would be, under the same circumstances—a sort of positive bystander effect. These studies also reveal that altruism is often related to the status of the actor, with higher-status individuals engaging in more altruistic behaviors (Liebe & Tutic, 2010).

10.5 Interpersonal Relationships

Altruism, by definition, goes beyond simple acts of warmth and kindness: It implies behavior where there is significant disadvantage to the doer and clear potential advantage to the receiver.

Many of our positive social behaviors, kind and selfless as they might seem, are not altruistic: They present us with no significant disadvantage. In fact, much of our behavior is governed by a desire to establish and maintain close relationships with others. Sometimes we are nice just because we want other people to like us: We are attracted to them and we want them to be attracted to us.

The Rules of Attraction

Interpersonal attraction, social psychologists tell us, seems to be strongly influenced by three things: proximity, similarity, and physical attraction.

Propinquity

Physical proximity (often referred to as **propinquity** in social psychology) is closely related to *similarity*. People in close proximity often attend the same churches, colleges, and clubs and go to the same beaches, bars, and bingos. These people are likely to be similar in a lot of important ways. And ties among individuals who live in close proximity tend to be more common and much stronger than among those more physically distant (Hipp & Perrin, 2009).

Similarity

Do opposites attract? Some early research speculated that people are attracted to each other on the basis of their differences. Submissive people might be attracted to dominant people. Each might fulfill certain needs the other has. But it is not as logical to assume that a highly aggressive individual will be attracted to a highly pacific individual; that an extrovert will naturally gravitate toward an introvert; that liberals and conservatives will love each other; that, to carry the argument to its illogical extreme, the more dissimilar two individuals are, the more they will love each other.

Research suggests that the opposite is more often true. Newcomb (1961) provided a house for 17 male university students so that he could study friendship patterns among them. Not surprisingly, roommates, regardless of similarity of interests and beliefs, tended to be attracted at the beginning. But as time passed and students got to know each other better, similarity gradually emerged as the most important factor in determining friendships.

A study of online attraction confirms these findings. Antheunis, Valkenburg, and Peter (2010) looked at interaction patterns and social attraction among 704 members of a social networking site very similar to Facebook, MySpace, and Friendster. They found that participants used three different strategies to reduce uncertainty about other members' attitudes, emotions, and behavior: *passive* strategies such as simply observing how the target person interacts with others; *active* strategies such as asking other people about the target person; and, most effective, *interactive* strategies where the two people interact directly. Interactive strategies often involve self-disclosure, which tends to elicit self-disclosure in the other person.

Results of this study indicate that in an online situation, knowing important things about the other person (reduction of uncertainty) is closely related to social attraction.

People who are similar in important ways tend to like each other more than those who are less similar. For this pair, the beads, the headband, and the dress are loud signals of similarity.

Furthermore, degree of attraction is closely related to how similar each person thinks the other is.

Physical Attractiveness

Physical attractiveness, too, is often an important variable. Walster, Aronson, Abrahams, and Rottman (1966) arranged for an elaborate "dating" experiment at the University of Minnesota involving 376 men and 376 women who were to attend a dance. Participants were unaware that the dance had been arranged for experimental purposes. They were simply told that they would be "computer matched" with a partner and were asked to fill out questionnaires for that purpose. Meanwhile, experimenters surreptitiously assigned them physical attractiveness ratings so as to divide them into three groups: ugly, average, and attractive. (In this age's more politically correct climate, it is unlikely that researchers would use the label *ugly* for those less physically attractive.)

Participants were then matched randomly except that no woman was matched with a shorter partner. Of the 376 pairs thus formed, all but 40 actually attended the dance. During the intermission, some 2 ½ hours after the start of the dance, subjects were asked to fill out an apparently anonymous questionnaire—which, of course, was not at all anonymous. It dealt with how much they liked their date, how attractive the date was, how comfortable the subject felt, how much the date seemed to like the subject, how similar the subject thought the date was in terms of attitudes and beliefs, how much effort each was putting into making sure that the other had a good time, and whether or not they were likely to date again. Actual frequency of subsequent dating was ascertained some 4 to 6 months later by contacting all subjects directly.

The most important finding from this study was that of all the measures employed (intelligence, self-acceptance, extroversion, and a number of other scores in student files based on standardized tests such as the MMPI), physical attractiveness was the only significant variable in determining degree of social attraction. More attractive males and females were much less attracted to those classified as "ugly" or "average." Although members of the least attractive group would , in general, date anybody, they too said they preferred those more attractive (Figure 10.13).

That physical attractiveness is perceived as exceptionally important in interpersonal attraction is underlined in a study by Toma and Hancock (2010), which found that online daters exaggerate their physical attractiveness in their self-descriptions. And the least attractive tend to exaggerate more than the more attractive.

Wilbur and Campbell (2010) presented female participants with descriptions of four prospective mates who varied in terms of physical attractiveness and ambition. They were asked to rate these men as potential short-term sexual partners, as casual dating

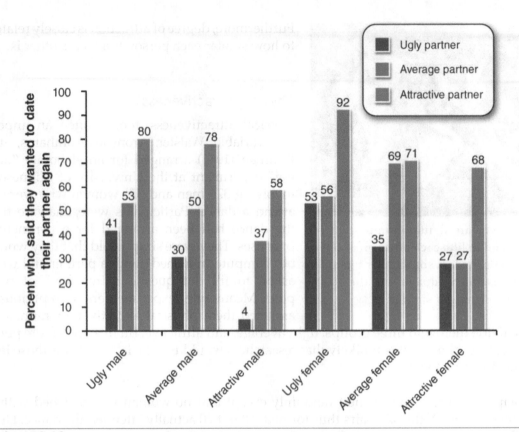

Figure 10.13

How important is physical attractiveness in dating behavior? Strikingly, the most attractive partners in a "random" dating study were those consistently more likely to be asked out again. (Data from E. Walster, V. Aronson, O. Abrahams, & L. Rottman. (1966). Importance of physical attractiveness in dating behavior. *Journal of Personality and Social Psychology, 4,* 508–516. Used by permission.)

partners, and as long-term romantic partners. In all cases, physical attraction determined the man's appeal; only for a long-term romantic relationship did degree of ambition also become a factor.

Liking and Loving

Freud (1914/1955) put it very simply: "[In] the last resort, we must begin to love in order not to fall ill, and we are bound to fall ill if, in consequence of frustration, we are unable to love" (p. 95).

How likely is it that we will fall ill if we cannot **love**? Science does not answer this question as confidently as have the poets. But then love was the province of the poet long before science claimed it. And even now, poets may know more about love than does science. Of the wonder and joy and all-consuming nature of love, the poets have had little doubt; about its practical value, they remain less certain. "True love," writes the poet Szymborska (1995), "Is it normal, is it serious, is it practical / What does the world get from two people who exist in a world of their own?" But we have little time for the poetry of love; here we deal only with its science.

Science provides us with ways of measuring, if not of completely understanding, love. For example, Rubin's (1970) Loving and Liking Scales provide a way of measuring interpersonal attraction. The scales are based on the assumption that those who like each other sense that they have things in common, evaluate each other positively, and appreciate each other's company. Items that indicate liking (but not loving) are items like *I think that _____ is unusually well adjusted*, or *I would highly recommend _____ for a responsible job.*

Loving implies deeper feelings, feelings of intense caring, strong attachment, and intimacy. Love brings with it a degree of emotional interdependence, a quality of exclusiveness and absorption. If you simply like someone, that person doesn't dominate your thoughts and your dreams; nor are you concerned that someone else might also like the same person. Love, on the other hand, often brings with it a measure of fierce possessiveness and the possibility of jealousy and pain—perhaps the possibility of ecstasy as well. Rubin (1970) measures love with items such as *I feel that I can confide in _____ about virtually everything* or *If I could never be with _____ , I would feel miserable.*

Physical attraction appears to be one of the most important factors at the beginning of a romantic relationship.

A Model of Love

Interpersonal attraction is no simple thing, Sternberg (1986) informs us. There are at least eight varieties of it: nonlove, romantic love, liking, fatuous love, infatuation, companionship, empty love, and consummate love. What differentiates these states from one another is the combination of **intimacy**, **passion**, and **commitment** involved in each. Accordingly, Sternberg has given us a **triangular theory of love**. But the triangle in this theory is not the classical male–male–female or female–female–male love triangle: It is the intimacy–passion–commitment triangle (Figure 10.14).

In this model, *intimacy* refers to emotions that bring people closer together—emotions such as respect, affection, and support. Feelings of intimacy are what lead two people to want to share things, perhaps to disclose personal, private experiences and feelings.

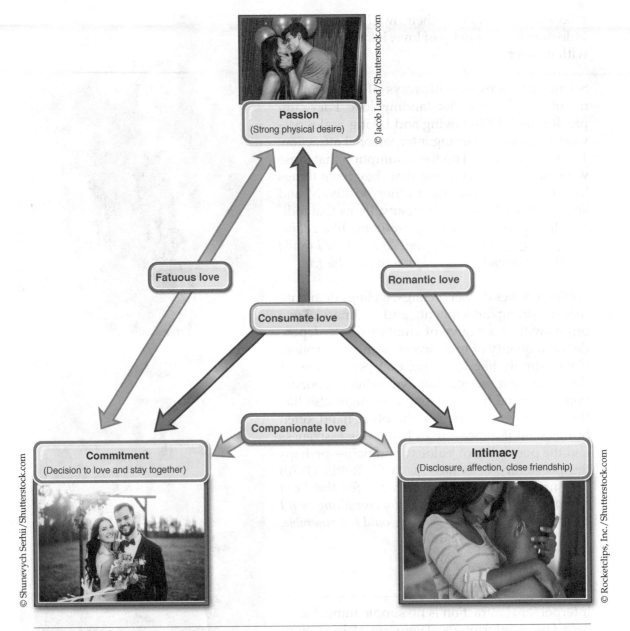

Figure 10.14

Sternberg's triangle of love. Different combinations of commitment, passion, and intimacy determine the nature of the love relationship.

Passion is a strong, sometimes almost overwhelming, desire to be with another person. Passion is often, although not always, sexual. Sternberg suggests that passion is a feeling that builds rapidly but then gradually subsides.

Commitment implies a decision-making process and may involve either a short-term or a long-term decision. On a short-term basis, commitment requires making the decision that one is in love. From a long-term point of view, commitment involves deciding to cultivate

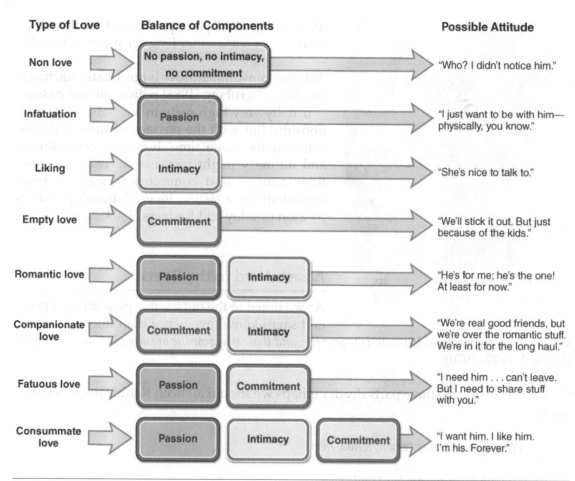

Type of Love	Balance of Components	Possible Attitude
Non love	No passion, no intimacy, no commitment	"Who? I didn't notice him."
Infatuation	Passion	"I just want to be with him—physically, you know."
Liking	Intimacy	"She's nice to talk to."
Empty love	Commitment	"We'll stick it out. But just because of the kids."
Romantic love	Passion Intimacy	"He's for me; he's the one! At least for now."
Companionate love	Commitment Intimacy	"We're real good friends, but we're over the romantic stuff. We're in it for the long haul."
Fatuous love	Passion Commitment	"I need him . . . can't leave. But I need to share stuff with you."
Consummate love	Passion Intimacy Commitment	"I want him. I like him. I'm his. Forever."

Figure 10.15

How can you tell whether you really are in love? One way is to analyze your relationship in terms of the Sternberg model, looking at the balance among passion (physical attraction and desire), intimacy (affection, mutual disclosure), and commitment (conscious decision to love, to share, to be together).

and maintain the loving relationship. In practice, this often implies a decision to share living arrangements and sometimes the raising of a family, either in marriage or otherwise.

Sternberg's (1986) theory of love holds that it is the particular combination of these three components—intimacy, passion, and commitment—that determines the nature of the relationship. As Figure 10.15 shows, for example, empty love involves commitment but is devoid of passion or of intimacy ("Okay, we'll stay together until the children are gone. Then adios!"). **Consummate love**, on the other hand, has all three components.

There is a pattern to the development of many relationships, Sternberg suggests. Two individuals might begin with nonlove—no passion, commitment, or intimacy. In time, nonlove might give way to infatuation, which has passion but no commitment or intimacy—or perhaps to romantic love, which now adds intimacy but is still short of commitment. Eventually, consummate love might evolve as commitment is brought into the

The ways of love, says Gibran, are hard and steep. Love carries no guarantees.

relationship. And perhaps the end result will be marriage or some other long-term commitment.

But even consummate love is not a static, unchanging thing. Sternberg (1986) points out that passion is usually very high early in a consummate relationship. But with the passage of time, it diminishes; at the same time, however, commitment and intimacy might increase. Research suggests that intimacy and commitment may be more important for a lasting love relationship than is passion (Madey and Rodgers, 2009).

A Last Word to the Poets

As we noted at the outset, it is possible that poets and sages know love better than does science. *To fear love*, wrote Bertrand Russell, *is to fear life, and those who fear life are already three parts dead* (Russell, 1929/1970).

So, if we are not to be three parts dead, perhaps we should all heed Kahlil Gibran's (1923) advice:

When love beckons to you, follow him,

Though his ways are hard and steep.

There is a good chance, if the philosophers and the poets are correct, that love will turn out to be the most important piece of the human puzzle.

Main Points

1. **Social Psychology:** The subject matter of social psychology deals with how thinking, feeling, and behavior are influenced by the real or imagined presence of others. It looks at how attitudes form, change, and influence behavior, and it looks at human interactions, including those that are antisocial, prosocial, friendly, and loving.
2. **Attitudes and Attitude Change:** Attitudes are emotion-laden beliefs with strong motivational components. They may be evident in stereotypes and personal opinions, and they often reflect the human tendency to conform to majority opinions. In spite of personal beliefs and opinions, there is a tendency to obey authority (the Milgram studies) and to assume socially expected roles (the Stanford prison experiment). Persuasion, cognitive dissonance, and attributions are powerful forces in attitude change.
3. **Antisocial Behaviors:** Aggression, defined as actions intended to cause harm, can range from assertive behavior to extreme violence, such as might be evident

in terrorism. It may be motivated by frustration, instinctual impulses (as in territoriality or possessiveness), the effects of observing aggression and violence in society (social learning), and biochemical factors (hormones, drugs, brain injury, or disease). Bystander apathy is another antisocial behavior.

4. **Prosocial Behaviors**: Altruism implies a behavior that has a definite cost for the giver but a clear advantage for the recipient. Among animals, it is often related to survival, mating, and protection of the young and of the tribe, flock, swarm, herd, or group. In sociobiological terms, it represents a sort of *genetic selfishness*.

5. **Interpersonal Relationships**: Interpersonal attraction is influenced by physical attraction, similarity, and proximity (the last two are closely related). Opposites don't attract; and physical attraction seems to be highly important in the early stages of establishing a relationship. Consummate love implies passion, intimacy, and commitment. Various other kinds of love are possible based on the balance that exists among these three factors.

Thoughts and Suggestions

What was the most interesting study that you read in this chapter? Why?

What are some example of group pressure that you personally see in your current surroundings? Could be in your neighborhood, school, class, or perhaps you see on social media or television and so on.

Can you think of a time you did something with a crowd of people that you later regretted, or became aware that what **you did was not really the "real you?"**

Suggested readings from Hock, R. R. (1999). *Forty studies that changed psychology* (3rd ed.). Upper Saddle River, NJ: Prentice Hall. (ISBN #: 0-13-922725-3):

- Reading 37: A Prison by Any Other Name
- Reading 38: The Power of Conformity
- Reading 39: To Help or Not to Help
- Reading 40: Obey at Any Cost

Study Terms

aggression

altruistic behaviors

attitude

attributions

biological altruism

bystander effect

cognitive dissonance

commitment

compliance

conformity

consummate love

dispositional attributions

ethologists

frustration

frustration-aggression hypothesis

interpersonal attraction

intimacy

love

opinions

overjustification

passion

persuasion

prejudices

propinquity

reciprocal altruism

situational attributions

social psychology

stereotypes

territoriality

triangular theory of love

Concluding Remarks

When first developing this book I had intended to write a concluding summary section. However, if you remember the preface of the book, I said that the students that use this book in the first year of publication would help me write the second edition of this book.

With that in mind, I will wait to write an official conclusion to this book until after the first year of using this book. Hopefully I will be older and wiser. I look forward to learning and growing along with the students I serve. Life is truly a never-ending journey of growth. An adventure into enlightenment. A Gift of God with many twists and turns and stumbles. Many mountain tops and valleys. Triumphs and tribulations. Through it all may we learn to be grateful, thankful, and growing in wisdom and understanding.

In closing, let me share some of my favorite teachings from the Great Teacher Jesus Christ whom I consider my personal Lord and Savior, Great Shepard and King.

But seek ye first the kingdom of God, and his righteousness; and all these things shall be added unto you. Jesus in Mathew 6:33

Ask, and it shall be given you; seek, and ye shall find; knock, and it shall be opened unto you: For every one that asketh receiveth; and he that seeketh findeth; and to him that knocketh it shall be opened. Jesus in Matthew 7:7,8

And ye shall know the truth, and the truth shall make you free. Jesus in John 8:32

For God so loved the world, that he gave his only begotten Son, that whosoever believeth in him should not perish, but have everlasting life. For God sent not his Son into the world to condemn the world; but that the world through him might be saved. Jesus in John 3:16,17

God bless you richly and sincerely,

David